ABRIDGED HOLINESS CLASSICS

John Fletcher's
Checks to Antinomianism

Abridged by

Rev. Peter Wiseman, S.T.D.

Printed in U.S.A.
1948

BEACON HILL PRESS

2923 Troost Ave.   Kansas City, Mo.

CONTENTS

I. FIRST CHECK TO ANTINOMIANISM

II. SECOND CHECK TO ANTINOMIANISM

III. THIRD CHECK TO ANTINOMIANISM

IV. FOURTH CHECK TO ANTINOMIANISM

IN A SERIES OF LETTERS TO MR. RICHARD HILL

INTRODUCTION

In giving to the public *Checks to Antinomianism by* Rev. John Fletcher, M.A., in an abridged edition, the question that may naturally be raised by the younger generation will be, "Who is Rev. John Fletcher?" Let us read what a few outstanding writers have to say about him. "Jean Guillaume De La Flechere," wrote Robert Southey, "was a man of rare talents, and rarer virtue. No age or country has ever produced a man of more fervent piety, and more perfect charity; no church has ever possessed a more apostolic minister. He was a man of whom Methodism may well be proud, as the most able of its defenders; and whom the Church of England may hold in remembrance, as one of the most pious and excellent of her sons." "Fletcher was a saint," said Isaac Taylor, "as unearthly a being as could tread the earth at all." Robert Hall exclaimed, "Fletcher is a seraph who burns with the ardour of divine love. Spurning the fetters of mortality, he almost habitually seems to have anticipated the rapture of the beatific vision." "I conceive Fletcher," said Dr. Dixon, "to be the most holy man who has been upon earth since the apostolic age." In his sermon on the death of Mr. Fletcher, the Rev. John Wesley, M.A., said, "Many exemplary men have I known, holy in heart and life, within fourscore years. But one equal to him, I have not known: one so inwardly and outwardly devoted to God. So unimpeachable a character in every respect, I have not found either in Europe or America. And I scarce expect to find another such, on this side eternity."

The Rev. John Fletcher was a scholar and a saint; a rare combination of intellectualism and spirituality; a keen debater and a great lover of men. This alone would make his work most valuable.

There may be those who think that *Fletcher's Checks* have had their day and should be allowed to pass out. Many there are, however, who think differently: many who know the value of these checks have been hoping for a reprint either in whole or in abridgement, chiefly because many of the errors dealt with by Mr. Fletcher are prevalent today.

The reader may notice at times an abruptness or lack of continuity in the paragraphing. This is due to the fact that sometimes whole paragraphs have been omitted. Then, there has been no reconstruction of Mr. Fletcher's sentences; that which has been considered most valuable and helpful has been selected. Naturally because of limited space much that is valuable had to be omitted but the best has been preserved. "The Fifth Check," because of the lack of space, and the fact that much of its subject matter had already been discussed, has been omitted entirely.

The publication of this immortal work by such a wonderful Christian character by the Nazarene Publishing House is a venture of faith and a labor of love. Every student for the Christian ministry and young preacher should read and study these checks; indeed, every lover of the truth of full salvation should do likewise; and every person should help scatter these books for the good they will do. Let God's people not fail in this.

As a young student for the Christian ministry I had to write an examination on *Fletcher's Checks*. After so many years, the reviewing of these checks in preparing this abridged edition has brought a new challenge to the study of sacred doctrines, and the fire of devotion in my soul has been fanned to a mighty flame. The sainted Fletcher is a challenge to the holiness movement to live "true holiness."

PETER WISEMAN

PREFACE

A COPY OF THE CIRCULAR LETTER
WHICH
GAVE OCCASION TO THIS VINDICATION;
TO WHICH IS ANNEXED
A COPY OF THE REV. MR. WESLEY'S MINUTES

"Sir: Whereas Mr. Wesley's conference is to be held at Bristol, on Tuesday, the 6th of August next, it is proposed by Lady Huntingdon, and many other Christian friends, (real Protestants,) to have a meeting at Bristol, at the same time, of such principal persons, both clergy and laity, who disapprove of the under written Minutes: and as the same are thought injurious to the very fundamental principles of Christianity, it is farther proposed that they go in a body to the said conference, and insist upon a formal recantation of the said Minutes; and in case of a refusal, that they sign and publish their protest against them. Your presence, sir, on this occasion, is particularly requested. But if it should not suit your convenience to be there, it is desired that you will transmit your sentiments on the subject to such persons as you think proper to produce them. It is submitted to you, whether it would not be right, in the opposition to be made to such a dreadful heresy, to recommend it to as many of your Christian friends, as well of the dissenters as of the established church, as you can prevail on, to be there, the cause being of so public a nature.

"I am, sir, your obedient servant,

"WALTER SHIRLEY."

"P.S. Your answer is desired, directed to the countess of Huntingdon, or the Rev. Mr. Shirley, or John Lloyd, Esq. in Bath; or Mr. James Ireland, merchant, Bristol; or to Thomas Powis, Esq. at Berwick, near Shrewsbury; or to Richard Hill, Esq. at Hawkstone, near Whitchurch, Shropshire. *Lodgings will be provided. Inquire at Mr. Ireland's, Bristol.*"

EXTRACTS FROM THE MINUTES
OF SOME CONVERSATIONS
BETWEEN THE REV. MR. WESLEY AND OTHERS,
AT A PUBLIC CONFERENCE, HELD IN LONDON, AUGUST 7, 1770,
AND PRINTED BY W. PINE, IN BRISTOL.

"Take heed to your doctrine."

"We said in 1744, 'We have leaned too much toward Calvinism.' Wherein?

"1. With regard to *man's faithfulness.* Our Lord himself taught us to use the expression. And we ought never to be ashamed of it. We ought steadily to assert, on his authority, that if a man is not 'faithful in the unrighteous mammon,' God will not 'give him the true riches.'

"2. With regard to *working for life.* This also our Lord has expressly commanded us. 'Labour,' Εργαζεσθε, literally, *'work* for the meat that endureth to everlasting life.' and in fact every believer, till he comes to glory, works *for,* as well as *from* life.

"3. We have received it as a maxim, that 'a man is to do nothing *in order to justification.*' Nothing can be more false. Whoever desires to find favour with God, should 'cease from evil, and learn to do well.' Whoever repents, should do 'works meet for repentance.' And if this is not *in order to* find favour, what does he do them for?

"Review the whole affair.

"1. Who of us is *now* accepted of God?

"He that now believes in Christ, with a loving, obedient heart.

"2. But who among those who never heard of Christ?

"He that feareth God, and worketh righteousness according to the light he has.

"3. Is this the same with 'he that is sincere?'

"Nearly, if not quite.

"4. Is not this 'salvation by works?'

"Not by the *merit* of works, but by works as a *condition*.

"5. What have we then been disputing about for these thirty years?

"I am afraid, *about words*.

"6. As to *merit* itself, of which we have been so dreadfully afraid: we are rewarded, *according to our works*, yea, *because of our works*. How does this differ from, *for the sake of our works*? And how differs this from *secundum merita operum*, 'as our works deserve?' Can you split this hair? I doubt, I cannot.

"7. The grand objection to one of the preceding propositions is drawn from matter of fact. God does in fact justify those who, by their own confession, 'neither feared God nor wrought righteousness.' Is this an exception to the general rule?

"It is a doubt whether God makes any exception at all. But how are we sure that the person in question never did 'fear God and work righteousness?' His own saying so is not proof: for we know how all that are convinced of sin undervalue themselves in every respect.

"8. Does not talking of a justified or sanctified *state* tend to mislead men? almost naturally leading them to trust in what was done in one moment? Whereas we are every hour and every moment pleasing or displeasing to God, *according to our works*: according to the whole of our inward tempers and our outward behaviour."

FIRST CHECK TO ANTINOMIANISM

LETTER I.

HONOURED AND REVEREND SIR: Before a judge passes sentence upon a person accused of theft, he hears what his neighbours have to say for his character. Mr. Wesley, I grant, is accused of what is worse than theft, *dreadful heresy;* and I know that whosoever maintains a dreadful heresy is a *dreadful heretic;* and that the Church of Rome shows no mercy to such. But may not "real Protestants" indulge, with the privilege of a felon, one whom they so lately respected as a brother? And may not I, an old friend and acquaintance of his, be permitted to speak a word in his favour, before he is branded in the forehead, as he has already been on the back?

This step, I fear, will cost me my reputation, (if I have any,) and involve me in the same condemnation with him whose cause, together with that of truth, I design to plead. But when humanity prompts, when gratitude calls, when friendship excites, when reason invites, when justice demands, when truth requires, and conscience summons, he does not deserve the name of a *Christian friend,* who, for any consideration, hesitates to vindicate what he esteems truth, and to stand by an aggrieved friend, brother, and father. Were I not, sir, on such an occasion as this to step out of my beloved obscurity, you might deservedly reproach me as a *dastardly wretch:* nay, you have already done it in general terms, in your excellent sermon on the fear of man. "How often," say you, "do men sneakingly forsake their friends, instead of gloriously supporting them against a powerful adversary, even when their cause is just, for reasons hastily prudential, for fear of giving umbrage to a superior party or interest?"

These generous words of yours, Rev. sir, together with the leave you give both Churchmen and Dissenters to direct to *you* their answers to your circular letter, are my excuse for intruding upon you by this epistle, and my apology for begging your candid attention, while I attempt to convince you that my friend's principles and Minutes are not heretical. In order to this, I shall lay before you, and the principal persons, both clergy and laity, whom you have, from all parts of England and Wales, convened at Bristol, by printed letters,—

I. A general view of the Rev. Mr. Wesley's doctrine.

II. An account of the commendable design of his Minutes.

III. A vindication of the propositions which they contain, by arguments taken from the Scripture, reason, and experience; and by quotations from eminent Calvinist divines, who have said the same things in different words.

And suppose you yourself, sir, in particular, should appear to be a strong assertor of the doctrines which you call a *dreadful heresy* in Mr. Wesley, I hope you will not refuse me leave to conclude, by expostulating with you upon your conduct in this affair, and recommending to you, and our other Christian friends, the forbearance which you recommend to others, in one of your sermons: "Why doth the narrow heart of man pursue with malice or rashness those who presume to differ from him?" Yea, and what is more extraordinary, those who agree with him in all essential points?

I. When, in an intricate case, a prudent judge is afraid to pass an unjust sentence, he inquires, as I observed, into the general conduct of the person accused, and by that means frequently finds out the truth which he investigates. As that method may be of service in the present case, permit me, sir, to lay before you a general view of Mr. Wesley's doctrine.

1. For above these sixteen years I have heard him frequently in his chapels, and sometimes in my church: I have familiarly conversed and corresponded with him, and have often perused his numerous works in verse and prose: and I can truly say that, during all that time, I have heard him, upon every proper occasion, steadily maintain *the total fall of man in Adam,* and his utter inability to recover himself, or take any one step toward his recovery, "without the grace of God preventing him, that he may have a good will, and working with him when he has that good will."

The deepest expressions that ever struck my ears on the melancholy subject of our natural depravity and helplessness, are those which dropped from his lips: and I have ever observed that he constantly ascribes to Divine grace, not only the good works and holy tempers of believers, but all the good thoughts of upright heathens, and the good desires of those professors whom he sees "begin in the Spirit and end in the flesh:" when, to my great surprise, some of those who accuse him of "robbing God of the glory of his grace, and ascribing too much to man's power," directly or indirectly maintain that Demas and his fellow apostates never had any grace; and that if once they went on far in the ways of God, it was merely by the force of fallen nature; a sentiment which Mr. Wesley looks upon as diametrically opposite to the humbling assertion of our Lord, "Without me ye can do nothing"; and which he can no more admit than the rankest Pelagianism.

2. I must likewise testify, that he faithfully points ont *Christ as the only way of salvation;* and strongly recommends faith as the only mean of receiving him, and all the benefits of his righteous life and meritorious death: and truth obliges me to declare, that he frequently expresses his detestation of the errors of modern Pharisees, who laugh at original sin, set up the powers of fallen man,

cry down the operation of God's Spirit, deny the absolute
necessity of the blood and righteousness of Christ, and
refuse him the glory of all the good that may be found
in Jew or Gentile. And you will not without difficulty,
sir, find in England, and perhaps in all the world, a minister who hath borne more frequent testimonies, either
from the pulpit or the press, against those dangerous
errors. All his works confirm my assertion, especially his
sermons on Original Sin, and Salvation by Faith, and
his mastery Refutation of Dr. Taylor, the wisest Pelagian
and Socinian of our age. Nor am I afraid to have this
testimony confronted with his Minutes, being fully persuaded that, when they are candidly explained, they
rather confirm than overthrow it.

3. The next fundamental doctrine in Christianity is
that of *holiness of heart and life;* and no one can here
accuse Mr. Wesley of leaning to the Antinomian delusion,
which "makes void the law through" a speculative and
barren "faith:" on the contrary, he appears to be peculiarly set for the defence of practical religion: for, instead
of representing Christ "as the minister of sin," with
Ranters, to the great grief and offence of many, he sets
him forth as a complete *Saviour from sin.* Not satisfied
to preach holiness begun, he preaches finished holiness,
and calls believers to such a degree of heart-purifying
faith, as may enable them to triumph in Christ, as "being
made to them of God, sanctification as well as righteousness."

It is, I grant, his misfortune (if indeed it be one) to
preach a fuller salvation than most professors expect to
enjoy here; for he asserts that Jesus can "make clean"
the inside as well as the *outside* of his vessels unto honour;
that he hath power on earth "to save his people from their
sins;" and that his blood "cleanses from all sin," from the
guilt and defilement both of original and actual corruption.
He is bold enough to declare, with St. John, that "if we

say we have no sin, *either by nature or practice*, we deceive ourselves, and the truth is not in us: but if we confess our sins, God is faithful and just to forgive us our sins, and to cleanse us from all unrighteousness." He is legal enough not to be ashamed of these words of Moses: "The Lord thy God will circumcise thine heart, and the heart of thy seed, to love the Lord thy God with all thine heart, and with all thy soul, that thou mayst live." And he dares to believe that the Lord can perform the words which he spoke by Ezekiel: "I will sprinkle clean water upon you, and you shall be clean: from ALL your filthiness and from ALL your idols will I cleanse you. A new heart also will I give you: I will take away the stony heart out of your flesh, and I will give you a heart of flesh; and I will put my Spirit within you, and cause you to walk in my statutes; and ye shall keep my judgments, and do them. I will also save you from *all* your uncleannesses." Hence it is that he constantly exhorts his hearers "to grow in grace, and in the knowledge of our Saviour"; till by a strong and lively faith they can continually "reckon themselves to be dead indeed unto sin, but alive unto God through Jesus Christ our Lord." He tells them, that "he who committeth sin, is the servant of sin";—that "our old man is crucified with Christ, that the body of sin might be destroyed, that henceforth we should not serve sin";—that "if the Son shall make us free, we shall be free indeed";—and that although "*the* law of the Spirit of life in Christ Jesus" will not deliver us from the innocent infirmities incident to flesh and blood, it will nevertheless make us "free from the law of sin and death," and enable us to say with holy triumph, "How shall we, that are dead to sin, live any longer therein?" In a word, he thinks that God can so "shed abroad his love in our hearts, by the Holy Ghost given unto us," as to "sanctify us wholly, soul, body, and spirit:" and enable us to rejoice evermore, pray without ceasing, and in every thing give thanks." And he is persuaded, that He who "can do far exceeding abundantly above all that we can ask or think," is able to fill us with the "perfect love which casts out fear; that we, being delivered out of the hands of our enemies," may have "the mind which was in Christ"; be righteous as the *man* Jesus was righteous; "walk as he also walked," and be in our measure, "as he was in the world:" he as the stock of the tree of righteousness, and we as the branches, "having our fruit" from him "unto holiness," and serving God without fear in true holiness and righteousness all the days of our life."

4. But this is not all: he holds also *general redemption,* and its necessary consequences, which some account *dreadful heresies.* He asserts with St. Paul, that "Christ, by the grace of God, tasted death for every man;" and this grace he calls *free,* as extending itself *freely* to all. Nor can he help expressing his surprise at those pious ministers who maintain that the Saviour keeps his grace, as they suppose he kept his blood, from the greatest part of mankind, and yet engross to themselves the title of *preachers of* FREE *grace!*

He frequently observes, with the same apostle, that "Christ is the Saviour of *all* men, but especially of them that believe"; and that "God will have *all* men to be saved," consistently with their moral agency, and the tenor of his Gospel.

With St. John he maintains that "God is love," and that "Christ is the propitiation not only for our sins, but also for the sins of the *whole world.*" With David he affirms that "God's mercy is over *all* his works:" and with St. Peter, that "the Lord is not willing that any should perish, but that *all* should come to repentance"; yea, that God, without hypocrisy, "commandeth *all* men, *every where,* to repent." Accordingly he says with the Son of God, "Whosoever will, let him come and take of the water of life freely"; and after his blessed example, as well as by his gracious command, he "preaches the Gospel TO *every creature*"; which he apprehends would be inconsistent with common honesty, if there were not a Gospel FOR *every creature*. Nor can he doubt of it in the least, when he considers that Christ is a king as well as a priest; that we are under a law to him; that those men who "will not have him to reign over them, shall be brought and slain before him"; yea, that he will "judge the secrets of men," according to St. Paul's Gospel, and take vengeance on all them that obey not his *own* Gospel, *and* be the author of eternal salvation to *none but* them that obey him.

5. As a consequence of the doctrine of general redemption, Mr. Wesley lays down two axioms, of which he never loses sight in his preaching. *The first* is, that ALL OUR SALVATION IS OF GOD IN CHRIST, and therefore OF GRACE;—all opportunities, invitations, inclination, and power to believe being bestowed upon us of mere grace;—grace most absolutely free: and so far, I hope, that all who are called Gospel ministers agree with him. But he proceeds farther; for, *secondly,* he asserts with equal confidence, that according to the Gospel dispensation, ALL OUR DAMNATION IS OF OURSELVES, by our obstinate unbelief and avoidable unfaithfulness; as we may "neglect so great salvation," desire to "be excused" from coming to the feast of the Lamb, "make light of" God's gracious offers, refuse to "occupy," bury our talent, and act the part of the "slothful servant"; or, in other words, "resist, grieve, do despite to," and "quench the Spirit of grace," *by our moral agency.*

The first of these evangelical axioms he builds upon such scriptures as these:—"In me is thy help. Look unto me and be saved. No man cometh unto me except the Father draw him. What hast thou that thou hast not received? We are not sufficient to think aright of ourselves, all our sufficiency is of God. Christ is exalted to give repentance. Faith is the gift of God. Without me ye can do nothing," etc., etc.

And *the second* he founds upon such passages as these: "This is the condemnation, that light is come into the world, and men loved darkness rather than light. Ye always resist the Holy Ghost. They rejected the counsel of God toward themselves. Grieve not the Spirit. Quench not the Spirit. My Spirit shall not always strive with man. Turn, why will ye die? Kiss the Son, lest ye perish. I gave Jezebel time to repent, and she repented not. The goodness of God leads [not *drags*,] thee to repentance, who after thy hardness and impenitent heart treasurest up wrath unto thyself. Their eyes have they closed, lest they should see, and be converted, and I should heal them. See that ye refuse not him that speaketh from heaven. I set before you life and death, choose life! Ye will not come unto me that ye might have life. I *would* have gathered you, and ye *would not*," etc., etc.

As to the *moral agency* of man, Mr. Wesley thinks it cannot be denied upon the principles of common sense and civil government; much less upon those of natural and revealed religion; as nothing would be more absurd than to bind us by laws of a civil or spiritual nature; nothing more foolish than to propose to us punishments and rewards; and nothing more capricious than to inflict the one or bestow the other upon us; if we were not *moral agents*.

He is therefore persuaded, the most complete system of divinity is that in which neither of those two axioms is superseded: He thinks it is bold and unscriptural to set up the one at the expense of the other, convinced that the prophets, the apostles, and Jesus Christ left us no such precedent; and that, to avoid what is termed *legality*, we must not run into refinements which they knew nothing of, and make them perpetually contradict themselves: nor can we, he believes, without an open violation of the laws of candour and criticism, lay a greater stress upon a few obscure and controverted passages, than upon a hundred plain and irrefragable Scripture proofs. He therefore supposes that those persons are under a capital mistake who maintain only the first Gospel axiom, and under pretence of securing to God *all* the glory of the salvation of *one* elect, give to perhaps *twenty* reprobates full room to lay *all* the blame of their damnation either upon their first parents, or their Creator. This way of making twenty *real* holes, in order to stop a *supposed* one, he cannot see consistent either with wisdom or Scripture.

Thinking it therefore safest not to "put asunder" the truths which "God has joined together," he makes all extremes meet in one blessed Scriptural medium. With the Antinomian he preaches, "God worketh in you both to will and to do of his good pleasure"; and with the Legalist he cries, "Work out, therefore, your own salvation with fear and trembling"; and thus he has all St. Paul's doctrine. With the Ranter he says, "God has chosen you, you are elect"; but, as it is "through sanctification of the Spirit and belief of the truth," with the disciples of Moses he infers, "make your calling and election sure, for if ye do these things ye shall never fall." Thus he presents his hearers with all St. Peter's system of truth, which the others had rent to pieces.

In short, he would think that he mangled the Gospel, and forgot part of his awful commission, if, when he has declared that "he who believeth shall be saved," he did not also add, that he "who believeth not shall be damned"; or, which is the same, that none perish merely for Adam's sin, but for their own unbelief, and wilful rejection of the Saviour's grace. Thus he advances God's glory every way, entirely ascribing to his mercy and grace all the salvation of the elect, and completely freeing him from the blame of directly or indirectly hanging the millstone of damnation about the neck of the reprobate. And this he effectually does, by showing that the former owe all they

are, and all they have, to creating, preserving, and redeeming love, whose innumerable bounties they freely
and continually receive; and that the rejection of the latter has absolutely no cause but their obstinate rejecting
of that astonishing mercy which wept over Jerusalem;
and prayed, and bled even for those that shed the atoning
blood—the blood that expiated all sin but that of final
unbelief.

I have now finished my sketch of Mr. Wesley's doctrine, so far as it has fallen under my observation during
above sixteen years' particular acquaintance with him and
his works. It is not my design, sir, to inquire into the
truth of his sentiments, much less shall I attempt to prove
them orthodox, according to the ideas that some *real
Protestants* entertain of orthodoxy. This only I beg leave
to observe: Suppose he is mistaken in all the scriptures
on which he founds his doctrine of Christian perfection
and general redemption, yet his mistakes seem rather to
arise from a regard for Christ's glory, than from enmity
to his offices; and all together do not amount to any heresy
at all; the fundamental doctrines of Christianity, namely,
*the fall of man, justification by the merits of Christ, sanc-
tification by the agency of the Holy Spirit,* and *the worship
of the one true God in the mysterious distinction of Father, Son, and Holy Spirit,* as it is maintained in the three
creeds, not being at all affected by any of his peculiar
sentiments.

But you possibly imagine, sir, that he has lately
changed his doctrine, and adopted a new system. If you
do, you are under a very great mistake; and to convince
you of it, permit me to conclude this letter by a paragraph of one which I received from him last spring: —
"I always did (for between these thirty and forty
years) clearly assert the total fall of man, and his utter
inability to do any good of himself: the absolute necessity
of the grace and Spirit of God to raise even a good thought

or desire in our hearts: the Lord's rewarding no works, and accepting of none, but so far as they proceed from his preventing, convincing, and converting grace, through the Beloved; the blood and righteousness of Christ being the sole meritorious cause of our salvation. And who is there in England that has asserted these things more strongly and steadily than I have done?"

Leaving you to answer this question, I remain, with due respect, Hon. and Rev. sir, your obedient servant, in the bond of a peaceful Gospel,   J. FLETCHER.

MADELEY, *July* 29, 1771.

LETTER II

HONOURED AND REVEREND SIR,—Having proved that Mr. Wesley's doctrine is not heretical, permit me to consider the propositions which close the Minutes of his last conference, on which, it seems, your charge of *dreadful heresy* is founded.

Mr. Wesley's propositions were to guard them and their hearers against Antinomian principles and practices, which spread like wild fire in some of his societies; where persons who spoke in the most glorious manner of Christ, and their interest in his complete salvation, have been found living in the greatest immoralities, or indulging the most unchristian tempers. Nor need I go far for a proof of this sad assertion. In one of his societies, not many miles from my parish, a married man, who professed being *in a state of justification and sanctification,* growing wise above what is written, despised his brethren as legalists, and his teachers as persons not clear in the Gospel. He instilled his principles into a serious young woman; and what was the consequence? Why they talked about "finished salvation in Christ," and "the absurdity of perfection in the flesh," till a perfect child was conceived and born; and, to save appearances, the mother swore it to a travelling man that cannot be heard of. Thus, to avoid legality, they plunged into hypocrisy, fornication, adultery, perjury, and the depth of Ranterism. Is it not hard, that a minister should be traduced as guilty of *dreadful heresy,* for trying to put a stop to such dreadful practices? And is it not high time that he should cry to all that regard his warnings, "Take heed to your doctrine"? As if he had said,

"Avoid all extremes. While on the one hand you keep clear of the Pharisaic delusion that slights Christ, and makes the pretended merit of an imperfect obedience the procuring cause of eternal life; see that on the other hand you do not lean to the Antinomian error, which, under pretence of exalting Christ, speaks contemptuously of obedience, and "makes void the law through a faith that *does not* work by love." As there is but a step between high Arminianism and self-righteousness, so there is but one between high Calvinism and Antinomianism. I charge you to shun both, especially the latter.

"You know, by sad experience, that at this time we stand particularly in danger of splitting upon the Antinomian rock. Many smatterers in Christian experience talk of *finished salvation in Christ,* or boast of being in a state of justification and sanctification, while they know little of themselves and less of Christ. Their whole behaviour testifies, that their hearts are void of humble love, and full of carnal confidence. They cry, *Lord! Lord!* with as much assurance and as little right as the foolish virgins. They pass for sweet Christians, dear children of God, and good believers; but their secret reserves evidence them to be only such believers as Simon Magus, Ananias, and Sapphira.

"Some, with Diotrephes, 'love to have the pre-eminence, and prate malicious words,' and not content therewith, 'they do not themselves receive the brethren, and forbid them that would,' and even cast them out of the Church as heretics. Some have 'forsaken the right way, and are gone astray, following the way of Balaam, who loved the wages of unrighteousness; they are wells without water, clouds without rain, and trees without fruit': with Judas they try to 'load themselves with thick clay,' endeavour to 'lay up treasures on earth, and make provision for the flesh to fulfil the lusts thereof.' Some, with the incestuous Corinthian, are led captive by fleshly lusts, and fall into the greatest enormities. Others, with the language of the awakened publican in their mouths, are fast asleep in their spirits; you hear them speak of the corruptions of their hearts, in as unaffected and airy a manner, as if they talked of freckles upon their faces. It seems they run down their sinful nature only to apologize for their sinful practices; or to appear great proficients in self-knowledge, and court the praise due to genuine humility.

"Others, quietly settled on the lees of the Laodicean state, by the whole tenor of their life say, 'they are rich and increased in goods, and have need of nothing'; utter strangers to 'hunger and thirst after righteousness,' they never importunately beg, never wrestle hard for the hidden manna. On the contrary, they sing a *requiem* to their poor dead souls, and say, 'Soul, take thine ease, thou hast goods laid up (in Christ) for many years, yea, for ever and ever'; and thus, like Demas, they go on talking of Christ and heaven, but loving their ease, and enjoying this present world.

"Yet many of these, like Herod, hear and entertain us gladly; but, like him also, they keep their beloved sin, pleading for it as a right eye, and saving it as a right hand. To this day their bosom corruption is not only alive, but indulged; their treacherous Delilah is hugged; and their spiritual 'Agag walks delicately,' and boasts that 'the bitterness of death is past,' and he shall never be 'hewed in pieces before the Lord': nay, to dare so much as to talk

of his *dying* before the body, becomes almost an un-
pardonable crime.

"Forms and fair shows of godliness deceive us: many,
whom our Lord might well compare to 'whited sepulchres,' look like angels of light when they are abroad,
and prove tormenting fiends at home. We see them weep
under sermons; we hear them pray and sing with the
tongues of men and angels; they even profess the faith
that removes mountains: and yet, by and by, we discover
they stumble at every mole hill; every trifling temptation
throws them into peevishness, fretfulness, impatience, ill
humour, discontent, anger, and sometimes into loud passion.

"Relative duties are by many grossly neglected: husbands slight their wives, or wives neglect and plague
their husbands: children are spoiled, parents disregarded,
and masters disobeyed: yea, so many are the complaints
against servants professing godliness, on account of their
unfaithfulness, indolence, pert answering again, forget-
fulness of their menial condition, or insolent expectations,
that some serious persons prefer those who have no knowledge of the truth, to those who make a high profession
of it.

"Knowledge is certainly *increased;* 'many run to and
fro' after it, but it is seldom experimental; the power of
God is frequently talked of, but rarely felt, and too often
cried down under the despicable name of *frames* and
feelings. Numbers *seek,* by hearing a variety of Gospel
ministers, reading all the religious books that are published, learning the best tunes to our hymns, disputing
on controverted points of doctrine, telling or hearing
Church news, and listening to, or retailing, spiritual scandal. But, alas! few *strive* in pangs of heart-felt convictions; few 'deny themselves and take up their cross daily';
few 'take the kingdom of heaven by *the holy* violence' of

wrestling faith, and agonizing prayer; few *see*, and fewer live in 'the kingdom of God, which is righteousness, peace, and joy in the Holy Ghost.' In a word, many say, 'Lo! Christ is here; and lo! he is there'; but few can consistently witness that '*the* kingdom of heaven is within them.'

"Many assert that 'the clothing of the king's daughter is of wrought gold'; but few, very few experience that she is 'all glorious within'; and it is well if many are not bold enough to maintain that she is *all full of corruptions*. With more truth than ever we may say,

> Ye different sects, who all declare,
> Lo! here is Christ, or Christ is there;
> Your stronger proofs divinely give,
> And show us where *the Christians* live:
> Your claims, alas! ye cannot prove,
> Ye want the genuine mark of *love*.

"The consequences of this high, and yet lifeless profession, are as evident as they are deplorable. Selfish views, sinister designs, inveterate prejudice, pitiful bigotry, party spirit, self-sufficiency, contempt of others, envy, jealousy, *making men offenders for a word*—possibly a Scriptural word too, taking advantage of each other's infirmities, magnifying innocent mistakes, putting the worst construction upon each other's words and actions, false accusations, backbiting, malice, revenge, persecutions, and a hundred such evils, prevail among religious people, to the great astonishment of the children of the world, and the unspeakable grief of the true Israelites that yet remain among us.

"But this is not all. Some of our hearers do not even keep to the great outlines of heathen morality: not satisfied practically to reject Christ's declaration, that 'it is more blessed to give than to receive,' they proceed to that pitch of covetousness and daring injustice, as not to pay their just debts; yea, and to cheat, and to extort, whenever they have a fair opportunity. How few of our societies are there where this, or some other evil, has not broken out, and given such shakes to the ark of the Gospel, that had not the Lord wonderfully interposed, it must long ago have been overset! And you know how to this day the name and truth of God are openly blasphemed among the baptized heathens, through the Antinomian lives of many, who 'say they are Jews when they are not, but *by their works declare* they are of the synagogue of Satan.' At your peril, therefore, my brethren, countenance them not: I know you would not do it designedly, but you may do it unawares; therefore 'take heed,'—more than ever 'take heed to your doctrine.' Let it be scripturally evangelical: give not the children's bread unto dogs: comfort not people that do not mourn. When you should give emetics do not administer cordials, and by that means strengthen the hands of the slothful and unprofitable servant. I repeat it once more, warp not to Antinomianism, and in order to this, *take heed, O! take heed to your doctrine.*"

Surely, sir, there is no harm in this word of exhortation; it is Scriptural, and Mr. Wesley's pen cannot make it heretical. Take we then heed to the design of the directions which follow:

It is evident, that, in order to keep his fellow labourers clear from Antinomianism, he directs them, FIRST, Not to *lean too much toward Calvinism;* and, SECONDLY, Not to *talk of a justified and sanctified state* so unguardedly as some, even Arminians do; which *tends to mislead men,* and relax their watchful attention to their internal and external works, that is, to *the whole of their inward tempers and outward behaviour.*

From the general tenor of these propositions, is it not evident that Mr. Wesley, (who is now among Gospel ministers, what St. James formerly was among the disciples, and Mr. Baxter among the Puritan divines, that is, the person peculiarly commissioned by the Bishop of souls to defend the Gospel against the encroachments of Antinomians,) aims at stemming the torrent of their delusions, and not at all at "injuring the fundamental principles of Christianity," or bringing "a dreadful heresy into the Church."

You may reply, that you do not so much consider what he *aims* at doing, as what he *has actually* done. Nay, sir, the intention is what a candid judge (much more a loving brother) should particularly consider. If aiming to kill a wild beast that attacks my friend, I unfortunately stab him, it is a "melancholy accident"; but he wrongs me much, who represents it as a "dreadful barbarity." In like manner, if Mr. Wesley has unhappily wounded the truth, in attempting to give the wolf in sheep's clothing a killing stroke, his mistake should rather be called "well-meant legality" than *dreadful heresy.*

You possibly reply, "Let any one look at these Minutes, and say, whether all the unawakened clergy in the land would not approve and receive them." And what if they did? Would the propositions be the worse barely for this? Is nothing Gospel but what directly shocks common sense? And is the apostles' creed dreadfully heretical, because all the carnal clergy of the Church of England, yea, and of the Church of Rome, receive it? At this strange rate we must give up the Bible itself, for all the Socinians receive it. Ashamed of taking farther notice of an argument by which every Papist might attack the reasonable simplicity of our communion service, and defend the gross absurdity of transubstantiation, I come to an objection of greater weight:

"Mr. Wesley contradicts himself. He has hitherto preached salvation by faith, and now he talks of *salvation by works, as a condition:* he has a thousand times offered a *free pardon* to the worst of sinners, and now he has the assurance to declare that a *man is to do something in order to justification.*" Where will you "find such incon-

sistencies?" Where! In the Old and New Testament, and
especially in the epistles of the great preacher of free
justification, and salvation by faith. There you will see
many such *seeming* inconsistencies as these: *Eternal life
is the gift of God through our Lord Jesus Christ.* "Charge
the rich to lay up in store for themselves a good foundation, that they may lay hold on eternal life: we are tem-
perate, to obtain an incorruptible crown." *By grace ye
are saved through faith.* "In so doing thou shalt save thyself. Work out your own salvation." *We are not sufficient
of ourselves to think any thing as of ourselves.* "The
Gentiles do by nature the things contained in the law."
God justifieth the ungodly and him that worketh not. "He
shall render to every man according to his works, even
eternal life to them who by patient continuance in well
doing, seek for glory." *God forbid that I should glory in
anything, save, in the cross of Christ.* "As the truth of
God is in me, no man shall stop me of this glorying," that
I have kept myself from being burdensome. *I am the
chief of sinners.* "I have lived in all good conscience before God until this day." *We rejoice in Christ Jesus, and
have no confidence in the flesh.* "Our rejoicing is this, the
testimony of our conscience, that in simplicity and godly
sincerity we have had our conversation in the world."
*Not by works of righteousness that we have done, but ac-
cording to his mercy he saved us: not of works, lest any
man should boast; for if it be of works, then it is no more
grace, otherwise work is no more work.* "I keep under
my body, lest I myself should be a cast-away: be not deceived; whatsoever a man soweth that shall he also reap:
he that soweth little shall reap little; he that soweth to
the Spirit, shall of the Spirit reap life everlasting." *I am
persuaded that neither death, nor life, neither things
present nor things to come, etc., shall be able to separate
us from the love of God which is in Christ Jesus.* Those
that fall away "crucify to themselves the Son of God

afresh, and put him to an open shame: for the earth which beareth thorns and briers is rejected, and is nigh unto cursing, whose end is to be burned. Some of the branches were broken off by unbelief, thou standest by faith; be not high minded, but fear; continue in God's goodness, otherwise thou also shalt be cut off."

Now, sir, permit me to beg you would lay your hand upon your heart, and say, whether malicious infidels have not a fairer show of reason to raise wicked men against St. Paul, than you have to raise good men against Mr. Wesley? And whether a grain of the candour with which you would reconcile the *seeming* contradictions of the great apostle would not be more than sufficient to reconcile the *seeming* inconsistencies of the great minister whom you have so warmly attacked?

Some persons indeed complain aloud that "Mr. Wesley, in his new scheme of salvation by works as a condition, fairly renounces Christ's blood and righteousness." I grant that the words "blood and righteousness" are not found in the Minutes, but "acceptance by believing in Christ" is found there; and he must be a caviller indeed, who asserts that he means a Christ without blood, or a Christ without righteousness. Besides, when he cuts off *the merit of works* from having any share in our salvation, far from forgetting the meritorious life and death of the Redeemer, he effectually guards them, and the Protestant ark, sprinkled with the atoning blood, from the rash touches of all merit mongers. Add to this, that Mr. Wesley has sufficiently declared his faith in the atonement, in thousands of sermons and hymns, some of which are continually sung both by him and the *real Protestants,* so that "out of their own mouth" their groundless charge may be refuted.

I remain, Rev. and dear sir, yours, etc.

J. FLETCHER.

LETTER III

HONOURED AND REVEREND SIR: We have seen how exceedingly commendable was Mr. Wesley's design in writing what you have extracted from his last Minutes; and how far from being unanswerable are the *general* objections which some have moved against them. Let us now proceed to a candid inquiry into the true meaning of the propositions. They are thus prefaced:

"We said in 1744, *We have leaned too much toward Calvinism.* Wherein?"

This single sentence is enough, I grant, to make some persons account Mr. Wesley a heretic. He is not a Calvinist! And what is still more dreadful, he has the assurance to say that he has *leaned too much toward Calvinism!* This will sound like a double heresy in their ears; but not in *yours,* sir, who seem to carry your anti-Calvinistical notions farther than Mr. Wesley himself. He never spoke more clearly to the point of free grace than you do, page 85, of your sermons: "God," say you, "never left himself without witness, not only from the visible things of the creation, but likewise from the inward witness, a spiritual seed of light sown in the soul of every son of man, Jew, Turk, or Pagan, as well as Christians, whose kindly suscitations whoever follows, will gladly perceive increasing gleams still leading farther on to nearer and far brighter advances, till at length a full and perfect day bursts forth upon his ravished eyes." In this single sentence, sir, you bear the noblest testimony to all the doctrines in which Mr. Wesley dissents from the Calvinists. You begin with GENERAL REDEMPTION, and end with PERFECTION: or, to use your own expression, you follow him "from the spiritual seed of light in a Turk," quite to the "full and perfect day, bursting forth upon the ravished eyes of the Pagan who follows the kindly suscitations" of Divine grace.

And far from making man a mere machine, you tell us, page 140, "it is true that faith is the gift of God, but the

exertion of that faith, when once given, lieth in *ourselves.*"
Mr. Wesley grants it, sir; but permit me to tell you that
the word *ourselves* being printed in italics, seems to convey rather more anti-Calvinism than he holds: for he is
persuaded that we cannot exert faith without a continual
influence of the same Divine power that produced it; it
being evident, upon the Gospel plan, that "without Christ
we can do nothing." From these and the like passages in
your sermons, I conclude, sir, that your charge of *dreadful
heresy* does not rest upon these words, "We have leaned
too much toward Calvinism." Pass we then to the next,
in which Mr. Wesley begins to show wherein he has con-
sented too much to the Calvinists.

"I. With regard to *man's faithfulness.* Our Lord himself taught us to use the expression. And we ought never
to be ashamed of it. We ought steadily to assert, on his
authority, that if a man 'is not faithful in the unrighteous
mammon, God will not give him the true riches.' "

Now, where does the heresy lie here? Is it in the word
man's faithfulness? Is there so much *faithfulness* to God
and man among professors, that he must be *opposed* by
all good men who dares to use the bare word? Do *real
Protestants* account "man's faithfulness" a grace of super-
erogation, and quoting Scripture a heresy? Or do they
slight what our Lord recommends in the plainest terms,
and will one day reward in the most glorious manner? If
not, why are they going to enter a protest against Mr.
Wesley because he is "not ashamed of Christ and his
words before an evil and adulterous generation," and will
not "keep back" from his immense flock any part of "the
counsel of God," much less a part that so many professors
overlook, while some are daring enough to lampoon it,
and others wicked enough to trample it under foot?

O, sir, if Mr. Wesley is to be cast out of your synagogue
unless he *formally recant* the passage he has quoted, and
which he says "we are not to be ashamed of"; what will

you do to the Son of God who spoke it? What to St. Luke who wrote it? And what to good Mr. Henry who thus comments upon it? "If we do not make a right use of the gifts of God's providence, how can we expect from him those present and future comforts which are the gifts of his spiritual grace? Our Saviour here compares these; and shows that though our faithful use of the things of this world cannot be thought to merit any favour at the hand of God, yet our unfaithfulness in the use of them may be justly reckoned a *forfeiture* of that grace which is necessary to bring us to glory. And that is it which our Saviour shows, Luke 16: 10-12, He that is unjust, *unfaithful,* in the least, is unjust, unfaithful also in *much.* The riches of this world are the *less;* grace and glory are the *greater.* Now, if we be unfaithful in the less, if we use the things of this world to other purposes than those to which they were given us, it may justly be feared we shall be so in the gifts of God's grace, that we will receive them also in vain, and therefore they will be denied us. He that is faithful in that which is least, is faithful also in much. He that serves God and does good with his money, will serve God and do good with the more noble and valuable talents of wisdom and grace, and spiritual gifts, and the earnest of heaven: but he that buries the one talent of this world's wealth, will never improve the five talents of spiritual riches."

You know, sir, what destruction this sin brought upon Achan, and by his means upon Israel: and you remember how Saul's avarice, and his "flying upon the spoil of the Amalekites" cost him his kingdom, together with the Divine blessing. You will perhaps, object that "they forfeited only temporal mercies." True, if they repented; but if their sin sealed up the hardness of their heart, then they lost all.

I can, however, mention two who indisputably forfeited both spiritual and eternal blessings: the one is the moral young man whose fatal attachment to wealth is mentioned in the Gospel. "Go," said our Lord to him, "sell all thou hast, give to the poor; come, follow me, and thou shalt have treasure in heaven." He was unfaithful in the "mammon of unrighteousness"; he would not comply with the proposal, and though "Jesus loved him," yet he stood firm to his word, he did not "give him the true riches." The unhappy wretch chose to have his good things in this world, and so lost them in the next.

The other instance is Judas. "He left all," at first, "to follow Jesus"; but when the devil placed him upon the high mountain of temptation, and showed him the horrors of poverty and the alluring wealth of this world, covetousness, his besetting sin, prevailed again: and as he carried the bag he turned thief, and made a private purse. You know, sir, that "the love of money" proved to him "the root of all evil"; and that on account of his "unfaithfulness in the mammon of unrighteousness" our Lord not only did "not give him the true riches," but took his every talent from him, his apostleship on earth, and one of the twelve thrones which he had promised him in common with the other disciples.

Some, I know, will excuse Judas by fathering his crime and damnation upon the decrees of God. But we who are not numbered among *real Protestants* think that sinners are reprobated as they are elected, that is, says St. Peter, "according to the foreknowledge of God." We are persuaded that because God's knowledge is *infinite* he foreknows future contingencies; and we think we should insult both his holiness and his omniscience if we did not believe that he could both foresee and foretell that Judas would be unfaithful, without necessitating him to be so, that the Scriptures might be fulfilled. We assert, then, that as Jesus loved the poor covetous young man, so he loved his poor covetous disciple. For had he hated him, he must have acted the base part of a dissembler, by show-

ing him for years as much love as he did the other apostles; an idea too horrid for a Christian to entertain, I
shall not say of "God made flesh," but even of a man that
has any sincerity or truth! Judas's damnation, therefore,
and the ruin of the young man, according to the second
axiom in the Gospel, were merely of themselves, by their
unbelief and "unfaithfulness in the mammon of unrighteousness": for "how could they believe," seeing they re-
posed their "trust in uncertain riches!"

Thus, sir, both the express declaration of our Lord,
and the plain histories of the Scripture agree to confirm
this fundamental principle in Christianity, that when God
works upon man he expects faithfulness from man; and
that when man, as a moral agent, grieves and quenches
the Spirit that strives to make him faithful, temporal and
eternal ruin are the inevitable consequence.

Thus far, then, the Minutes contain a great, evangelical
truth, and not a shadow of heresy. Let us see whether the
dreadful snake lurks under the second proposition.

"II. We have leaned too much toward Calvinism; (2)
With regard to *working for life*. This also our Lord has
expressly commanded us. *Labour* (Εργαζεσθε, literally,
work) *for the meat that endureth to everlasting life*. And
in fact every believer, till he comes to glory, works *for* as
well as *from* life."

Here Mr. Wesley strikes at a fatal mistake of all Antinomians, many honest Calvinists, and not a few who are
Arminians in sentiment, and Calvinists in practice. All
these, when they see that man is by nature dead in trespasses and sins, lie easy in the mire of iniquity, idly waiting till, by an irresistible act of omnipotence, God pulls
them out without any striving on their part. Multitudes
uncomfortably stick here, and will probably continue to
do so till they receive and heartily embrace that part of
the Gospel which is now, alas! called *heresy*. Then shall
these poor prisoners in giant Despair's castle find the key

of their dungeon about them, and perceive that "the word is nigh them, yea, in their mouth and in their heart; stirring up the gift of God within them, and in hope believing against hope," they will happily "lay hold on eternal life, and apprehend," by the confidence of faith, "him that has apprehended them" by convictions of sin.

But now, instead of imitating Lazarus, who, when the Lord had called him and restored life to his putrefying body, "came forth" out of his grave, though he was "bound hand and foot"; these mistaken men indolently wait till the Lord drags them out, not considering that it is more than he has promised to do. On the contrary, he reproves by his prophet, those that "do not stir themselves up to lay hold on him"; and deciding the point himself, says, "Turn ye at my reproof: behold, I will pour out my Spirit upon you; because I called and ye refused, I stretched out my hands unto you, and no man regarded, I will mock when your fear cometh."

Should you object, "that the case is not similar, because the Lord gave life to the dead body of Lazarus, whereas our souls are *dead in sin by nature.*" True, sir, *by nature;* but does not *"grace* reign" to control nature? And "as by the offence of one, judgment came upon all men to condemnation; even so, by the righteousness of one, is not the free gift come upon all men to justification of life?" According to the promise made to our first parents, and of course to all men then contained in their loins, is not "the seed of the woman *always* nigh," both to reveal and "bruise the serpent's head?" Is not Christ "the light of men—the light of the world—come into the world? Shineth he not in the darkness of our nature, even when the darkness comprehends him not? And is not this "light the life," the spiritual "life of men?" Can this be denied, if the "light is Christ," and if "Christ is the resurrection and the life," who came that "we might have life, and that we might have it more abundantly?"

In this scriptural view of free grace, what room is there for the ridiculous cavil that "Mr. Wesley wants the dead to work for life?" God, of his infinite mercy in Jesus Christ, gives to *poor sinners,* naturally dead in sin, *a talent* of free, preventing quickening grace, which "reproves them of sin"; and when it is followed, of "righteousness and judgment." This, which some Calvinists call *common grace,* is granted to all without any respect of persons; so that even the poor Jew, Herod, if he had not preferred the smiles of his Herodias to the convincing light of Christ which shone in his conscience, would have been saved as well as John the Baptist; and that poor heathen, Felix, if he had not hardened his heart in the day of his visitation, would have sweetly experienced that Christ had as much tasted death for him as he did for St. Paul. The living light visited them; but they, not "working while it was day," or refusing to "cut off the right hand," which the Lord called for, fell at last into that "night wherein no man can work; their candlestick was removed, their lamp went out." They quenched their "smoking flax," or, in other words, *their talent* unimproved was justly "taken from them." Thus, though once through grace they could work, they died while they lived; and so were, as says St. Jude, "twice dead," *dead* in Adam by that sentence, "In the day that thou eatest thereof thou shalt surely die"; and *dead* in themselves, by personally renouncing Christ the life, or rejecting the light of his convincing Spirit.

This being premised, I ask, Where is the *heresy* in this paragraph of the minutes.

"The heresy," say you, "does not consist in asserting that the believer works *from,* but *for* life!" Does it indeed? Then the Lord Jesus is the *heretic;* for Mr. Wesley only repeats what he spoke about seventeen hundred years ago: "Labour," says he, Εργαζεσθε, "work for the meat that endureth to everlasting life." Enter therefore "your protest against" St. John's Gospel, if Christ will not "formally recant it"; and not against the Minutes of his servant who dares not "take away from his Lord's words," for fear "God should take away his part out of the book of life!"

But if the Son of God be a heretic for putting the unbelieving Jews upon *working* by that dreadful word, Εργαζεσθε, St. Paul is undoubtedly an arch-heretic for corroborating it by a strong preposition: Κατεργαζεσθε says he to the Philippians, *work out*—and what is most astonishing, "work out your own salvation." *Your own salvation!* Why, Paul, this is even worse than *working for life;* for *salvation* implies a deliverance from all guilt, sin, and misery; together with obtaining the life of grace here, and the life of glory hereafter. Ah! poor legal apostle, what a pity is it thou didst not live in our evangelical age! Some, by explaining to thee the mystery of "finished salvation," or by "protesting in a body against thy dreadful heresy," might have saved "the fundamental doctrines of Christianity"; and the Richard Baxter of our age would not have had thee to bear him out in his Pharisaical and Papistical delusions!

Here you reply, that "St. Paul gives God all the glory, by maintaining that 'It is he who works in us both to will and to do of his good pleasure.'" And does not Mr. Wesley do the same? Has he not for near forty years steadily asserted that all power to think a good thought, much more to will or do a good work, is from God, by mere grace, through the merits of Jesus Christ and the agency of the Holy Spirit? If any dare to deny it, myriads of witnesses who have heard him preach, and thousands of printed sermons, hymns, and tracts dispersed through the three kingdoms will prove it.

But let us come closer to the point. Is not Christ "the bread that came down from heaven to give life to the world?" Is he not "the meat that endureth to everlasting

life?" "the meat which" he directs even the poor Caper-
naites "to work for"? Must we not *come* to him for that
meat? Is not "coming" to Christ a "work" of the heart?
Yea, "the work of God?" The work that God peculiarly
calls for? John 6:28, 29. Does not our Lord complain of
those who will not work for life, that is, "come unto him
that they might have life, or that they might have it more
abundantly?" And must not every believer "do this
work"—come to Christ for life, yea, and live upon him
every day and every hour?

Again, sir, consider these scriptures, "He that believeth hath everlasting life: he that hath the Son hath life."
Compare them with the following complaint: "None stir-
reth up himself to lay hold on God"; and with the charge
of St. Paul to Timothy, "Lay hold on eternal life." And
let us know whether "stirring up one's self to lay hold on
the God of our life," and actually "laying hold on eternal
life," are not "works," and works *for,* as well as *from* life!
And whether believers are dispensed from these works
till they come to glory!

Once more: please to tell us if praying, using ordinances, "running a race, taking up the cross, keeping under
the body, wrestling, fighting a good fight," are not works;
and if all believers are not to do them till death brings
them a discharge? If you say that "they do them *from*
life and not *for* life," you still point blank oppose our
Lord's express declaration.

Perhaps some suppose the expression of working *for*
life implies the working in order to *merit* or *purchase* life.
But, as our Lord's words convey no such idea, so Mr.
Wesley takes care positively to exclude it, by those words,
"not by the merit of works": for he knows that "eternal
life is the gift of God"; and yet with St. Paul he says,
"Labour to enter into rest, lest ye fall after the example
of Israel's unbelief": and with the great anti-Crispian
divine, Jesus Christ, he cries aloud, "Strive *to walk* in the

narrow way; agonize to enter in at the strait gate that
leads to life."

I pass to the third instance which he produces of his
having leaned too much toward Calvinism:

"III. We have received it as a maxim, *that a man is to
do nothing in order to justification.* Nothing can be more
false. Whoever desires to find favour with God, should
'cease from evil, and learn to do well.' Whoever repents,
should 'do works meet for repentance.' And if this be not
in order to find favour, what does he do them for?"

To do Mr. Wesley justice, it is necessary to consider
what he means by "justification." And, First, He does not
mean that general benevolence of our merciful God toward
sinful mankind, whereby, through the Lamb slain from
the foundation of the world, he casts a propitious look
upon them, and freely makes them partakers of "the light
that enlightens every man that cometh into the world."
This general loving kindness is certainly previous to any
thing we can do to find it; for it always prevents us, saying
to us in our very infancy, *Live;* and when we turn from
the paths of life, still crying, "Why will ye die?" In consequence of this general mercy, our Lord says, "Let little
children come unto me: for of such is the kingdom of
heaven." Much less does Mr. Wesley understand what
Dr. Crisp calls "eternal justification," which, because I do
not see it in the Scripture, I shall say nothing of.

But the "justification" he speaks of, as something that
we must "find," and "in order to which something must
be done," is either *that public and final* JUSTIFICATION
which the Lord mentions in the Gospel, "By thy words
thou shalt be justified, and by thy words thou shalt be condemned." And in this sense no man in his wits will find
fault with Mr. Wesley's assertion; as it is evident that we
must absolutely "do something," that is, speak good words,
in order to be "justified by our words." Or he means FOR-
GIVENESS, *and the* WITNESS *of it;* that wonderful transac-

tion of the Spirit of God, in a returning prodigal's conscience, by which the forgiveness of his sin is proclaimed
to him through the blood of sprinkling. This is what Mr.
Wesley and St. Paul generally mean. It is thus that "being justified by faith we have peace with God through our
Lord Jesus Christ."

And now, do not Scripture, common sense, and experience, show that "something must be done in order to
attain or find," though not to *merit* and *purchase* this
justification?

Please to answer the following questions founded upon
the express declarations of God's word: "To him that or-
dereth his conversation aright will I show the salvation
of God." Is "ordering our conversation aright," doing
nothing? "Repent ye, and be converted, that your sins
may be blotted out." Are "repentance and conversion"
nothing? "Come unto me, all ye that are heavy laden, and
I will give you rest," I will justify you. Is "coming" doing
nothing? "Cease to do evil, learn to do well. Come now,
let us reason together, and though your sins be red as
crimson they shall be white as snow," you shall be justified. Is "ceasing to do evil and learning to do well," doing
nothing? "Seek the Lord while he may be found, call upon
him while he is near. Let the wicked forsake his way, and
the unrighteous man his thoughts; and let him return unto
the Lord, and he will have mercy upon him, and to our
God, for he will abundantly pardon." Is "seeking, calling,
forsaking one's way, and returning to the Lord," a mere
nothing? "Ask, and you shall receive; seek, and you shall
find; knock, and it shall be opened unto you." Be "violent,
take even the kingdom of heaven by force." Is "seeking,
asking, knocking, and taking by force," doing absolutely
nothing? Please to answer these questions; and when
you have done, I will throw one or two hundred more of
the like kind in your way.

Let us now see whether reason is not for Mr. Wesley as well as Scripture. Do you not maintain that *believing* is necessary in order to our justification? If you do, you subscribe Mr. Wesley's *heresy;* for "believing" is not only "doing something," but necessarily supposes "a variety of things." "Faith cometh by hearing," and sometimes by *reading,* which implies "attending the ministry of the word, and searching the Scriptures," as the Bereans did. It likewise presupposes at least "the attention of the mind, and consent of the heart to a revealed truth"; or "the consideration, approbation, and receiving of an object proposed to us." Nay, it implies "renouncing worldly, and seeking Divine honour." For, says our Lord, "How can you believe who receive honour one of another, and seek not the honour that cometh of God only?" And if none can believe in Christ unto salvation, but those who give up seeking worldly honours, by a parity of reason they must give up following fleshly lusts, and putting their trust in uncertain riches. In a word, they must own themselves sick, and renounce their physicians of no value, before they can make one true application to the invaluable Physician. What a variety of things is, therefore, implied in "believing," which we cannot but acknowledge to be previous to justification! Who can then, consistently with reason, blame Mr. Wesley for saying *"something* must be done in order to justification?"

When the poor woman has lost her "piece of silver, she lights a candle," says our Lord, "she sweeps the house, and searches diligently till she find it." Mr. Wesley asks, "If she do not do ALL this *in order to find it,* what does she do it for?" At this the alarm is taken; and the post carries, through various provinces, printed letters against old Mordecai; and a synod is called together to *protest* against the dreadful error!

Having defended Mr. Wesley's third proposition from Scripture and common sense, permit me to do it also from

experience. And here I might appeal to the most established persons in Mr. Wesley's societies; but as their
testimony may have little weight with you, I waive it, and
appeal to all the accounts of *sound* conversions that have
been published since Calvin's days. Show me one, sir,
wherein it appears that a mourner in Sion found the above
described justification, without *doing* some previous
"works meet for repentance." If you cannot produce one
such instance, Mr. Wesley's doctrine is supported by the
printed experiences of all the converted Calvinists, as
well as of all the believers in his own societies. Nor am I
afraid to appeal even to the experience of your own
friends. If any one of these can say, with a good conscience, that he found the above described justification
without first stopping in the career of outward sin, without praying, seeking, and confessing his guilt and misery,
I promise to give up the Minutes. But if none can make
such a declaration, you must grant, sir, that experience is
on Mr. Wesley's side, as much as reason, revelation, the
best Calvinists, and yourself. I say *yourself:*

Give me leave to produce but one instance: page 76 of
your sermons, you address those "who see themselves destitute of that knowledge of God which is eternal life," the
very same thing that Mr. Wesley calls justification; and
which you define, "a home-felt knowledge of God, by the
experience of his *love* being *shed abroad in our hearts by
the Holy Ghost given unto us: the Spirit of God bearing
witness with our spirits that we are the children of God"*;
and you recommend to them "to *seek* and *press* after it."
Now, sir, "seeking and pressing after it" is certainly "doing something in order to find it."

I say to two beggars, "Hold out your hand; here is an
alms for you." The one complies, and the other refuses.
Who in the world will dare to say that my charity is no
more *a free gift,* because I bestow it only upon the man
that held out his hand? Will nothing make it *free* but

my wrenching his hand open, or forcing my bounty down his throat? Again: the king says to four rebels, "Throw down your arms; surrender, and you shall have a place both in my favour and at court." One of them obeys, and becomes a great man; the others, upon refusal, are caught and hanged. What sophister will face me down that the pardon and place of the former are not *freely* bestowed upon him, because he did something in order to obtain them? Once more:

The God of providence says, "If you plough, sow, harrow, fence, and weed your fields, I will give the increase, and you shall have a crop." Farmers obey: and are they to believe that because they do so many things toward their harvest, it is *not the free gift* of Heaven? Do not all those who fear God know that their ground, seed, cattle, strength, yea, and their very life, are the gifts of God? Does not this prevent their claiming a crop as a *debt;* and make them confess, that though it was suspended on their ploughing, etc., it is the *unmerited bounty of Heaven?*

Apply this, sir, to the present case; and you will see that our *doing something in order to justification* does not in the least hinder it from being a *free gift;* because whatever we do in order to it, we do it "by the grace of God" preventing us, that we may have a good will, and working with us when we have that good will; all being a free, most absolutely free grace through the merits of Christ. And, nevertheless, so sure as a farmer, in the appointed ways of Providence, shall have no harvest if he does nothing toward it; a professor in the appointed ways of grace, (let him *talk* of "finished salvation" all the year round,) shall go without justification and salvation, unless he do something toward them. (My comparison is scriptural:) "He that now goeth on his way weeping," says the psalmist, "and beareth forth good seed, shall doubtless come again with joy, and bring his sheaves with him." "Be not deceived," says the apostle, "whatsoever a man soweth, that shall he also reap; and he *only* that soweth to the Spirit shall of the Spirit reap life everlasting." David, therefore, and St. Paul must be proved enemies to free grace before Mr. Wesley can be represented as such: for they both did something in order to justification; they both "sowed in tears," before they "reaped in joy"; their doctrine and experience went hand in hand together.

J. FLETCHER.

LETTER IV

HONOURED AND REVEREND SIR: If the three first propositions of the Minutes are Scriptural, Mr. Wesley may well begin the remaining part, by desiring the preachers in his connection to emerge, along with him, from under the noisy billows of prejudice, and to struggle quite out of the muddy streams of Antinomian delusions which have so long gone over our heads, and carried so many souls down the channels of vice, into the lake that burneth with fire and brimstone. Well may he entreat them to "review the whole affair."

And why should this modest request alarm any one? Though error dreads a revisal, truth, you know, cannot but gain by it.

Mr. Wesley says in this REVIEW,

"I. *Who is now accepted of God? He that now 'believes in Christ with a loving, obedient heart.'*"

Excellent answer! Worthy of St. Paul and St. James; for it sums up in one line the epistles of both. In the FIRST part of it, ("he that now believes in Christ,") you see St. Paul's Gospel calculated for lost sinners, who now fly from the Babel of self righteousness and sin, and find "all things" in Christ "ready" for their reception. And in the SECOND part, ("with a loving and obedient heart,") you see the strong bulwark raised by St. James to guard the truth of the Gospel against the attacks of Antinomian and Laodicean professors. Had he said, "He that shall believe

the next hour is *now* accepted," he would have bestowed
upon present unbelief the blessing that is promised to
present faith. Had he said, "He that believed a year ago
is *now* accepted of God," he would have opened the kingdom of heaven to apostates, contrary to St. Paul's declarations to the Hebrews. He therefore very properly says,
"He that *now* believes:" for it is written, "He that believeth," (not he that *shall* believe, or he that *did* believe,)
"hath everlasting life."

What fault can you then find with Mr. Wesley here?
Surely you cannot blame him for proposing Christ as the
object of the Christian's faith, or for saying that the *believer* hath a loving and obedient heart; for he speaks of
the *accepted man,* and not of him who *comes for acceptance.*

"II. *But who among those that never heard of Christ?
He that feareth God and worketh righteousness, according to the light he has.*"

And where is the error here? Did not St. Peter begin
his evangelical sermon to Cornelius by these very words,
prefaced by some others that make them remarkably em-
phatical? "Of a truth I perceive that God is no respecter
of persons; but in every nation he that feareth God and
worketh righteousness is accepted of him." Surely, sir,
you will never insist upon a formal recantation of a plain
scripture.

FIRST OBJECTION. But perhaps you object to those
words which Mr. Wesley has added to St. Peter's declaration, "according to the light he hath."

ANSWER. What, should it be "according to the light
he has *not?*" Are not there people enough among us who
follow the wicked servant that intimated his Lord "was
a hard and austere man, reaping where he had not sown,
and gathering where he had not strewed?" Must Mr.
Wesley increase the number? Or would you have him
insinuate that God is more cruel than Pharaoh, who

granted the poor Israelites daylight, if he allowed them *no straw* to make bricks; that he requires a heathen to work without any degree of *light,* without a *day* of visitation, in the Egyptian darkness of a merely natural state. And that he will then damn and torment him everlastingly, either for not doing, or for marring his work? O, sir, like yourself, Mr. Wesley is too evangelical to entertain such notions of the God of love.

"At this rate," say some, "a heathen may be saved without a Saviour. His *fearing God and working righteousness* will not go for the blood and righteousness of Christ." Mr. Wesley has no such thought. Whenever a heathen is accepted, it is merely through the merits of Christ; although it is in consequence of his *fearing God and working righteousness.* "But how comes he to see that God is to be feared, and that righteousness is his delight?" Because a beam of our Sun of righteousness shines in his darkness. All is therefore of grace; the light, the works of righteousness done by that light, and acceptance in consequence of them.

SECOND OBJECTION. "Mr. Wesley, by allowing the possibility of a righteous heathen's salvation, goes point blank against the eighteenth article of our Church, which he has solemnly subscribed."

ANSWER. This assertion is groundless. Mr. Wesley, far from presuming to say that a heathen "can be saved by the law or sect that he professes, if he frames his life according to the light of nature," cordially believes that all the heathens who are saved, attain salvation through the name, that is, through the merits and Spirit of Christ; by framing their life, not according to I know not what light naturally received from fallen Adam, but according to the supernatural light which Christ graciously affords them in the dispensations they are under.

THIRD OBJECTION. "However, if he does not impugn the eighteenth article, he does the thirteenth, which says, that 'works done before justification, or before the grace of Christ and the inspiration of his Spirit, forasmuch as they proceed not from faith in Christ, are not pleasant to God, yea, have the nature of sin.'"

ANSWER. Nay, this article does not affect Mr. Wesley's doctrine; for he constantly maintains that if the works of a Melchisedec, a Job, a Plato, a Cornelius, are accepted, it is only because they follow the general justification above mentioned, (which is possibly what St. Paul calls the "free gift that comes upon all men to justification of life," Rom. 5: 18,) and because they proceed FROM "the grace of Christ, and the inspiration of his Spirit," they are not therefore done BEFORE that grace and inspiration, as are the works which the article condemns.

FOURTH OBJECTION. "But 'all that is not of faith is sin, and without faith it is impossible to please God.'"

ANSWER. True: therefore, "he that cometh to God must believe that he is, and that he is a rewarder of them that diligently seek him." Cornelius had undoubtedly this faith, and a degree of it is found in all sincere heathens. For Christ, the Light of men, visits all, though in a variety of degrees and dispensations. He said to the carnal Jews that believed not on him, "Yet a little while the light is with you; walk while ye have the light, lest darkness come upon you. While ye have the light, believe in the light, that ye may be the children of the light." All the heathens that are saved are then saved by a lively faith in Jesus, "the Light of the world"; or to use our Lord's own words, by "believing in the light" of their dispensation, before the day of their visitation is past, before total "darkness comes upon them," even the night when "no man can work."

FIFTH OBJECTION. "But if heathens can be saved without the Gospel, what need is there of the Christian dispensation?"

ANSWER, (1.) None of them were ever saved without a beam of the internal light of the Gospel, which is preached "in ϵν every creature under heaven," Col. 1:23. (2.) The argument may be retorted. If sinners could be saved under the patriarchal dispensation, what need was there of the Mosaic? If under the Mosaic, what need of John's baptism? If under the baptism of John, what need of Christianity? Or to answer by a comparison: If we see our way by starlight, what need is there of moonshine? If by moonshine, what need of the dawn of day? If by the dawn of day, what need of the rising sun?

The brightness of Divine dispensations, like the light of the righteous, "shines more and more unto the perfect day." And though a heathen may be saved in his low dispensation, and attain unto a low degree of glory, which the apostle compares to the shining of a star, ("for in my Father's house," says Christ, "there are *many mansions*,") yet it is an unspeakable advantage to be saved from the darkness attending his uncomfortable dispensation, into the full enjoyment of the "life and immortality brought to light by the *explicit* Gospel." Well might then the angel say to Cornelius, who was already accepted according to his dispensation, that Peter should "tell him words whereby he should be saved"; saved from the weakness, darkness, bondage, and tormenting fears attending his present state, into that blessed state of light, comfort, liberty, power, and glorious joy, where "he that is feeble is as David, and the house of David as God, or as the angel of the Lord."

Having thus briefly answered the objections that are advanced against St. Peter's and Mr. Wesley's doctrine, proceed we to the third query, in the review of the whole affair.

"III. *Is this the same with, he that is sincere? Nearly, if not quite.*"

In the name of charity where is the error of this answer? Where the shadow of heresy? Do you suppose by—*he that is sincere,* Mr. Wesley means "a carnal, unawakened wretch who boasts of his imaginary sincerity?" No, sir, he means "one who, in God's account, and not barely in his own, sincerely and uprightly follows the light of his dispensation." Now, if you expose Mr. Wesley as guilty of heresy, for using this word once, what protests will you enter against St. Paul for using it over and over? How will you blame him for desiring the Ephesians, (according to the beautiful reading of our margin,) to "be sincere in love!" αληθευοντες εν αγαπη. Or for wishing nothing greater to his dear Philippians, than that they might be "sincere in the day of Christ!" O, sir, to fear, and much more, to love the Lord "in sincerity," is a great and rare thing! Eph. 6:24. We find every where too much of the "old leaven of malice," and too little of "the unleavened bread of sincerity and truth," I Cor. 5:8. Think not therefore that Mr. Wesley betrays the cause of God, because he thinks that "to be sincere," and to "fear God and work righteousness," are expressions nearly, if not quite, synonymous.

But you do not perhaps find fault with Mr. Wesley for setting accepted heathens too low, but too high, by giving them the character of being sincere. For you know that our translators render the Hebrew word *tamim* sometimes "sincere," at other times "upright, undefiled," and most commonly "perfect." As in these sentences, "Noah was a *perfect* man, Job was a *perfect* man," etc. May not then Mr. Wesley secretly bring in his abominable doctrine of PERFECTION, under the less frightful expression of *sincerity?* Of this more by and by.

In the meantime, I shall close my vindication of the second and third query by the sentiments of two unquestionable Protestants on the present subject. The one is Mr. Henry, in his comment on St. Peter's words: "God,"

says he, "never did, nor ever will reject an honest Gentile who fears God and worships him, and works righteousness; that is, is just and charitable toward all men,
who lives up to the light he has, in a sincere devotion and
regular conversation. Wherever God finds an *upright*
man, he will be found an *upright* God, Psalms 18: 25. And
those that have not the knowledge of Christ, and therefore cannot have an explicit regard to him, may yet receive grace for his sake, 'to fear God and work righteousness'; and wherever God gives grace to do so, as he did to
Cornelius, he will, through Christ, accept the work of his
own hands." Here, sir, you have the very doctrine of
Mr. Wesley quite down to the heretical word *sincere.*

The other divine, sir, is yourself. You tell us in your
sermon on the same text, that "we cannot but admire and
adore God's universal tenderness and pity for every people and nation under heaven, in that 'he willeth not the
death of any single sinner,' but accepteth every one into
Gospel covenant with him, 'who feareth him and worketh
righteousness,' according to the light imparted to him."

Now, sir, where is the difference between your *orthodoxy* and Mr. Wesley's *heresy?* He asserts, God accepts
"him that *fears God and works righteousness* according
to the light he has." Mr. Henry says, "him that lives up
to the light he has"; and you, sir, "him *who feareth God
and worketh righteousness* according to the light imparted
to him." If Mr. Wesley must share the fate of Shadrach
for his heresy, I doubt Mr. Henry will have that of Me-
shech, and you, of Abednego; for you are all three in the
same honourable condemnation.

But Mr. Wesley, foreseeing that some will be offended
at St. Peter's evangelical declaration concerning the acceptance of sincere heathens who work righteousness,
proposes and answers the following objection:

"IV. *Is not this salvation by works? Not by the merit
of works, but by works as a condition."*

In the former part of this answer Mr. Wesley freely grants all you can require to guard the Gospel against the Popish doctrine of making satisfaction for sin, and meriting salvation by works:· for he maintains, that, though God accepts the heathen who work righteousness, yet it is not through the merit of his works, but solely through that of Christ. Is not this the very doctrine of our Church, in her eleventh article, which treats of justification? "We are accounted righteous before God only for the *merit of our Lord Jesus Christ* by faith, and not for our own works, or *deservings.*"

If you say, that "his heresy does not consist in exploding the merit of works in point of salvation, but in using that legal expression, *salvation by works as a condition*"; I answer, that as I would not contend for the word *trinity*, because it is not in the Bible; no, nor yet for the word *perfection*, though it is there; neither would I contend for the expression, *salvation by works, as a condition:* but the *thing* Mr. Wesley means by it is there in a hundred different turns and modes of expression. Therefore it is highly worth contending for: and so much the more, as it is, next to the doctrine of the atonement, the most important part of "the faith once delivered unto the saints."

St. Paul, the evangelical Paul, says the same thing in a variety of expressions: "If any man love not the Lord Jesus, let him be anathema." If *love*, the noblest work of the heart, does not take place, the fearful curse will: "If ye live after the flesh, ye shall die"; but "if ye through the Spirit do mortify the deeds of the body, ye shall live." *Spiritual mortification* is here the condition. "Without holiness no man shall see the Lord." Here *holiness* is the condition. "Be not deceived, neither fornicators, nor covetous, nor drunkards, nor thieves, nor revilers, shall inherit the kingdom of God." Here ceasing from *fornication, drunkenness*, etc., is the same condition.

St. John is in the same condemnation as Mr. Wesley, for he declares, "There shall in no wise enter into the New Jerusalem any thing that defileth, neither whatsoever worketh abomination, or maketh a lie." Here the condition is, *not working abominations,* etc. "Whosoever hateth his brother is a murderer," and "ye know that no murderer hath eternal life." Here the condition is, *ceasing from hatred,* the murder of the heart.

St. Peter is equally deep in the heresy. In a variety of expressions he describes the misery and fatal latter end of those "who escape the pollution of the world, through the knowledge of the Lord Jesus, and are again entangled therein," through the non-performance of this condition, *"If ye do these things, ye shall never fall."*

As for St. James, I need not quote him. You know that, when Luther was in his heat, he could have found it in his heart to tear this precious epistle from among the sacred books, and burn it as *an epistle of straw.* He thought the author of it was an enemy to *free grace,* and abettor of Popish tenets, an antichrist. It is true, the scales of prejudice fell at last from his eyes; but, alas! it was not till he had seen the Antinomian boar lay waste the Lord's flourishing vineyard all over Protestant Germany. Then was he glad to draw against him St. James's despised sword; and I shall be happily mistaken, sir, if you are not obliged one day to make use of the *heretical Minutes,* as he did of the epistle of straw.

How justly does Mr. Wesley ask next:

"V. *What have we then been disputing about for these thirty years? I am afraid, about words."*

Pardon me, sir, if here also I cannot, with you cry *heresy!* Far from doing it, I admire the candour of an aged servant of God, who, instead of stiffly holding, and obstinately maintaining an old mistake, comes down as a little child, and freely acknowledges it before a respect-

able body of preachers, whose esteem it is his interest
to secure. O how many are there that look upon Mr.
Wesley as a rotten threshold, and themselves as pillars in
the temple of God, who would not own themselves mistaken for the world!

He says, "I am afraid we have disputed about words":
perhaps he might have said, "I am very sure of it." How
many disputes have been raised these thirty years among
religious people, about those works of the heart which
St. Paul calls "repentance toward God, and faith in our
Lord Jesus Christ!" Some have called them *the only way*
or *method* of receiving salvation, others *the means* of salvation, others *the terms* of it. Some have named them
duties or *graces* necessary to salvation, others *conditions*
of salvation, others *parts* of salvation, or *privileges* annexed to it; while others have gone far round about, and
used I know not what far-fetched expressions and ambigu-
ous phrases to convey the same idea. I say *the same idea;*
for if all maintain that although *repentance* and *works
meet for it,* and *faith working by love,* are not meritorious,
they are nevertheless absolutely necessary; that they are
a thing *sine qua non,* all are agreed; and that if they *dispute,* it must be, as Mr. Wesley justly intimates, *about
words.*

Let us leave them to the uneasy workings of their unaccountable panic, to consider the next article of the
Minutes.

"VI. *As to merit itself, of which we have been so
dreadfully afraid: We are rewarded according to our
works, yea, because of our works. How does this differ
from, for the sake of our works? And how differs this
from secundum merita operum? 'as our works deserve?'
Can you split this hair? I doubt, I cannot.*"

If Mr. Wesley meant that we are saved by the *merit of
works,* and not by the alone merits of Christ, you might
exclaim against his proposition as erroneous; and I would

echo back your exclamation. But as he flatly denies it, No. 4, in those words, "not by the merit of works," and has constantly asserted the contrary for above thirty years, we cannot, without monstrous injustice, fix that sense upon the word *merit* in this paragraph.

The latter assertion is not less evident from the repeated declarations of God: "BECAUSE thou hast kept the word of my patience, I also will keep thee from the hour of temptation, which shall come upon all the world." Rev. iii, 10. "BECAUSE Phinehas was zealous for his God," in killing Zimri and Cosbi, "behold I give unto him my covenant of peace, and he shall have it, and his seed after him, even the covenant of an everlasting priesthood." And again: "BECAUSE thou hast done this, and hast not withheld thy son, by myself have I sworn that in blessing I will bless thee, *because* thou hast obeyed my voice." Now, says Mr. Wesley, "How differs this from, 'I will bless thee, for the sake of thy obedience to my voice?' And how differs this from *secundum merita obedientiœ?* 'as thy obedience deserves?' " And by comparing the difference of these expressions to *the splitting of a hair,* or to a metaphysical subtilty, he very justly insinuates that we have been too dreadfully afraid of the word *merit.* Surely, sir, you will not divest yourself of the candour that belongs to a Christian, to put on the bitter zeal of a bigot. You will not run, for fear of Popery, into the very spirit of it, by crying, *Heresy! heresy!* before you have maturely considered the question: or, if you have done so once, you will do it no more. And if Mr. Wesley should ever propose again "the splitting of a hair," I hope you will remember that equity (to say nothing of brotherly love) requires you to split the hair *first* yourself, before you can with decency stir up people far and near against him, for modestly doubting whether he can do it or no.

I own, I believe there is such a dignity in every thing in which the Son of God has a hand, that the Father, who is always well pleased with him and his works, cannot but look upon it with peculiar complacency. Even a "cup of water given in his *dear* name," that is, by the efficacy of his loving Spirit, hath that in it which "shall in no wise lose its reward;" for it has something of the love of the God-man, Jesus Christ, which merits all the approbation and smiles of the Father.

In our well-meant zeal against Popery we have been driven to an extreme, and have not done *good works* justice. "I am the Vine," says Jesus, "and ye are the branches: he that abideth in me bringeth forth much fruit. Herein is my Father glorified, that ye bear much fruit." What! is the Father glorified in the fruit of believers? And shall this fruit be represented to us always grub-eaten, and rotten at the core? Do we honour either the Vine or the husbandman, while one hour we speak wonders of the Vine and its fruit, and the next represent the branches and their fruit as full of deadly poison? O God of mercy and patience, forgive us, for we know not what we do! We even think we do thee service. O give us *genuine,* and save us from *voluntary,* humility!

Having explained and vindicated the sixth article of the Minutes, I proceed to the

"VII. *The grand objection to one of the preceding propositions is drawn from matter of fact. God does, in fact, justify those who, by their own confession, neither 'feared God, nor wrought righteousness.' Is this an exception to the rule? It is a doubt, if God make any exception at all. But how are we sure that the person in question never did 'fear God and work righteousness?' His own saying so is not proof: for we know how all that are convinced of sin undervalue themselves in every respect.*"

Do you think, sir, the "heresy" of this proposition consists in intimating that God does, in fact, justify those

who fear him, and not those who make asolutely no stop
in the downward road of open sin and flagrant iniquity?
If it does, I am sure the sacred writers are heretics to a
man. See the account we have of conversions in the
Scripture; please to remember what Mr. Wesley means
by justification, and then answer the following questions: —

Did not the prodigal son "come to himself," repent,
and return to his father, before he received the kiss of
peace? Did not the woman that was a sinner forsake her
wicked course of life before our Lord said to her, "Go in
peace, thy sins are forgiven thee?"

Again: was not the woman of Samaria convinced of
sin, yea, of "all that ever she did," before our Lord revealed himself to her, to enable her to believe unto
justification? Did not Zaccheus evidence his *fear of God*,
yea, and "work righteousness," by hearty offers of resti-
tution, before Christ testified that he was "a son of Abraham"? Did not St. Paul express his fear of God, and
readiness to work righteousness, when he cried out, "Lord,
what wouldst thou have me to do?" Yea, did he not produce "fruit meet for repentance," by praying three days
and three nights, before Ananias was sent to direct him
"how to wash away his sins?" Did not the eunuch and
Cornelius fear God? Did not David himself, whom the
apostle mentions as a grand instance of justification without the merit of works, fear God from his youth? And
when he had wrought folly in Israel, was he not humbled
for his sin, before he was washed from it? Did he not
confess his crime, and say, "I have sinned," before Nathan said by Divine commission, "The Lord hath put
away thy sin?"

Does not St. Paul himself carry Mr. Wesley's "heresy"
so far as to say, "Whosoever among you feareth God, to
you is the word of this salvation sent?" Acts 13:26. Must
we so understand Rom. 4:5, as to make him contradict,

point blank, his own declarations, his own experience, and the account of all the above mentioned conversions? Certainly not. Those words, "God justifies the ungodly, and him that worketh not, but believeth in Jesus," when candidly explained, agree perfectly with Mr. Wesley's doctrine. (1) By "the ungodly," the apostle does not mean "the wicked that does not forsake his way"; but the man who, before he believed to justification, was ungodly, and still remains ungodly in the eye of the law of works, needing daily forgiveness by grace, even after he is made godly in a Gospel sense. (2) By "him that worketh not" St. Paul does not mean a lazy, indolent wretch, who, without any reluctance, follows the stream of his corrupt nature; but "a penitent," who, whatever works he does, has no dependence upon them, esteems them as nothing, yea, "as dung and dross *in comparison of* the excellency of Christ"; and, in short, one who does not work to merit or purchase his justification, but comes to receive that invaluable blessing as a free gift. (3) That this is the meaning of the apostle is evident from his adding, that he who "worketh not," yet "believeth." For if he took the word "worketh not," in an absolute sense, he could never make it agree with "believing," which is certainly a *work*, yea, a work of our noblest part; for "with the heart man believeth to righteousness." Add to this, sir, that justifying faith, as I observed before, never comes without her forerunner, conviction; nor conviction of sin without suitable tempers or inward works. "There is nothing," says Dr. Owen, "that I will more firmly adhere to in this whole doctrine, than the necessity of convictions previous to true believing; as also displacency, sorrow, fear, a desire of deliverance, with other necessary effects of true convictions." St. Paul, therefore, is consistent with himself, and Mr. Wesley with St. Paul.

Again: if God justify sinners merely as "ungodly," and people that "work not," why should he not justify *all*

sinners; for they are all ungodly, and there is "none of
them that does good, no, not one?" Why did not the
Pharisee, for example, go to his house justified as well as
the publican? You will probably answer, that "he was
not convinced of sin." Why, sir, this is just what Mr. Wesley maintains. Express yourself in St. Peter's words, "He
did not *fear God"; or in those of John the Baptist, "He
did not *bring forth fruits meet for repentance."*

Should some ask, "What *works meet for repentance*
did the woman caught in adultery do, before our Lord
justified her?" I would ask, in my turn, how do they know
that the Lord justified her? Do they conclude it from those
words, "Neither do I condemn thee?" Does not the context show, that as the Pharisees had not condemned her to
be stoned, according to the Mosaic law, neither would our
Lord take upon himself to pass sentence upon her, according to his declaration on another occasion, "I am not sent
to condemn the world, but that the world through me
might be saved?" This by no means implies, that the
world is justified in St. Paul's sense, Rom. 5:1. But supposing she was justified, how do you know that our Lord's
words, writing, looks, and grace, had not brought her to
godly shame and sorrow, that is, to "the fear of God,"
and "the working of *internal* righteousness," before he
gave her the peace that passes all understanding?

After all, Mr. Wesley says, with modesty and wisdom,
"It is a doubt whether God makes any exception at all":
and it lies upon you to show there is in these words any
thing contrary to the humility of the true Christian, and
orthodoxy of the sound divine. But please to remember,
that if you judge of orthodoxy according to the works of
Dr. Crisp, we will take the liberty to appeal to the word
of God.

But you make, perhaps, Mr. Wesley's heresy in this
proposition consist in his refusing to take the word of
persons convinced of sin, when they say they never

"feared God nor wrought righteousness." "For we know," says he, "how all that are convinced of sin, undervalue themselves in every respect."

Had Mr. Wesley imagined that some Christian friends (O my God, deliver me from such friendship!) would leave no stone unturned to procure a copy of his Minutes, in order to find some occasion against him, he would probably have worded this with more circumspection. But he wrote for real friends; and he knew such would at once enter into his meaning, which is, that "persons deeply convinced of sin are apt, very apt, to form a wrong judgment both of their state and performances, and to think the worst of themselves in every respect, that is, both with regard to what Divine grace does in them, and by them."

And this is so obvious a truth, that he must be a novice indeed in Christian experience who doubts of it for a moment; and a great lover of disputing, who will make a man an offender for so true an assertion. Do not we daily see some, in whom the arrows of conviction stick fast, who think they are as much past recovery as Satan himself? Do not we hear others complain, "they grow worse and worse," when they only discover more and more how bad they are by nature? And are there not some, who bind upon themselves heavy burdens of their own making, and when they cannot bear them, are tormented in their consciences with imaginary guilt; while others are ready to go distracted through groundless fears of having committed the sin against the Holy Ghost? In a word, do we not see hundreds, who, when they have reason to hope well of their state, think there is no hope for them? In all these respects do they not act like Jonah in the whale's belly, and complain, "I am cast out of thy sight?" And have not they need to encourage themselves in their God, and say, "Why art thou cast down, O my soul?"

But let your conscience speak, sir, on this matter. When some deep mourners have complained to you of their misery, danger, and desperate state, did you never drop a word of comfort to this effect—"You undervalue yourselves; you write too bitter things against yourselves; your case is not so bad as your unbelieving fears represent it: God's thoughts are not as your thoughts. Many, like the foolish virgins, think themselves sure of heaven, when they stand on the brink of hell; and many think they are just dropping into it, who are not far from the kingdom of God."

Yea, and as it is with real seekers, so it is with real believers. Did not they undervalue, yea, degrade themselves, by the remains of their unbelief; or, which is the same, did they live up to their dignity, and every where consider themselves as "members of Christ, children of God, and inheritors of the kingdom of heaven," "what manner of persons," yea, what angels "would they be in all holy conversation!"

One more article remains, and if it does not contain "the dreadful heresy," which hitherto we have looked for in vain, the Minutes are, from first to last, scripturally orthodox, and you have given Churchmen and dissenters a false alarm.

"VIII. Does not talking of a justified and sanctified state tend to mislead men? Almost naturally leading them to trust in what was done in one moment? whereas we are every hour, and every moment, pleasing or displeasing to God, according to our works—according to the whole of our inward tempers and outward behaviour."

To do this proposition justice, and prevent misunderstandings, I must premise some observations.

1. Mr. Wesley is not against persons talking of justification and sanctification in a Scriptural sense: for when he "knows the tree by the fruits," he says himself to his

flocks, as St. Paul did to the Corinthians, "Some of you are sanctified and justified." Nor does he deny that God justifies a penitent sinner in a moment, and that in a moment "he can manifest himself" unto his believing people "as he does not to the world, and give them an inheritance among them that are sanctified, through faith in Jesus." His objection respects only the idea entertained by some, and countenanced by others, that when God forgives us our sins, he introduces us into a state where we are unalterably fixed in his blessed favour, and for ever stamped with his holy image; so that it matters no longer whether the tree is barren or not, whether it produces good or bad fruit; it was set at such a time, and therefore it must be a "tree of righteousness" still. A conclusion directly contrary to the words of our Lord and his beloved disciple: "By their fruits ye shall know them. He that sinneth is of the devil. Every branch in me that beareth not fruit, [much more that beareth evil fruit,] my Father taketh away."

2. Permit me, sir, to observe also, that Mr. Wesley has many persons in his societies, (and would to God there were none in ours!) who profess they were justified or sanctified in a moment; but instead of trusting in the living God, so trust to what was done in that moment, as to give over "taking up their cross daily, and watching unto prayer with all perseverance." The consequences are deplorable; they slide back into the spirit of the world; and their tempers are no more regulated by the meek, gentle, humble love of Jesus. Some inquire with the heathens, "What shall we eat, and what shall we drink," to please ourselves? Others evidently, "love the world, lay up treasures on earth," or ask, "wherewith shall we be *fashionably* clothed?" Therefore "the love of the Father is not in them." And not a few are "led captive by the devil at his will"; influenced by his unhappy suggestions, they harbour bitterness, malice, and revenge; none is in

the right but themselves, and "wisdom shall die with them."

Now, sir, Mr. Wesley cannot but fear it is not well with persons who are in any of these cases. Though every body should join to extol them as "dear children of God," he is persuaded that "Satan has beguiled them as he did Eve"; and he addresses them as our Lord did the angel of the Church of Sardis, "I know thy works, that thou hast a name that thou livest, and art dead, [or dying:] repent, therefore, and strengthen the things which remain, that are ready to die; for I have not found thy works perfect before God." Mr. Wesley hath the word of prophecy, which he thinks more sure than the opinion of a world of professors; and, according to that word, he sees that "they who are led by the Spirit of God are the sons of God," and that God's Spirit does not lead into the vanities of the world, or indulgences of fleshly lusts, any more than into the pride or malice of Satan. Nor does he think that those are not "under the law" who can merrily laugh at the law, and pass jests upon Moses, the venerable servant of God. But with St. Paul he asserts, that when people are "under grace, and not under the law, sin hath not dominion over them." With our Lord he declares, "He who committeth sin, is the servant of sin"; and with his prophet, that "God is of purer eyes than to behold iniquity" with the least degree of approbation. In short, he believes that God, being unchangeable in his holiness, cannot but always "love righteousness and hate iniquity"; and that, as the heart is continually working either iniquity or righteousness, and as God cannot but be pleased at the one, and displeased at the other, he is continually pleased or displeased with us, according to the workings of our hearts, and the fruits which they outwardly produce.

Perhaps you object to the word "every moment." But why should you, sir? If it be not *every moment,* it is *never.* If God do not approve holiness, and disapprove sin every moment, he never does it, for he changes not. If he do it only now and then, he is such a one as ourselves; for even wicked men will approve righteousness and condemn unrighteousness by fits and starts. I may every moment harbour malice in my heart, and so commit internal murder. If God winks at this one instant, why not two? And so on to days, months, and years? Does the *duration* of moral evil constitute sin? May not I be guilty of the greatest enormity in the twinkling of an eye? And is it not the ordinary property of the most horrid crimes, such as robbery and adultery, that they are soon finished?

Do not say, sir, that this doctrine sets aside "salvation by faith." It is highly consistent with it. He that, in God's account, does the best works, has the most faith, most of the sap of eternal life that flows from the heavenly Vine. And he that has most faith has most of Christ's likeness, and is of course most pleasing to God, who cannot be pleased but with Christ and his living image. On the other hand, he that in God's account does the worst works, and has the worst tempers, has most unbelief. He that has most unbelief, is most "like his father, the devil"; and must consequently be most displeasing to him that accepts us "in the Beloved," and not "in the wicked one."

Having premised these obstructions, I come closer to the point, and assert that if we are not every moment pleasing or displeasing to God, according to the works of our hearts and hands, you must set your seal to the following absurdities:

(1) "God is angry with the wicked all the day," and yet there are moments in which he is not angry at them. (2) Lot *pleased* God as much in those moments in which he got drunk and committed incest with his daughters, as in the day he exercised hospitality toward the disguised angels. (3) David did not *displease* God more

when he committed adultery with Bathsheba, and im-
brued his hands in her husband's blood, than when he
danced before the ark, or composed the 103d Psalm. (4)
Solomon was as acceptable to God in the moment when
"his wives turned away his heart after other gods," as
when he chose wisdom, and his speech pleased the Lord,
when he went after the goddess Ashtaroth, and built a
high place to bloody Moloch, as when he represented our
Melchisedec, and dedicated the temple. (5) Again: you
must set your seal to these propositions of Dr. Crisp:
"From the time thy transgressions were laid upon Christ,
thou ceasest to be a transgressor to the last hour of thy
life; so that now thou art not an idolater, thou art not a
thief, etc.; thou art not a sinful person, whatsoever sin
thou commitest." (6) In short, sir, you must be of the
sentiment of the wildest Antinomian I ever knew, who,
because he had once a bright manifestation of pardon, not
only concludes that he is safe, though he lives in open sin,
but asserts God would no more be *displeased* with him
for whoring and stealing, than for praying and receiving
the sacrament.

Again: It is an important truth, that we may please
God for a time, and yet afterward displease him. St. Paul
mentions those who, by putting away a good conscience,
"concerning faith made shipwreck," and therefore pleased
God no longer, "seeing that without faith it is impossible
to please him."

I know one, sir, who was burned as "a dreadful heretic,"
that did not go farther in this heresy than you do. And
that is good Bishop Latimer, my second witness. He not
only affirmed that "Christ shed as much blood for Judas
as he did for Peter," but roundly asserted, "We may one
time be in the book, and another out; as it appeareth by
David, who was written in the book of life; but when he
sinned with a high hand, [which, by the by, we may do
every moment,] he, at the same time, was out of the favour

of God, until he had repented; out of Christ, who is the book in which all believers are written." (*Latimer's Sermon on the Third Sunday after Epiphany.*)

Thus, sir, have I looked out for "the heresy," the dreadful heresy of Mr. Wesley's Minutes, by bringing all the propositions they contain to the touchstone of Scripture and common sense; but, instead of finding it, I have found the very marrow of the Gospel of Christ, so far as it is opposed to Dr. Crisp's Antinomian Gospel; which at this time would overflow our little Sion, if God did not sit above the water floods, and say to the proudest billows of error, "Hitherto shall ye come, and no farther." I have showed that the Minutes contain nothing but what is truly scriptural, and nothing but what the best Calvinist divines have themselves directly or indirectly asserted; except perhaps the sixth proposition concerning *the merit of works;* and with respect to this, I hope I have demonstrated, upon rational and evangelical principles, that Mr. Wesley, far from "bringing in a damnable heresy," has done the Gospel justice, and Protestantism service, by candidly giving up an old prejudice, equally contrary to Scripture and good sense, a piece of bigotry which hath long hardened the Papists against the doctrine of "salvation by the merit of Christ," and hath added inconceivable strength to the Antinomian delusion among us. One difficulty remains, and that is, to account for your attacking Mr. Wesley, though you could not wound him without stabbing yourself. Reserving my reflections upon this amazing step for another letter, I remain your astonished servant, in the bonds of a peaceful Gospel,

J. FLETCHER.

LETTER V

HONOURED AND REVEREND SIR: Having vindicated both some important doctrines of the Gospel, and an eminent servant of Christ, from the charge of "dreadful heresy";

I will not take the liberty of a friend to expostulate a little with *you.*

When Brutus, among other senators, rushed upon Caesar, the venerable general, as he wrapped himself in his mantle, just said, "And art thou also among them? Even thou, my son?" May not Mr. Wesley address you sir, in the same words, and add, "If a body of men must be raised to attack me, let some zealous followers of Dr. Crisp, some hot-headed vindicator of reprobation and eternal justification blow the trumpet, and put himself at their head: but let it not be *you,* who believe with me that we are moral agents; that God is love; that Jesus tasted death for every man; and that the Holy Spirit shall not always strive with sinners. If you do not regard my reputation, consider at least your own; and expose me not as a heretic for advancing propositions, the substance of which you have avowed before the sun."

But had those propositions at length appeared to you unsound, yea, and had you never maintained them yourself, should you not, as a Christian and a brother, have written to him, acquainted him with your objections, and desired him to solve them and explain himself, or you should be obliged publicly to expose him?

Was this condescension more than was due from you, sir, and our other friends, to a gray-headed minister of Christ; an old general in the armies of Emmanuel; a father who has children capable of instructing even masters in Israel; and one whom God made the first and principal instrument of the late revival of internal religion in our Church?

Instead of this friendly method, as if you was a Barak, "commanded by the Lord God of Israel, you call together the children of Naphtali and Zebulun": you convene, from England and Wales, clergy and laity, Churchmen and Dissenters, to meet you at Bristol, where they are, it seems, to be entertained in good and free quarters. And for what grand expedition? Why, on a day appointed you are to march up "in a body," not to attack Sisera and his iron chariots, but an old Caleb, who, without meddling with you, quietly goes on to the conquest of Canaan; not to desire in a friendly manner, after a fair debate of every proposition that appears dangerous, and upon previous conviction that what is exceptionable may be given up, but to do what I think was never done by nominal, much less by "real Protestants"—O let it not be told in Rome, lest the sons of the inquisition rejoice!—This mixed, this formidable body, is to "insist upon" Mr. Wesley, and the preachers in his connection, "formally recanting" their Minutes, as appearing "injurious to the very fundamental principles of Christianity, and being dreadfully heretical." And this, (astonishing!) without the least inquiry made into their meaning and design—without a shadow of authority from our superiors in Church or state—without an appeal to "the law and to the testimony"—without form of process—without judge or jury—without so much as allowing the poor "heretics," (who are condemned six weeks before they can possibly be heard,) to answer for themselves!

As I was fortunate enough to stop, some months ago, such rash proceedings in Wales, permit me, sir, to bear my testimony against them in England, and to tell you they exceed the late transactions in Edmund Hall. The six students, against whom wrath was gone forth, were allowed to say what they could in their own defence before they were sentenced, as unfit members of a literary society. Likewise the vice-chancellor had the statutes of the university of Oxford, seeming to countenance his proceedings: but what statute of the university of Jesus can you produce, even to save appearances? Surely not that which the Papists made use of, "Compell them to come in"; for I am persuaded, that although clergy and laity,

Churchmen and Dissenters, are convened to go in a body
to Mr. Wesley's conference, you mean no external compulsion. Much less are you authorized to "insist" upon
his owning himself "a heretic," by these words of the
apostle, "As much as lieth in you, live peaceably with all
men, and esteem ministers highly in love for their work's
sake." Neither by his command, "A heretic, after the first
and second admonition, reject," etc.; for you have neither
proved Mr. Wesley a *heretic*, nor *once admonished* him
as such.

PREFACE

The publication of the *Vindication of Mr. Wesley's Minutes* having been represented by some persons as an act of injustice, the following letter is made public to throw some light upon that little event, and serve as a preface to the SECOND CHECK TO ANTINOMIANISM.

To the Rev. Mr. John Wesley.

"REV. AND DEAR SIR: As I love open dealing, I send you the substance, and almost the very words, of a private letter I have just written to Mr. Shirley, in answer to one, in which he informs me he is going to publish his Narrative. He is exceedingly welcome to make use of any part of my letters to Mr. Ireland, concerning the publication of my Vindication, and you are equally welcome to make what use you please of this. Among friends all things are, or should be, common.

"I am, Rev. and dear sir, yours, etc.,   J. FLETCHER.

"MADELEY, *Sept.* 11, 1771."

To the Hon. and Rev. Mr. Shirley

"REV. AND DEAR SIR: It is extremely proper, nay, it is highly necessary, that the public should be informed how much like a minister of the Prince of Peace, and a meek, humble, loving brother in the Gospel of Christ you behaved at the conference. Had I been there, I would gladly have taken upon me to proclaim these tidings of joy to the lovers of Zion's peace. Your conduct at that time of love is certainly the best excuse for the hasty step you had taken; as my desire of stopping my Vindication, upon hearing it, is the best apology I can make for my severity to you.

"I am not averse at all, sir, to your publishing the passages you mention, out of my letters to Mr. Ireland.

They show my peculiar love and respect for you, which I shall at all times think an honour, and at this juncture shall feel a peculiar pleasure, to see proclaimed to the world. They apologize for my calling myself *a lover of quietness,* when I unfortunately prove *a son of contention:* and they demonstrate, that I am not altogether void of the fear that becomes an awkward, unexperienced surgeon, when he ventures to open a vein in the arm of a person for whom he has the highest regard. How natural is it for him to tremble, lest by missing the intended vein, and pricking an unseen artery, he should have done irreparable mischief, instead of a useful operation.

"But while you do me the kindness of publishing those passages, permit me, sir, to do Mr. Wesley the justice of informing him I had also written to Mr. Ireland, that 'whether my letters were suppressed or not, the Minutes *must* be vindicated—that Mr. Wesley owed it to the Church, to the *real Protestants,* to all his societies, and to his own aspersed character—and that, after all, the controversy did not seem to me to be so much, whether the Minutes should stand, as whether the Antinomian gospel of Dr. Crisp should prevail over the practical Gospel of Jesus Christ.'

"I must also, sir, beg leave to let my vindicated friend know, that in the very letter where I so earnestly entreated Mr. Ireland to stop the publication of my letters to you, and offered to take the whole expense of the impression upon myself, though I should be obliged to sell my last shirt to defray it, I added, that 'if they were published, I must look upon it as a *necessary evil* or *misfortune';* which of the two words I used I do not justly recollect. *A misfortune* for you and me, who must appear inconsistent to the world: you, sir, with your Sermons, and I with my title page; and nevertheless *necessary* to vindicate misrepresented truth, defend an eminent minister of Christ, and stem the torrent of Antinomianism.

"It may not be improper also, to observe to you, sir, that when I presented Mr. Wesley with my Vindication, I begged he would correct it, and take away whatever might be unkind or too sharp; urging that, though I meant no unkindness, I was not a proper judge of what I had written under peculiarly delicate and trying circumstances, as well as in a great hurry; and did not therefore dare to trust either my pen, my head, or my heart. He was no sooner gone, than I sent a letter after him, to repeat and urge the same request; and he wrote me word he had 'expunged every tart expression.' *If he has,* (for I have not yet seen what alterations his friendly pen has made,) I am reconciled to their publication; and *that he has* I have reason to hope from the letters of two judicious London friends, who calmed my fears lest I should have treated you with unkindness.

"One of them says, 'I reverence Mr. Shirley for his candid acknowledgment of his hastiness in judging. I commend the Calvinists at the conference for their justice to Mr. Wesley, and their acquiescence in the declaration of the preachers in connection with him. But is that declaration, however dispersed, a remedy adequate to the evil done, not only to Mr. Wesley, but to the cause and work of God? Several Calvinists, in eagerness of malice, had dispersed their calumnies through the three kingdoms. A truly excellent person herself, in her mistaken zeal, had represented him as *a Papist unmasked, a heretic, an apostate.* A clergyman of the first reputation informs me a *Poem on His Apostasy* is just coming out. Letters have been sent to every serious Churchman and Dissenter through the land, together with the Gospel Magazine. Great are the shoutings, *And now that he lieth, let him rise up no more!* This is all the cry. His dearest friends and children are staggered, and scarce know what to think. You, in your corner, cannot conceive the mischief that has been done, and is still doing. But your letters, in the hand of Providence, may answer the good ends you proposed by writing them. You have not been too severe to dear Mr. Shirley, moderate Calvinists themselves being judges; but very kind and friendly to set a good mistaken man right, and probably to preserve him from the like rashness as long as he lives. Be not troubled, therefore, but cast your care upon the Lord.'

"My other friend says, 'Considering what harm the Circular Letter has done, and what a useless satisfaction Mr. Shirley has given by his vague acknowledgement, it is no more than just and equitable that your letters should be published.'

"Now, sir, as I never saw that *acknowledgment,* nor the *softening* corrections made by Mr. Wesley in my Vindication; as I was not informed of some of the above mentioned particulars when I was so eager to prevent the publication of my letters; and as I have reason to think, that through the desire of an immediate peace, the festering wound was rather skinned over than probed to the bottom; all I can say about this publication is, what I wrote to our common friend, namely, that 'I must look upon it as a necessary *evil.*'

"I am glad, sir, you do not direct your letter to Mr. Olivers, who was so busy in publishing my Vindication; for, by a letter I have just received from Bristol, I am informed he did not hear how desirous I was to call it in, till he had actually given out before a whole congregation it would be sold. Beside, he would have pleaded with smartness that he never approved of the patched-up peace, that he bore his testimony against it at the time it was made, and had a personal right to produce *my* arguments, since both parties refused to hear *his* at the conference.

"If your letter is friendly sir, and you print it in the same size with my Vindication, I shall gladly buy ten pounds' worth of the copies, and order them to be stitched with my Vindication, and given gratis to the purchasers of it; as well to do you justice as to convince the world that we make a loving war; and also to demonstrate how much I regard your respectable character, and honour your dear person. Mr. Wesley's heart is, I am persuaded, too full of brotherly love to deny me the pleasure of thus showing you how sincerely I am, Rev. and dear sir, your obedient servant,   JOHN FLETCHER.

"MADELEY, *September* 11, 1771."

SECOND CHECK TO ANTINOMIANISM

LETTER I

HONOURED AND REVEREND SIR: I cordially thank you for the greatest part of your Narrative. It confirms me in my hopes that your projected opposition to Mr. Wesley's Minutes proceeded in general from zeal for the Redeemer's glory. And as such a zeal, though amazingly mistaken, had certainly something very commendable in it, I sincerely desire your Narrative may evidence your *good meaning,* as some think my Vindication does your *mistake.*

In my last private letter I observed, Rev. sir, that if your Narrative was *kind,* I would buy a number of copies, and give them gratis to the purchasers of my books, that they might see all you can possibly produce in your defence, and do you all the justice your proper behaviour at the conference deserves. But as it appears to me there are some important mistakes in that performance, I neither dare recommend it *absolutely* to my friends, nor wish it in the religious world the *full* success you desire.

I do not complain of its severity; on the contrary, considering the sharpness of my fifth letter, I gratefully acknowledge it is *kinder* than I had reason to expect. But permit me to tell you, sir, I look for *justice* to the Scriptural arguments I advance in defence of truth, before I look for *kindness* to my insignificant person; and could much sooner be satisfied with the former than with the latter alone. As I do not admire the fashionable method of advancing general charges without supporting them by particular proofs, I shall take the liberty of pointing out some mistakes in your Narrative, and by that means endeavour to do justice to Mr. Wesley's declara-

75

tions, your own sermons, my Vindication, and above all,
to the cause of practical religion.

Waiving the repetition of what I said in my last, touching the publication of my Five Letters to you, I object
first to your putting a wrong colour upon Mr. Wesley's
declaration. You insinuate, or assert, that he, and fifty-
three of the preachers in conference with him, give up
the doctrine of "justification by works in the day of judgment." "It appears," say you, "from their subscribing the
declaration," notwithstanding Mr. Olivers' remonstrances,
"that they do not maintain a second justification by
works."

Surely, sir, you wrong them. They might have objected to some of Mr. Olivers' expressions, or been displeased with his readiness to enter the lists of dispute;
but certainly so many judicious and good men could never
so betray the cause of practical religion, as tamely to renounce a truth of that importance. If they had, one step
more would have carried them full into Dr. Crisp's eternal
justification, which is the very center of Antinomianism;
and without waiting for the return of the next conference,
I would bear my *legal* testimony against their *Antinomian*
error. Mr. Wesley I reverence as the greatest minister
I know, but would not follow him one step farther than
he follows Christ. Were he really guilty of rejecting the
evangelical doctrine of a second justification by works,
with the plainness and honesty of a Suisse I would address him, as I beg you will permit me to address you.

I. *Neither you, Rev. sir, nor any divine in the world,
have, I presume, a right to blot out of the sacred records
those words of Jesus Christ, St. James, and St. Paul:*
"Blessed are they that do his commandments, that they
may have right to the tree of life. Not every one that says
to me, *Lord! Lord!* shall enter into the kingdom of heaven,
but he that does the will of my Father. Be ye therefore
doers of the word, and not hearers only, deceiving your

own selves. For we are under the law to Christ. Not the hearers of the law shall be just before God, but the doers of the law shall be justified. Every man's work shall be made manifest: for the day shall declare it, because it shall be revealed by fire, and the fire shall try every man's work of what sort it is." His very words shall undergo the severest scrutiny. "I say unto you, [O how many will insinuate the contrary!] that every idle word that men shall speak they shall give account thereof in the day of judgment, for by thy words shalt thou [then] be justified, and by thy words shalt thou [then] be condemned."

Can you say, sir, that the justification mentioned by our Lord in this passage is the same as that which St. Paul speaks of as the present privilege of all believers, and has no particular reference to "the day of judgment" mentioned in the preceding sentence? Or will you intimate our Lord does not declare we shall be justified in the last day by *works,* but by *words?* Would this evasion be judicious? Do not all professors know that *words* are *works* in a theological sense; as being both the signs of the "workings" of our hearts, and the positive "works" of our tongues? Will you expose your reputation as a divine, by trying to prove, that although we shall be justified by the *works* of our tongues, those of our hands and feet shall never appear for or against our justification? Or will you insinuate that our Lord "recanted" the legal sermons written Matt. 5, and 12? If you do, his particular account of the day of judgment, chapter 25, which strongly confirms and clearly explains the doctrine of our second justification by works, will prove you greatly mistaken, as will also his declaration to St. John, above forty years after, "Behold, I come quickly, and my reward is with me, to give to every man as his work [not faith] shall be."

O, if faith alone turn the scale of justifying evidence at the bar of God, how many bold Antinomians will claim relation to Christ, and boast they are interested in his

imputed righteousness! How many will say, with the
foolish virgins, " 'Lord! Lord! we are of faith, and Abraham's children. In thy name' we publicly opposed all legal
professors, traduced their teachers as enemies to thy *free
grace;* and, 'to do thee service,' made it our business to
expose the righteousness, and cry down the good works of
thy people; therefore 'Lord! Lord! open to us!' " But, alas!
far from thanking them for their pains, without looking
at their boasted faith, he will dismiss them with a "Depart from me, ye that work iniquity!" As if he said—

"Depart, ye that made the doctrine of my atonement a
cloak for your sins, or 'sewed' it as a 'pillow under the
arms of my people,' to make them sleep in carnal security,
when they should have 'worked out their salvation with
fear and trembling.' You profess to know me, but I dis-
own you. My sheep I know: them that are mine I know.
The seal of my holiness is upon them all: the motto of it,
(*Let him that nameth the name of Christ depart from
iniquity,*) is deeply engraven on their faithful breasts—
not on yours, ye 'carnal, ye sold under sin!'

" 'And why called ye me, Lord! Lord! and did not the
things which I said?' Why did you even use my righteousness as a breastplate, to stand it out against the word of
my righteousness; and as an engine to break both tables
of my law, and batter down my holiness? Your heart condemns you, ye 'sinners in Zion! Ye salt without savour!'
Ye believers without charity! And am not I 'greater than
your heart?' And 'know' I not 'your works?' Yes, 'I know
that the love of God is not in you,' for you despised one of
these my brethren. How could you think to deceive me,
'the Searcher of hearts and Trier of reins?' And how did
you dare to call yourselves by my name? As if you were
my people? my dear people? mine elect? Are not all my
peculiar people 'partakers of my holiness,' and 'zealous
of good works? Have not I chosen to myself the man that
is godly,' and protested that 'the ungodly shall not stand

in the judgment, nor sinners,' though in sheep's clothing, 'in the congregation of the righteous?' And say I not to the wicked, though he should have been one of my people, *Lo ammi, Thou art none of my people now.* 'What hast thou to do with taking my covenant in thy mouth?' You denied me in works, and did not wash your hearts from iniquity in my blood; therefore, according to my word, 'I deny you,' in my turn, 'before my Father and his holy angels.' Perish your hope, ye hypocrites: and utter darkness be your portion, 'ye double minded! Let fearfulness surprise you,' ye tinkling cymbals! Let the fall of your Babels crush you, ye towering professors of my humble faith! Fly, 'ye clouds without water; ye chaff,' fly before the blast of my righteous indignation! 'Ye workers of iniquity! Ye Satans transformed into angels of light! 'Ye cursed, depart!' "

II. *Nor is our Lord singular in his doctrine of justification, or condemnation, by works in the day of judgment.* If it is a heresy, the patriarchs, prophets, and apostles are as great heretics as their Master. Enoch, quoted by St. Jude, prophesied, that when the Lord shall "come to execute judgment upon all men," he will "convince the ungodly among them of all their ungodly deeds and hard speeches." This *conviction* will no doubt be in order to condemnation; and this condemnation will not turn upon unbelief, but its effects, "ungodly deeds and hard speeches." Solomon confirms the joint testimony of Enoch and St. Jude where he says, "He that knoweth the heart, shall render to every man according to his works"; and again, "Know, O young man, that for all these things, for all thy ways, God shall bring thee into judgment."

St. Paul, the great champion for faith, is particularly express upon this anti-Crispian doctrine. "The Lord," says he, "in the day of wrath and revelation of the righteous judgment of God, will render to every man according to his *deeds;* to them that *continue in well doing,*" (here is the true perseverance of the saints!) "eternal life! Indignation upon every soul of man that *does* evil, and glory to every man who *worketh* good; for there is no respect of persons with God. We shall all appear before the judgment seat of Christ, that every one may receive the things *done* in the body," not according to that he hath *believed,* whether it be true or false, but "according to that he hath *done,* whether it be good or bad." St. Peter asserts, that the Father, "without respect of persons, judgeth according to every man's *work.*" And St. John, who, next to our Lord, gives us the most particular description of the day of judgment, concludes it by these awful words: "And the dead were judged out of the things written in the books, according to their *works.*" It is not once said, "according to their *faith.*"

III. *This doctrine is so obvious in the Scriptures, so generally received in all the Churches of Christ, and so deeply engraven on the consciences of sincere professors, that most eminent ministers or all denominations perpetually allude to it;* yourselves, sir, not excepted, as I could prove from your sermons if you had not recanted them. How often, for instance, has that great man of God, the truly reverend Mr. Whitefield, said to his immense congregations, "You are warned; I am clear of your blood; I shall rise as a swift witness against you, or you against me, in the terrible day of the Lord! O, remember to clear me then!" or words to that purpose. And is not this just as if he had said, "We shall all be 'justified or condemned in the day of judgment' by what we are now *doing:* I by my preaching, and you by your hearing?"

And say not, sir, that "such expressions were only *flights of oratory,* and prove nothing." If you do, you "touch the apple of God's eye." Mr. Whitefield was not a *flighty orator,* but spoke the words of soberness and truth, with Divine pathos, and floods of tears declarative of his sincerity.

Instead of swelling this letter into a volume, (as I easily might,) by producing quotations from all the sober Puritan divines, who have directly or indirectly asserted a second justification by works, I shall present you only with two passages from Mr. Henry. On Matt. 12:37, he says, "Consider how strict the judgment will be on account of our words. 'By thy words thou shalt be justified or condemned'—a common rule in men's judgment, and here applied to God's. Note the constant tenor of our discourse, according as it is gracious or not gracious, will be an evidence for us, or against us, at that day. Those that 'seemed to be religious, but bridled not their tongue,' will then be found to have put a cheat upon themselves with a vain religion. It concerns us to think much of the day of judgment, that it may be a check upon our tongues." And again:

Upon those words, Rom. 2:13, "Not the hearers of the law are just before God, but the doers of the law shall be justified"; the honest commentator says, "The Jewish [Antinomian] doctors bolstered up their followers with an opinion that all that were Jews, [the elect people of God,] how bad soever they lived, should have a glorious place in the world to come. This the apostle here opposes. It was a very great privilege that they had the law, but not a saving privilege, *unless they lived up to the law they had.* We may apply it to the Gospel: it is not hearing, but *doing that will save us,*" John 13:17; James 1:22.

IV. *These testimonies will, I hope, make you weigh with an additional degree of candour the following arguments, which I shall produce as a logician, lest any should be tempted to call me a bold metaphysician, or almost a magician:*

The voice that St. John heard in heaven did not say, "Blessed are the dead that die in the Lord, for their FAITH follows them": no, it is *their works.* Faith is the hidden root, hope the rising stalk, and love, together with good works, the nourishing corn: and as the king's agents, who fill a royal granary, do not take in the roots and stalks, but the pure wheat alone; so Christ takes neither faith nor hope into heaven, the former being gloriously absorbed in sight, and the latter in enjoyment.

If I may compare faith and hope to "the chariot of Israel and the courser thereof," they both bring believers to the everlasting doors of glory, but do not enter in themselves. Not so *love* and *good works;* for love is both the nature and element of saints in glory; and good works necessarily follow them, both in the books of remembrance which shall then be opened, and in the objects and witnesses of those works, who shall then be all present; as it appears from the words of our Lord, "You have done it," or "You have not done it, to one of the least of these my brethren"; and those of St. Paul to his dear converts, "You shall be 'my joy and my crown' in that day." Thus it is evident, that although *faith* is the temporary measure according to which God deals out his mercy and grace in this world, as we may gather from that sweet saying of our Lord, "Be it done to thee according to thy FAITH"; yet *love* and *good works* are the eternal measures, according to which he distributes justification and glory in the world to come. On these observations, I argue,

We shall be justified in the last day by the grace and evidences which shall then remain.

Love and good works, the fruits of faith, shall then remain.

Therefore we shall then be justified by love and good works, that is, not by faith, but by its fruits.

V. *This doctrine, so agreeable to Scripture, the sentiments of moderate Calvinists,* and the dictates of reason, "recommends" itself likewise "to every man's conscience in the sight of God." Who, but Dr. Crisp, could (after a calm "review of the whole affair," affirm, that in the day of judgment, if I am accused of being actually a hypocrite, Christ's sincerity will justify me, whether it be found in me or not?

Again: suppose I am charged with being a drunkard, a thief, a whoremonger, a covetous person; or a fretful, impatient, ill-natured man; or, if you please, a proud bigot, an implacable zealot, a malicious persecutor, who, notwithstanding fair appearances of godliness, would raise disturbances even in heaven if I were admitted there: will Christ's sobriety, honesty, chastity, generosity: or will his gentleness, patience, and meekness, justify me from such dreadful charges? Must not I be found really sober, honest, chaste, and charitable? Must I not be inherently gentle, meek, and loving? Can we deny this without flying in the face of common sense, breaking the strongest bars of scriptural truth, and opening the flood gates to the foulest waves of Antinomianism? If we grant it, do we not grant a second justification by works? And does not St. Paul grant, or rather insist upon as much, when he declares, that "without holiness no man shall see the Lord?"

VI. *You will probably ask, what advantage the Church will reap from this doctrine of a second justification by works?* I answer, that, under God, it will rouse Antinomians out of their carnal security, stir up believers to follow hard after holiness, and reconcile fatal differences among Christians, and seeming contradictions in the Scripture.

1. It will *re-awaken Antinomians,* who fancy "there is no condemnation to them," whether they "walk after the Spirit" in love, or "after the flesh" in malice; whether they forsake all" to follow Christ, or like Judas and Sapphira "keep back part" of what should be the Lord's without reserve. Thousands boldly profess justifying faith, and perhaps eternal justification, who reverence the commandments of God just as much as they regard the scriptures quoted in Mr. Wesley's Minutes.

The Gospel cries to them, "Repent and believe!" and just as if God was to be the penitent, believing sinner, they carelessly reply, "The Lord must do all; repentance and faith are his works, and they will be done in the day of his power"; and so without resistance they decently follow the stream of worldly vanities and fleshly lusts. St. Paul cries, "If ye live after the flesh, ye shall die." "We know better," answer they, "there are neither *ifs* nor conditions in all the Gospel." He adds, "This one thing I do, leaving the things that are behind, I press toward the mark for the prize of my high calling in Christ Jesus— the crown of life. Be ye followers of me. Run also the race that is set before you." "What!" say they, would you have us *run* and *work for life?* Will you always harp upon that legal string, *Do! do!* instead of telling us that we have nothing to do, but to believe that all is done?" St. James cries, *"Show your faith by your works; faith without works is dead* already, much more that which is accompanied by bad works." "What!" say they, "do you think the lamp of faith can be put out as a candle can be extinguished, by not being suffered to shine? We orthodox hold just the contrary: we maintain both that faith can never die, and that living faith is consistent not only with the omission of good works, but with the commission of the most horrid crimes." St. Peter bids them "give all diligence to make their election sure, by adding to their faith virtue," etc. "Legal stuff!" say they, "The covenant is well ordered in all things and sure; neither will our virtue save us, nor our sins damn us." St. John comes next, and declares, "He that sinneth is of the devil." "What!" say they, "do you think to make us converts to Arminianism, by thus insinuating that a man can be a child of God today, and a child of the devil tomorrow?" St. Jude advances last, and charges them to "keep themselves in the love of God"; and they supinely reply, "We can do nothing." Beside, "We are as easy and as safe without a frame as with one."

2. This doctrine is not less proper to *animate feeble believers in their pursuit of holiness.* O if it were clearly preached and steadily believed—if we were fully persuaded, we shall soon "appear before the judgment seat of Christ," to answer for every thought, word, and work, for every business we enter upon, every sum of money we lay out, every meal we eat, every pleasure we take, every affliction we endure, every hour we spend, every idle word we speak, yea, and every temper we secretly indulge—if we knew we shall certainly "give account" of all the chapters we read, of all the prayers we offer, all the sermons we hear or preach, all the sacraments we receive; of all the motions of Divine grace, all the beams of heavenly light, all the breathings of the Spirit, all the invitations of Christ, all the drawings of the Father, reproofs of our friends, and checks of our own consciences—and if we were deeply conscious, that every neglect of duty will rob us of a degree of glory, and every wilful sin of a jewel in our crown, if not of our crown itself; what humble, watchful, holy, heavenly persons should we be! How serious and self denying! How diligent and faithful! In a word, how angelical and divine, "in all manner of conversation!"

Ye who hold the doctrine of perfection without "going on to perfection," and ye who explode it as a pernicious delusion, and inconsistently publish hymns of solemn prayer for it, how would you agree, from the bottom of your reawakened hearts, to sing together, in days of peace and social worship, as you have carelessly sung asunder,

> O for a heart to praise our God!
>   A heart from sin set free!
> A heart in every thought renew'd,
>   And fill'd with love divine!

> *Perfect,* and right, and pure, and good,
> A copy, Lord, of thine.
> Bigotry from us remove,
> *Perfect* all our souls in love, etc.

3. I observed that this doctrine will likewise *reconcile seeming contradictions in the Scriptures, and fatal differences among Christians.* Take one instance of the former: What can those who reject a second justification by works make of the solemn words of our Lord, already quoted, "By thy words thou shalt be justified, *or* by thy words thou shalt be condemned?" Matt. 12:37. And by what art can they possibly reconcile them with St. Paul's assertions, Rom. 4:5, "To him that worketh not, but believeth on him that justifieth the ungodly, his faith is imputed to him for righteousness?" and 5:1, "Being justified by faith, we have peace with God through our Lord Jesus Christ." Accept an example of the latter. In the Antinomian days of Dr. Crisp arose the honest people we call Quakers. Shocked at the general abuse of the doctrine of *justification by faith,* they rashly inferred it never could be from God; and seeing none "shall be justified *in glory* but the doers of the law," they hastily concluded there is but one justification, namely, the being made inherently just, or the being sanctified, and then declared holy. Admit our doctrine, and you have both parts of the truth—that which the Antinomians hold against the Quakers, and that which the Quakers maintain against the Antinomians. Each alone is dangerous; both together mutually defend each other, and make up the scriptural doctrine of justification, which is invincibly guarded on the one hand by FAITH against Pharisees, and on the other by WORKS against Antinomians. Reader, may both be thy portion! So shalt thou be eternally reinstated both in the *favour* and *image* of God.

VII. *But while I enumerate the benefits which the Church will reap from a practical knowledge of our second*

*justification by works, an honest Protestant, who has more
zeal for, than acquaintance with the truth, advances, with
his heart full of holy indignation, and his mouth of objections, which he says are unanswerable.* Let us consider
them one by one.

FIRST OBJECTION. "Your Popish, antichristian doctrine
I abhor, and could even burn at a stake as a witness
against it. Away with your new-fangled Arminian tenets!
I am for old Christianity; and with St. Paul, 'determined
to know nothing *for justification* but Christ, and him crucified.' "

ANSWER. Do you, indeed? Then I am sure you will not
deny both Jesus Christ and St. Paul in this old Christian
doctrine; for Christ says, "By thy words shalt thou be
justified"; and St. Paul declares, "Not the hearers, but the
doers of the law (of Christ) shall be justified." Alas, how
often are those who say they "will know" and have "nothing but Christ," the first to "set him at nought" as a
prophet, by railing at his holy doctrine: or to reject him
as a king, by trampling upon his royal proclamations! But
"I wot that through ignorance they do it, as do their
rulers."

SECOND OBJECTION. "This legal doctrine robs God's
dear children of their comforts and Gospel liberty, binds
Moses' intolerable burden upon their free shoulders, and
'entangles them again in the *galling* yoke of bondage.' "

ANSWER. If God's dear children have got into a false
liberty of doing the devil's works, either by "not going
into the vineyard" when they have said, "Lord, I go," or
by "beating their fellow servants" there, instead of working with them; the sooner they are robbed of it the better: for if they continue thus free, they will ere long be
"bound hand and foot, and cast into outer darkness." It
is the very spirit of Antinomianism to represent God's
"commandments as grievous," and the keeping of his law
"as bondage." Not so the dutiful children of God: "Their

hearts" are never so much "at liberty," as when they "run the way of his commandments, and so fulfil the law of Christ." Keep them from obedience, and you keep them "in the snare of the devil, promising liberty *to others,* while they themselves are the servants of corruption."

Again: you confound the heavy yoke of the circumcision and ceremonial bondage, with which the Galatians once entangled themselves, with the "easy yoke of Jesus Christ." The former was intolerable, the latter is so "light a burden," that the only way to "find rest unto our souls is to take it upon us." St. Paul calls a dear brother his "yoke fellow." You know the word BELIAL in the original signifies "without yoke." They are *sons of Belial* who shake off the Lord's yoke; and though they should boast of their *election* as much as the Jews did, Christ himself will say concerning them, "Those mine enemies that *refused my yoke,* and would not that I should reign over them bring hither, and slay them before me!" So inexpressibly dreadful is the end of lawless liberty!

THIRD OBJECTION. "Your doctrine is the damnable error of the Galatians, who madly left Mount Sion for Mount Sinai, made Christ the *Alpha,* and not the *Omega,* and after 'having begun in the Spirit *would be* made perfect by the flesh.' This is *the other Gospel* which St. Paul thought so diametrically contrary to his own, that he wished the teachers of it, though they were 'angels of God,' might be even 'accursed and cut off.' "

ANSWER. You are under a capital mistake: St. Paul could never be so wild as to curse himself, anathematize St. James, and wish the Messiah to be again cut off: for he himself taught the Romans, that "the doers of the law shall be justified." St. James evidently maintains a justification by works; and our Lord expressly says, "By thy words thou shalt be justified." Again: the apostle, if he had foreseen how his Epistle to the Galatians would be abused to Antinomian purposes, gives us in it the most powerful antidotes against that poison. Take two or three instances. (1) He exhorts his fallen converts to the ful-filling of all the law: "Love one another," says he, "for all the law is fulfilled in this one word, *Thou shalt love thy neighbour as thyself";* because none can "love his neigh-bour as himself," but he that "loves God with all his heart." How different is this doctrine from the bold Anti-nomian cry, "We have nothing to do with the law!" (2) He enumerates the works of the flesh, "adultery, hatred, variance, wrath, strife, envyings, heresies, etc.; of which," says he, "I tell you before, as I have told you in time past, that they who do such things" shall not be justified in the day of judgment, or, which is the same thing, "shall not inherit the kingdom of God." How different a Gospel is this from that which insinuates, "impenitent adulterers may be dear children of God, even while such, and in a very safe state, and quite sure of glory!" And (3) As if this awful warning were not enough, he point blank cautions his readers against the Crispian error: "Be not deceived," says he, "Whatever a MAN (not *whatever* CHRIST) soweth, that shall he also reap. He that soweth to the flesh shall reap corruption, and he that soweth to the Spirit shall reap life everlasting." How amazingly strong therefore must your prejudice be, which makes you produce this epistle to thrust love and good works out of the important place allotted them in all the word of God! And no where more than in this very epistle!

FOURTH OBJECTION. "Notwithstanding all you say, I am persuaded you are in the dreadful heresy of the Gala-tians; for they were, like you, for 'justification by the works of the law'; and St. Paul resolutely maintained against them the fundamental doctrine of *justification by faith.*"

ANSWER. If you once read over the Epistle to the Galatians without prejudice, and without comment, you will see, that (1) They had returned "to the beggarly elements of this world," by superstitiously "observing days, months, times, and years." (2) Imagining they "could not be saved except they were circumcised," they submitted even to that grievous and bloody injunction. (3) Exact in their useless ceremonies, and fondly hoping to be justified by their partial observance of Moses' law, they well nigh forgot the merits of Christ, and openly trampled upon his law, and "walked after the flesh." Stirred up to contentious zeal by their new teachers, they despised the old apostle's ministry, hated his person, and "devoured one another." In short, they trusted partly in the merit of their superstitious performances, and partly in Christ's merits; and on this preposterous foundation they "built the hay" of Jewish ceremonies, and "the stubble" of fleshly lusts. With great propriety, therefore, the apostle called them back, with sharpness, to the only sure foundation, the merits of Jesus Christ; and wanted them to "build upon it gold and precious stones," all the works of piety and mercy that spring from "faith working by love."

Now which of these errors do we hold? Do we not preach present justification *by faith,* and justification at the bar of God *according to what a man soweth,* the very doctrine of this epistle? And do we not "secure the foundation," by insisting that both these justifications are equally through *the merits of Christ,* though the second, as our church intimates in her twelfth article, is by the evidence of works?

FIFTH OBJECTION. "However, your Pharisaic doctrine flatly contradicts the Gospel summed up by our Lord, Mark 16: 16, 'He that believeth shall be saved, and he that believeth not shall be damned.' Here is not one word about works. All turns upon faith."

ANSWER. Instead of throwing such hints, you might as well speak out at once, and say that Christ in these words flatly contradicts what he had said, Matt. 12: 37, "By thy words thou shalt be justified, or by thy words thou shalt be condemned." But drop your prejudices, and you will see that the contradiction is only in your own ideas. We steadily assert, as our Lord, that "he who believeth," or "endureth unto the end believing," (for the word implies both the reality and the continuance of the action,) "shall *infallibly* be saved"; because faith, which continues living, "works" to the last "by love" and good works, which will infallibly justify us in the day of judgment. For when faith is no more, love and good works will evidence, (1) That we were grafted into Christ by true faith: (2) That we did not "make shipwreck of the faith"; that we were not "taken away as branches in him which bear not fruit, *but* abode fruitful branches in the true Vine." And (3) That we are still in him by HOLY LOVE, the precious and eternal fruit of true persevering faith. How bad is that cause which must support itself by charging an imaginary contradiction upon the Wisdom of God, Jesus Christ himself!

SIXTH OBJECTION. "Your doctrine exalts man, and by giving him room to boast, robs Christ of the glory of his grace. 'The top stone' is no more 'brought forth with shouting, Grace! Grace!' but, Works! Works! 'unto it!' And the burden of the song in heaven will be—Salvation to our works! and no more, Salvation to the Lamb!"

ANSWER. I no less approve your godly jealousy, than I wonder at your groundless fears. To calm them, permit me once more to observe, (1) That this doctrine is Christ's, who would not be so unwise as to side with our self-righteous pride, and teach us to rob him of his own glory. It is absurd to suppose Christ would be thus against Christ, for even Satan is too wise "to be against Satan." (2) Upon our plan, as well as upon Crisp's scheme, free grace has absolutely *all the glory*. The love and good works by which we shall be justified in the day of judgment, are the fruits of faith, and "faith is the gift of God." Christ is the great object of faith, the Holy Ghost, called the

Spirit of faith, the power of believing, the means, opportunities, and will to use that power, are all the rich presents of God's free grace.

SEVENTH OBJECTION. "How will the converted thief,
that that did no good works, be justified by works?"

ANSWER. (1) We mean by works "the whole of our
inward tempers and outward behaviour"; and how do
you know *the outward behaviour* of the converted thief?
Did not his reproofs, exhortations, prayers, patience, and
resignation, evidence the liveliness of his faith, as there
was time and opportunity? (2) Can you suppose his
inward temper was not love to God and man? Could he
go into paradise without being born again? Or could he
be born again and not love? Is it not said, "He that loveth
is born of God"; consequently, he that is born of God
loveth? Again: does not he who "loveth, fulfill all the
law," and do as says Augustine, all good works in one?
And is not "the fulfilling of the law of Christ" work
enough to justify the converted thief by that law?

EIGHTH OBJECTION. "You say, that your doctrine 'will
make us zealous of good works'; but I fully discharge it
from that office: for 'the love of Christ constraineth us to
abound in every good word and work.'"

ANSWER. (1) St. Paul, who spoke those words with
more feeling than you, thought the contrary; as well as
his blessed Master, or they would never have taught this
doctrine. You do not, I fear, evidence the temper of *a
babe* when you are so exceedingly "wise above what"
Christ preached, and "prudent above what" the apostle
"wrote." (2) If the love of Christ in professors is so *constraining* as you say, why do good works and good
tempers bear so little proportion to the great talk we hear
of its irresistible efficacy? And why do those who have
tasted it "return to sin as dogs to their vomit?" Why can
they even curse, swear, and get drunk? Be guilty of
idolatry, murder, and incest? (3) If love alone is always

sufficient, why did our Lord work upon his disciples' hearts, by the hope of "thrones and a kingdom," and by the fear of a "worm that dieth not, and a fire that is not quenched?" Why does the apostle stir up believers to "serve the Lord with godly fear," by the consideration that "he is a consuming fire?" Illustrating his assertion by this awful warning, "If they (Korah and his company) escaped not," but were consumed by fire from heaven, because they "refused him (Moses) that spake on earth; much more shall not we escape, if we turn away from him that speaketh from heaven!"

NINTH OBJECTION. "All the formal and Pharisaical ministers, who are sworn enemies to Christ and the Gospel of his grace, preach your legal doctrine of *justification by works in the day of judgment.*"

ANSWER. And what do you infer from it? That the doctrine is false? If the inference be just, it will follow there is neither heaven nor hell; for they publicly maintain the existence of both. But suppose they now and then preach our doctrine without zeal, without living according to it, or without previously preaching the fall, and a present *justification by faith in Christ,* productive of peace and power, what can be expected from it? Would not the doctrine of the atonement itself be totally useless, if it were preached under such disadvantages? The truth is, such ministers are only for the roof, and you, it seems, only for the foundation. But a roof, unsupported by solid walls, crushes to death; and a foundation without a roof is not much better than the open air. Therefore, "wise master builders," like St. Paul, are for having both in their proper places. Like him, when the foundation is well laid, "leaving the first principles of the doctrine of Christ, they go on to perfection"; nor will they forget, as they work out their salvation, to shout, Grace! Grace! to the last slate that covers in the building; or to "the top stone," the key that binds the solid arch.

TENTH OBJECTION. "Should I receive and avow such a doctrine, the generality of professors would rise against me; and while the warmest would call me a *Papist, an antichrist,* and what not; my dearest Christian friends would pity me as an unawakened Pharisee, and fear me as a blind legalist."

ANSWER. "Rejoice, and be exceeding glad when all men (the godly not excepted) shall say all manner of evil of you falsely for Christ's sake,"—for preferring Christ's holy doctrine to the loose tenets of Dr. Crisp: and remember, that, in our Antinomian days, it is as great an honour to be called *legal* by fashionable professors, as to be branded with the name of *Methodist* by the sots who glory in their shame.

VIII. As I would hope my objector is either satisfied or silenced, before I conclude, permit me a moment, Rev. sir, to consider the two important objections which you directly, or indirectly, make in your Narrative.

1. "I should tremble," say you, (page 21,) "lest some bold metaphysician should affirm, that a second justification by works is quite consistent with what is contained in Mr. Wesley's declaration; but that it is expressed in such *strong and absolute terms* as must *for ever* put the most exquisite refinements of metaphysical distinctions *at defiance.*"

ANSWER. "For ever at *defiance!*" You surprise me, sir: I, who am as perfect a stranger to *"exquisite refinements"* as to Dr. Crisp's *eternal justification,* defy you (pardon a *bold* expression to a *bold metaphysician*) ever to produce out of Mr. Wesley's declaration, I shall not say (as you do) "strong and absolute terms," but one single word or tittle denying or excluding a second justification by works; and I appeal both to your second thoughts and to the unprejudiced world, whether these three propositions of the declaration, "We have no trust, or confidence, but in the alone merits of Christ *for* justification in the day of judgment. Works have no part in *meriting or purchasing* our justification from first to last, *either in whole, or in part.*

Who does not see, that, "to be justified by the *evidence* of works," and "to be justified by the *merit* of works," are no more phrases of the same import than *minutes* and *heresy* are words of the same signification? The latter proposition contains the error strongly guarded against, both in the declaration and the Minutes: the former contains an evangelical doctrine, as agreeable to the declaration and Minutes as to the Scriptures; a doctrine of which we were too sparing when we "leaned too much toward Calvinism," but to which, after the example of Mr. Wesley, we are now determined to do justice.

2. Your second objection is not so formal as the first; it must be made up of broad hints scattered through your Narrative, and they amount to this: "Your pretended difference between justification by the *merit* of works, by the *evidence* of works, and between a first and a second justification, is founded upon the *subtilties of metaphysical distinctions.* If what you say wears the aspect of truth, it is because *you give a new turn to error, by the almost magical power of metaphysical distinctions,*" pages 16, 20, 21.

Give me leave, sir, to answer this objection by two appeals, one to the most ignorant collier in my parish, and the other to your own sensible child; and if they can at once understand my meaning, you will see that my "metaphysical distinctions," as you are pleased to call them, are nothing but *the dictates of common sense.* I begin with the collier.

Thomas, I stand here before the judge, accused of having robbed the Rev. Mr. Shirley, near Bath, last month, on such an evening; can you speak a word for me? Thomas turns to the judge, and says, "Please your honour, the accusation is false, for our parson was in Madeley Wood;

and I can make oath of it, for he even reproved me for
swearing at our pit's mouth that very evening." By his
evidence, the judge acquits me. Now, sir, ask cursing
Tom whether I am acquitted and *justified*, by his *merits*,
or by the simple *evidence* he has given, and he will tell you,
"Ay, to be sure by the *evidence;* though I am no scholar,
I know very well that if our Methodist parson is not
hanged, it is none of my deservings." Thus, sir, an ignorant collier, as great a stranger to *your metaphysics* as you
are to *his mandrel,* discovers at once a material difference
between justification by the *evidence,* and justification
by the *merits* of a witness.

My second appeal is to your sensible child. By a plain
comparison I hope to make him at once understand, both
the difference there is between our first and second
justification, and the propriety of that difference. The
lovely boy is old enough, I suppose, to follow the gardener
and me to yonder nursery. Having shown him the operation of *grafting,* and pointing at the crab tree newly
grafted, "My dear child," would I say, "though hitherto
this tree has produced nothing but crabs, yet by the skill
of the gardener, who has just fixed in it that good little
branch, it is now made an *apple tree:* I *justify* and warrant it such. (Here is an emblem of our *first* justification
by faith!) In three or four years, if we live, we will come
again and see it: if it thrives and 'bears fruit,' *well;* we
shall then by that mark justify it a second time, we shall
declare that it is a *good* apple tree indeed, and fit to be
transplanted from this wild nursery into a delightful or-
chard. But if we find that the old crab stock, instead of
nourishing the graft, spends all its sap in producing wild
shoots and sour crabs; or if it is a 'tree whose fruit
withereth, without fruit, twice dead, (dead in the graft
and in the stock,) plucked up by the root,' or quite
cankered, far from declaring 'it a good tree,' we shall pass
sentence of condemnation upon it, and say, 'Cut it down;

why cumbereth it the ground? For every tree that bring-eth not forth good fruit is hewn down and cast into the fire.'" Here is an emblem of our *second* justification *by works*, or of the condemnation that will infallibly over-take those Laodicean professors and wretched apostates, whose faith is not shown by works, where there is time and opportunity.

I am, with due respect, Hon. and Rev. sir, your obedi-ent servant, in the bond of the practical Gospel of Christ,

THE VINDICATOR

LETTER II

HONOURED AND REVEREND SIR: Having endeavoured in my last to do justice to the practical Gospel of Christ, and Mr. Wesley's awful declarations, I pass on to the other mistakes of your Narrative. That which strikes me next is "the public recantation of your *useful* sermons, in the face of the whole world." (Page 22.)

I. *O! sir, what have you done!* Do you not know that your sermons contain not only the legally evangelical doc-trine of the Minutes, but likewise all the doctrine which moderate Calvinists esteem as the marrow of the Gospel? And shall all be treated alike? "Wilt thou also destroy the righteous with the wicked? That be far from thee to do after this manner!" Thus did a good man formerly plead the cause of a *wicked* city, and thus I plead that of your good sermons, those twelve valuable, though unripe fruits of your ministerial labours. Upon this plea the infamous city would have been spared, had only "ten" good men been found in it. Now, sir, spare a valuable book for the sake of a "thousand" excellent things it contains. But if you are inflexible, and still wish it "burned," imitate, at least, the kind angels who sent Lot out of the fiery over-throw, and except all the evangelical pages of the unfor-tunate volume.

Were it not ridiculous to compare wars which cost us only a little ink, and our friends a few pence, to those which cost armies their blood, and kingdoms their treasures, I would be tempted to say to you, Imitate the Dutch in their last effort to balance the victory, and secure the field. When they are pressed by the French, rather than yield, they break their dykes, let in the sea upon themselves, and lay all their fine gardens and rich pastures under water: but before they have recourse to that strange expedient, they prudently save all the valuable goods they can. Why should you not follow them in their prudential care, as you seem to do in their bold stratagem? When you publicly lay your useful book under the bitter waters of an anathema, why do you save absolutely nothing? Why must Gospel truths, more precious than the wealth of Holland and the gold of Ophir, lie for ever under the severe scourge of your recantation? Suppose you had "recanted" your third sermon, *The way to eternal life,* in opposition to mysticism; and "burned" the fourth, *Salvation by Christ for Jews and Gentiles,* in honour of Calvinism, could you not have spared the rest?

If you say, you may do what you please with your own; I answer, Your book, publicly exposed to sale, and bought perhaps by thousands, is, in one sense, no more your own; it belongs to the purchasers, before whom you lay, I fear, a dangerous example: for when they shall hear that the author has "publicly recanted it in the face of the whole world," it will be a temptation to them to slight the Gospel it contains, and perhaps to ridicule it "in the face of the whole world."

You add, "It savours too strongly of mysticism." Some passages are a little tainted with Mr. Law's capital error, and you might have pointed them out: but if you think mysticism is intrinsically bad, you are under a mistake. One of the greatest Mystics, next to Solomon, is Thomas a Kempis, and a few errors excepted, I would no more burn his "Imitation of Jesus Christ," than *the Song of Solomon,* and Mr. Romaine's edifying "Paraphrase of the 107th Psalm."

You urge also, your sermons "savour too much of *free will.*" Alas! sir, can you recant "free will?" Was not your will as *free* when you recanted your sermons as when you composed them? Is there not as much free will expressed in this one line of the Gospel as in all your sermons, "I would have gathered you, and ye would not?" Do not "free-will offerings, with a holy worship," delight the Lord more than *forced,* and, if I may be allowed the expression, *bond-will* services? Is not the free will with which the martyrs went to the stake as worthy of our highest admiration, as the mysticism of the Canticles is of our deepest attention? If all that strongly "savours of free will" must be "burned," ye heavens! what Smithfield work will there be in your lucid plains! Woe to saints! Woe to angels! for they are all free-willing beings—all full of free will. Nor can you deny it, unless you suppose they are *bound* by irresistible decrees, as the heathens fancied their deities were *hampered* with the adamantine chains of an imaginary something they called "fate": witness their *Fata vetant,* and *Fata jubent,* and *ineluctabile Fatum.*

Pardon, Rev. sir, the oddity of these exclamations. I am so grieved at the great advantage we give infidels against the Gospel, by making it ridiculous, that I could try even the method of Horace, to bring my friends back from the fashionable refinements of Crisp, to the plain truth as it is in Jesus.

> *Ridiculum acri*
> *Fortius ac melius stultas plerumque secat res.*

Nor is this the only bad tendency of your new doctrine: for by exploding the freedom of the will, you rob us of free agency. You afford the wicked, who determine to continue in sin, the best excuse in the world to do it without either shame or remorse; you make us mere machines, and indirectly reflect upon the wisdom of our Lord, for saying to a set of Jewish machines, "I would, and ye would not." But what is still more deplorable, you inadvertently represent it an unwise thing in God to judge the world in righteousness; and your *new* glass shows his vindictive justice in the same unfavourable light, in which England saw two years ago the behaviour of a great monarch, who was exposed in the public papers, for unmercifully cutting with a whip, and tearing with spurs, the horses worked in a tapestry of his royal apartment, because they did not prance and gallop at his nod.

If a commendable, but immoderate fear of Pelagius' doctrine drove you into that of Augustine, the oracle of all the Dominicans, Thomists, Jansenists, and all other Roman Catholic predestinarians, you need not go so far beyond him as to recant all your sermons, because you mention perhaps three or four times, the freedom of our will, in the whole volume. "Let no one," says judicious Melancthon, "be offended at the words free will, (*liberum arbitrium*,) for St. Augustine himself uses it in many volumes, and that almost in every page, even to the surfeit of the reader."

The most ingenius Calvinist that ever wrote against free will is, I think, Mr. Edwards, of New England. And his fine system turns upon a comparison by which it may be overturned, and the freedom of the will demonstrated.

The will, says he, (if I remember right,) is like an even balance which can never turn without a weight, and must *necessarily* turn with one. But whence comes the weight that *necessarily* turns it? From the understanding, answers he; the last dictate of the understanding necessarily turns the will. And is the understanding also necessarily determined? Yes, by the effect which the objects around us necessarily have upon us, and by the circumstances in which we necessarily find ourselves; so that from first to last, our tempers, words, and actions, necessarily follow each other, and the circumstances that give them birth, as the second, third, and fourth links of a chain follow the first, when it is drawn along. Hence the eternal, infallible, irresistible, universary concatenation of events both in the moral and material world. This is, if I mistake not, the scheme of that great divine, and he spends no less than four hundred and fourteen large pages in trying to establish it.

I would just observe upon it, that it makes the First Cause or First Mover, the only *free Agent* in the world; all others being necessarily bound with the chain of his decrees, drawn along by the irresistible motion of his arm, or, which is the same, entangled in *forcible* circumstances unalterably fixed by his immutable counsel.

And yet, even upon this scheme, you needed not, sir, be so afraid of free will; for if the will be like an even balance, it is free in itself, though it is only with what I beg leave to call "a mechanical freedom"; for an even balance, you know, is *free* to turn either way.

But with respect to our ingenious author's assertion, that the will cannot turn without a weight, because an even balance cannot, I must consider it as a mere begging the question, if not as an absurdity. What is a balance but *lifeless matter?* And what is the will but *the living, active soul, springing up in its willing capacity, and self-exerting, self-determining power?* O how tottering is the mighty fabric raised, I shall not say upon such a fine spun metaphysical speculation, but upon so weak a foundation as a comparison, which supposes that two things, so widely different as spirit and matter, a *living soul* and *a lifeless balance,* are exactly alike with reference to self determination! Just as if a spirit, made after the image of the living, free, and powerful God, was no more capable of determining itself, than a horizontal beam supporting two equal copper bowls by six silken strings!

I am sorry, sir, to dissent from such a respectable divine as yourself; but, as I have no taste for new refinements, and cannot even conceive how far actions can be *morally* good or evil, any farther than our free will is concerned in them, I must follow the universal experience of mankind, and side with the author of the sermons against the author of the Narrative concerning the freedom of the will.

Nor is this freedom derogatory to free grace: for as it was free grace that gave an upright free will to Adam at his creation; so whenever his fallen children think or act aright, it is because their free will is mercifully prevented, touched, and so far rectified by free grace.

However, it must be granted, that many fashionable professors, and the large book of Mr. Edwards, are for you: but when you maintained *the freedom of the will,* Jesus Christ and the Gospel were on your side. To the end of the world this plain, peremptory assertion of our Lord, "I would and ye would not," will alone throw down the sophisms, and silence the objections of the most subtle philosophers against free will. When I consider what it implies, far from supposing that the will is a lifeless pair of scales, necessarily turned by the least weight, I see it is such a strong, self-determining power, that it can resist the effect of the most amazing weights; keep itself inflexible under all the warnings, threatenings, miracles, promises, entreaties, and tears of the Son of God; and remain obstinately unmoved under the strivings of his Holy Spirit. Yes: put in one scale the most stupendous weights, for instance, the hopes of heavenly joys, and the dread of hellish torments; and only the gaudy feather of honour, or the breaking bubble of worldly joy, in the other; if the will casts itself into the light scale, the feather or bubble will instantly preponderate. Nor is the power of the rectified will less wonderful; for though you should put all the kingdoms of the world and their glory in the one scale, and nothing but "the reproach of Christ" in the other; yet, if the will *freely* leap into the infamous scale, a crown of thorns easily outweighs a thousand golden crowns, and a devouring flame makes ten thousand thrones kick the beam.

Thus it appears the will can be persuaded, but never forced. You may bend it by moral suasions; but if you do this farther than it freely gives way, you *break,* you absolutely *destroy* it. A will forced, is no more a *will;* it is mere *compulsion;* freedom is not less essential to it than moral agency to man. Nor do I go, in these observations upon the freedom of the will, one step farther than honest John Bunyan, whom all the Calvinists so deservedly admire. In his "Holy War" he tells us, "There is but one *Lord Will-be Will* in the town of Man's-soul": whether he serves Diabolus or Shaddai, he is *Lord Will-be Will* still, "a man of great strength, resolution, and courage, whom in his occasion no one can turn," if he does not freely turn, or yield to be turned.

I hope, sir, these hints upon the harmlessness of mysticism, and the important doctrine of our free agency, will convince you, and the purchasers of your sermons, that you have been too precipitate in "publicly recanting them in the face of the whole world," especially *the ninth.*

If you ask, why I particularly interest myself in behalf of that one discourse, I will let you into the mystery. At the first reading I liked and adopted it: I cut it out of the volume in which it was bound, put it in my sermon case, and preached it in my church. The title of it is, you know, "Justification by Faith"; and, among several striking things on the subject, you quote twice this excellent passage out of our homilies: "Justification by faith implies a sure trust and confidence which a man hath in God, that by the *merits* of Christ his sins are forgiven, and he is reconciled to the favour of God." O sir, why did you not except it in your recantation, both for the honour of our Church and your own?

Were I to print and disperse such an advertisement as this: "Eight years ago I preached in my church a sermon, entitled *Justification by Faith,* composed by the honourable and reverend Mr. Shirley, to convince Papists and Pharisees that we are accepted through the alone *merits* of Christ: but I see better now; *I wish this sermon had been burned, and I publicly recant it in the face of the whole world*"; how would the Popish priest of Madeley rejoice! And how will that of Loughrea triumph when he hears *you* have actually done it in your Narrative! What will your Protestant parishioners, to whom your book is dedicated, say, when the surprising news reaches Ireland? And what will the world think, when they see you warmly plead in August for *Justification by faith,* as being "the foundation that must by all means be secured"; and publicly recant, in September, your own excellent sermon on "Justification by Faith?"

Indeed, sir, though I admire your candour in acknowledging there are some exceptionable passages in your discourses, and your humility in readily giving them up, I can no more approve of your readiness in making, than in insisting upon "formal recantations." We cannot be too careful in dealing in that kind of ware; and it is extremely dangerous to do it by wholesale; as by that mean we may give up, or *seem* to give up, "before the whole world," precious truths, delivered by Christ himself, and brought down to us in streams of the blood of martyrs.

Among some blunt expostulations that Mr. Wesley erased in my Fifth Letter, as being too severe, he kindly but unhappily struck out this: "Before you could with candour insist upon 'a recantation' of Mr. Wesley's Minutes, should you not have recanted yourself the passages of your own sermons where the same doctrines are maintained; and have sent your recantation through the land, together with your Circular Letter?" Had this been published, it might have convinced you of the unseasonableness of your "recantation." Thus, this *second hasty step* would have been prevented; and if I dwell so long upon it now, believe me, sir, it is chiefly to prevent a *third.*

And, now your sermons are recanted, is the Vindication of Mr. Wesley's Minutes invalidated? Not at all; for you have not yet recanted the Bath Hymnbook, nor can you ever get Mr. Henry, Mr. Williams, and a tribe of other anti-Crispian, though Calvinist divines, now in glory, to recant with you; much less the prophets, apostles, and Christ himself, on whose irrefragable testimony we chiefly rest our doctrine.

II. *As I have pleaded out the cause of free will against bound will or that of your sermons against your Narrative, and am insensibly come to the Vindications, give me leave, sir, to speak a word also for that performance and the author of it.*

You say he has "*attempted* a vindication of the Minutes"; but do not some people think he has likewise *executed* it? And have you proved he has not?

You reply, "There would be a great impropriety in my giving a full and particular answer to those letters, because the author did all he could to revoke them, and has given me ample satisfaction in his letters of submission." Indeed, sir, you quite mistook the nature of that "submission"; it had absolutely no reference to the *arguments* of the Vindication; it only respected the *polemic dress* in which the vindicator had put them. You might have been convinced of it by this paragraph of his letter of submission: "I was going to preach when I had the news of your happy accommodation, and was no sooner out of church than I wrote to beg my Vindication might not appear in the *dress* in which I had put it. I did not then, nor do I yet, repent having written upon the Minutes; but, *as matters are now,* I am very sorry I did not write in a general manner, without taking notice of the Circular Letter, and mentioning your dear name." He begs, therefore, you will not consider his letter of submission as a reason for not giving "a full or particular answer" to his *arguments*. On the contrary, if you can prove they want solidity, *a letter of thanks* shall follow his "letter of submission": if he is wrong, he sincerely desires to be set right.

You add, however, that he has "broken the Minutes into sentences and half sentences; and by refining upon each of the detached particles, has given a new turn to the whole." But he appeals to every impartial reader whether he has not, like a candid man, first considered them all together, and then every one asunder. He begs to be informed, whether an artist can better inquire into the goodness of a watch, than by making first his observations on the whole movement in general, and then by taking it to pieces, that he may examine every part with greater attention. And he desires you would show, whether what you are pleased to call "a new turn," is not preferable to the *heretical turn* some persons give them; and whether it is not equally, if not better adapted to the literal meaning of the words, as well as more agreeable to the Antinomian state of the Church, the general tenor of the propositions, and the system of doctrine maintained by Mr. Wesley for near forty years?

In your last page you take your friendly leave of the vindicator, by saying, you "desire in love to cast a veil over all apparent mistakes of his judgment on this occasion"; but as he is not conscious of "all these apparent mistakes," he begs you would in love take off "the veil" you have cast upon them, that he may see, and rectify at least those which are capital.

III. *And that you may not hastily conclude he was "mistaken" in his Vindication of that article that touches upon merit, he embraces this opportunity of presenting you with another quotation from the* JOHN WESLEY *of the last century, he means Mr. Baxter, the most judicious divine, as well as the greatest, most useful, and most laborious preacher of his age.*

In his "Catholic Theology," answering the objections of an Antinomian, he says: "*Merit* is a word, I perceive, you are against; you may therefore choose any other of the same signification, and we will forbear this rather than offend you. But yet tell me, (1) What, if the words $\alpha\xi\iota o\varsigma$ and $\alpha\xi\iota\alpha$ were translated *deserving* and *merit*, would it not be as true a translation as *worthy* and *worthiness*, when it is the same thing that is meant? (2) Do not all the ancient teachers of the Churches, since the apostles, particularly apply the names $\alpha\xi\iota\alpha$ and *meritum* to believers? And if you persuade men that all these teachers were Papists, will you not persuade most that believe you to be Papists too? (3) Are not *reward,* and *merit* or *desert*, relative words, as *punishment* and *guilt, master* and *servant, husband* and *wife?* And is there any reward which is not *meriti prœmium,* "the reward of some merit?" Again:

"Is it not the second article of our faith, and next to 'believing there is a God,' that 'he is the rewarder of them that diligently seek him?' When you thus extirpate faith and godliness, on pretence of crying down *merit,* you see what *overdoing* tends to. And indeed by the same reason that men deny a reward to duty, (the faultiness being pardoned through Christ,) they would infer there is no punishment for sin; for if God will not do good to the righteous, neither will he do evil to the wicked; he becomes like the god of Epicurus, he does not trouble himself about us, nor about the merit or demerit of our actions. But David knew better: 'The Lord,' says he, 'plentiously rewardeth the proud doers; and verily there is a reward for the righteous, for there is a God that judgeth the earth'; that sees matter of praise or dispraise, rewardable-

ness or worthiness of punishment, in all the actions of
men." This is, sir, all Mr. Baxter and Mr. Wesley mean
by *merit* or *demerit;* and if the vindicator be wrong in
thinking they are both in the right, please to remove "the
veil" that conceals his "mistake."

IV. *As one of his correspondents desires him to explain himself a little more upon the article of the Minutes
which respects undervaluing ourselves; and as you probably place the arguments he has advanced upon that head
among his "apparent mistakes," he takes likewise this opportunity of making some additional observations on that
delicate, subject.*

How we can "esteem every man better than ourselves,"
and ourselves "the chief of sinners," or "the least of
saints," seems not so much a calculation for the understanding, as for the lowly, contrite, and loving heart. It
puzzles the former, but the latter at once makes it out.
Nevertheless, the seeming contradiction may, perhaps, be
reconciled to reason by these reflections:

1. If friendship brings the greatest monarch down
from his throne, and makes him sit on the same couch
with his favourites; may not brotherly love, much more
powerful than natural friendship; may not humility, ex-
cited by the example of Christ washing his disciples' feet;
may not a deep regard for that precept, "He that will be
greatest among you, let him be the least of all," sink the
true Christian to the dust, and make him lie in spirit at
the feet of every one?

2. A well-bred person uncovers himself, bows, and
declares, even to his inferiors, that he is their "most
humble servant." This affected civility of the world is but
an apish imitation of the genuine humility of the Church;
and if those who customarily speak humble words without
meaning, may yet be honest men, how much more the
saints, who have "truth written in their inward parts,"
and "speak out of the abundance of their *humble* hearts!"

3. He who walks in the light of Divine love, sees something of God's spiritual, moral, or natural image in all men, the worst not excepted; and at the sight, that which is merely creaturely in him, (by a kind of spiritual instinct found in all who are "born of the Spirit,") directly bows to that which is of God in another. He imitates the captain of a first rate man of war, who, upon seeing the king or queen coming up in a small boat, forgetting the enormous size of his ship, or considering it is the king's own ship, immediately strikes his colours; and the greater vessel, consistently with wisdom and truth, pays respect to the less.

4. The most eminent saint, having known more of the workings of corruption in his own breast, than he can possibly know of them in that of any other man, may, with great truth, (according to his present views and former feelings of the internal evil he has overcome,) call himself "the chief of sinners."

5. Nor does he know, but if the feeblest believers had all his talents and graces, with all his opportunities of doing and receiving good, they would have made far superior advances in the Christian life; and in this view also, without hypocritical humility, he prefers the least saint to himself. Thus, although, according to the humble light of *others,* all true believers certainly "undervalue," yet, according to *their own* humble light, they make a true estimate of "themselves."

V. The vindicator having thus solved a problem of godliness, which you have undoubtedly ranked among his "apparent mistakes," he takes the liberty of presenting you with a list of some of *your own* "apparent mistakes on this occasion."

1. In the very letter in which you recant your Circular Letter, you desire Mr. Wesley to "give up the fatal errors of the Minutes," though you have not yet *proved* they contain one; you still affirm, "They appear to you

evidently subversive of the fundamentals of Christianity,"
that is, in plain English, still "dreadfully heretical"; and
you produce a letter which asserts, also, without
shadow of proof, that the "Minutes were given for the es-
tablishment of another foundation than that which is
laid"; that they are "repugnant to Scripture, the whole
plan of man's salvation under the new covenant of grace,
and also to the clear meaning of our Established Church,
as well as to all other Protestant Churches."

2. You declare in your Narrative that, "when you
cast your eye over the Minutes, you are just where you
were," and assure the public, that "nothing inferior to an
attack upon the foundation of our hope, through the all-
sufficient sacrifice of Christ, could have been an object
sufficient to engage you in its defence." Thus, by continu-
ing to insinuate such an ATTACK was really made, you
continue to wound Mr. Wesley in the tenderest part.

3. Although Mr. Wesley and fifty-three of his fellow
labourers have let you quietly "secure the foundation,"
(which, by the by, had only been shaken in your own
ideas, and was perfectly secured by these express words
of the Minutes, "not by the merit of works," but by "believing in Christ,") yet, far from allowing them to *secure the superstructure* in their turn, which would be
nothing but just, you begin already a contest with them
about "our second justification by works in the day of
judgment."

4. Instead of frankly acknowledging the rashness of
your step, and the greatness of your mistake, with respect
to the Minutes, you make a bad matter worse, by treating
the Declaration as you have treated them; forcing upon it
a dangerous sense, no less contrary to the Scriptures, than
to Mr. Wesley's meaning, and the import of the words.

5. When you speak of the dreadful charges you have
brought against the Minutes, you softly call them "mis-
constructions you *may seem* to have made of their mean-

ing." (Page 22, line 4.) Nor is your "acknowledgment" much stronger than your "may seem"; at least it does not appear, to many, adequate to the hurt done by your Circular Letter to the practical Gospel of Christ, and the reputation of his eminent servant, thousands of whose friends you have grieved, offended, or stumbled; while you have confirmed thousands of his enemies in their hard thoughts of him, and in their unjust contempt of his ministry.

6. And, lastly, far from candidly inquiring into the merit of the arguments advanced in the Vindication, you represent them as mere "metaphysical distinctions"; or cast, as a veil over them, a friendly submissive *letter of condolence,* which was never intended for the use to which you have put it.

Therefore the vindicator, who does not admire a peace founded upon a "may seem" on your part, and on Mr. Wesley's part upon a "declaration," to which you have already fixed a wrong unscriptural sense of your own, takes this public method to inform you, he thinks his arguments in favour of Mr. Wesley's anti-Crispian propositions rational, scriptural, and solid; and once more he begs you would remove the veil you have hitherto "cast over all the apparent mistakes of his judgment on this occasion," that he may see whether the *Antinomian* gospel of Dr. Crisp is preferable to the *practical* Gospel which Mr. Wesley endeavours to restore to its primitive and Scriptural lustre.

VI. Having thus finished my remarks upon the mistakes of your Narrative, I gladly take my leave of controversy for this time. Would to God it were for ever! I no more like it than I do applying a caustic to the back of my friends; it is disagreeable to me, and painful to them; and nevertheless, it must be done, when their health and mine is at stake.

J. FLETCHER

LETTER III

HONOURED AND REVEREND SIR: If I mistake not the
workings of my heart, a concern for St. James' "pure and
undefiled religion" excites me to take the pen once more,
and may account for the readiness with which I have met
you in the dangerous field of controversy. You may possibly think mere partiality to Mr. Wesley has inspired me
with that boldness; and others may be ready to say as
Eliab, "We know the pride and naughtiness of thy heart.
Thou art come down that thou mightest see the battle."
But may I not answer with David, "Is there not a cause?"

Is it not highly necessary to make a stand against
Antinomianism? Is not that gigantic "man of sin" a more
dangerous enemy to King Jesus, than the champion of the
Philistines was to King Saul? Has he not defied more than
forty days the armies and arms, the people and truths of
the living God?

Multitudes indeed still keep the field, still make an
open profession of godliness. But how few of these "endure hardship as good soldiers of Jesus Christ!" How
many have already cast away "the shield of *Gospel* faith,
the faith which works by love!" What numbers dread the
cross, the heavenly standard they should steadily bear, or
resolutely follow! While in pompous speeches they extol
the cross of Jesus, how do they, upon the most frivolous
pretence, refuse to "take up" their own! Did the massy
staff of Goliath's spear seem more terrible to the fright-
ed Israelites than *the daily cross* of those dastardly followers of the Crucified? What Boanerges can spirit them up,
and lead them on "from conquering to conquer"? Who
can even make them look the enemy in the face? Alas!
"in their hearts they are *already* gone back to Egypt.
Their faces are *but half* Sion ward." They give way—they
"draw back"; O may it not be "to perdition!" May not the
king of terrors overtake them in their retreat, and make
them as great monuments of God's vengeance against

cowardly soldiers, as Lot's wife was in his indignation against halting racers!

But setting allegory aside, permit me, sir, to pour my fears into your bosom, and tell you with the utmost plainness my distressing thoughts of the religious world.

For some years I have suspected there is more imaginary than "unfeigned faith" in most of those who pass for believers. With a mixture of indignation and grief have I seen them carelessly follow the stream of corrupt nature, against which they should have manfully wrestled. And by the most preposterous mistake, when they should have exclaimed against their *Antinomianism*, I have heard them cry out against "the *legality* of their wicked hearts; which" they said "still suggested they were to *do something* in order to salvation." Glad was I, therefore, when I had attentively considered Mr. Wesley's Minutes, to find they were levelled at the very errors which give rise to an evil I had long lamented in secret, but had wanted courage to resist and attack.

I. *This evil is Antinomianism;* that is, any kind of doctrinal or practical *opposition to God's law,* which is the perfect rule of right, and the moral picture of the God of love, drawn in miniature by our Lord in these two exquisite precepts, "Thou shalt love God with all thy heart, and thy neighbour as thyself."

As "the law is good, if a man use it lawfully," so *legality* is excellent, if it be evangelical. The external respect shown by Pharisees to the law is but feigned and hypocritical legality. Pharisees are no more truly legal, than Antinomians are truly evangelical. "Had ye believed Moses," says Jesus to people of that stamp, "ye would have believed me": but in your hearts you hate his law as much as you do my Gospel.

We see no less Gospel in the preface of the Ten Commandments, "I am the Lord thy God," etc., than we do legality in the middle of our Lord's sermon on the mount,

"I say, Whosoever looketh on a woman to lust after her, hath already committed adultery in his heart." Nevertheless, the latter "has in all things the pre-eminence" over the former. For if "the law," shortly prefaced by the Gospel, "came by Moses"; *grace*, the gracious, the full display of the Gospel, *and truth*, the true explanation and fulfilling of the law, "came by Jesus Christ."

This evangelical law should appear to us "sweeter than the honeycomb, and more precious than fine gold." We should continually spread the tables of our hearts before our heavenly Lawgiver, beseeching him to write it there with his own finger, the powerful Spirit of life and love. But alas! God's commandments are disregarded; they are represented as the needless or impracticable sanctions of that superannuated legalist, Moses; and if we express our veneration for them, we are looked upon as people who are always strangers to the Gospel, or are fallen into the Galatian state.

Not so David. He was so great an admirer of God's law, that he declares the godly man "doth meditate therein day and night." He expresses his transcendent value for it, under the synonymous expressions of *law, words, statutes, testimonies, precepts,* and *commandments,* in almost every verse of the 119th Psalm. And he says of himself, "O how I love thy law! It is my meditation all the day!"

St. Paul was as evangelically legal as David; for he knew the law is as much contained in the Gospel, as the tables of stone, on which the moral law was written, were contained in the ark. He therefore assured the Corinthians, that "though he had all faith," even that which is most uncommon, and performed the greatest wonders, it would "profit him nothing," unless it was accompanied by "charity," unless it "worked by love," which is "the fulfilling of the law"; the excellency of faith arising from the excellent end it answers in producing and nourishing love.

Should it be objected, that St. Paul says to the Galatians, "I through the law am dead to the law, that I might live to God"; and to the Romans, "Ye are become dead to the law by the body of Christ": I answer, in the apostle's days, that expression, *the law,* frequently meant "the whole Mosaic dispensation"; and in that sense every believer is dead to it, dead to all that Christ has not adopted. For, (1) He is dead to the *Levitical law,* "Christ having abolished in himself the law of ordinances. Touch not, taste not, handle not." (2) He is dead to the *ceremonial law,* which was only "a shadow of good things to come," a typical representation of Christ and the blessings flowing from his sacrifice. (3) He is dead to the *curse* attending his past violations of the *moral law;* for "Christ hath delivered us from the curse of the law, being made a curse for us." And *lastly,* he is dead to the hopes of recommending himself to God by the *merit* of his obedience to the moral law; for in point of *merit,* he "is determined to know nothing but Christ and him crucified."

To make St. Paul mean more than this, is, (1) To make him maintain that no believer can sin: for if "sin is the transgression of the law," and "the law is dead and buried," it is plain, no believer can sin, as nobody can transgress a law which is abolished: for "where no law is, there is no transgression." (2) It is to make him contradict St. James, who exhorts us to "fulfil the royal law, according to the Scripture, Thou shalt love thy neighbour as thyself." And, (3) It is to make him contradict himself: for he charges the Galatians "by love to serve one another; all the law being fulfilled in one word, even in this, Thou shalt love thy neighbour as thyself." And he assures the Hebrews, that under the new covenant, believers, far from being "without *God's* laws, have them written in their hearts; God *himself* placing them in their minds."

And did our Lord side with Antinomians? Just the reverse. Far from repealing the two above mentioned royal precepts, he asserts, that "on them hang all the law and the prophets"; and had the four Gospels been then written, he would no doubt have represented them as subservient to the establishing of the law, as he did the book of Isaiah, the evangelical prophet. Such high thoughts had he of the law, that when a lawyer expressed his veneration for it, by declaring that "the love of God, and our neighbour, was more than all whole burnt offerings and sacrifices, Jesus, seeing that he had answered discreetly, said unto him, Thou art not far from the kingdom of God."

The Gospel itself terminates in the fulfilling of the commandments. For as the curse of the law, like the scourge of a severe schoolmaster, drives, so the Gospel, like a loving guide, brings us to Christ, the great Law Fulfiller, in whom we find inexhaustible treasures of pardon and power; of pardon for past breaches of the law, and of power for present obedience to it. Nor are we sooner come to him than he magnifies the law, by his precepts, as he formerly did by his obedience unto death. "If ye love me," says he, "keep my commandments." "This is his commandment, that we should love one another; and he that loveth another hath fulfilled the law "

Again: the Gospel displays Jesus' dying love, that by "believing" it "we may" love him, that is, "have everlasting life," the life of *love* which *abideth* when the life of faith is no more. Hence St. John sums up Christianity in these words, "We love him because he first loved us!" And what is it to love Jesus, but to fulfil the whole law at once, to love God and man, the Creator and the creature, united in one divinely human person!

Did the Son of God "magnify the law," that we might vilify it? Did he "make it honourable," that we might make it contemptible? Did he "come to fulfil it," that we might be discharged from fulfilling it according to our capacity? That is, discharged from loving God and our neighbour? Discharged from the employment and joys of heaven? No: the "Word was *never* made flesh" for this dreadful end. None but Satan could have become incarnate to go upon such an infernal errand as this! Standing, therefore, upon the rock of evangelical truth, we ask, with St. Paul, "Do we then make void the law through faith? God forbid! Nay, we establish the law." We point sinners to that Saviour in and from whom they may continually have the law-fulfilling power; "that the righteousness of the law may be fulfilled in us, who walk not after the flesh but after the Spirit."

Such are the glorious and delightful views which the Scriptures give us of the law, disarmed of its curse in Christ; the law of holy, humble love, so strongly enforced in the discourses, and sweetly exemplified in the life and death of the "Prophet like unto Moses!" So amiable, so precious is the book of the law, when delivered to us by Jesus, sprinkled with his atoning blood, and explained by his loving Spirit! And so true is St. Paul's assertion, "We are not without law to God, but under the law of Christ!"

Do not imagine, Rev. sir, I thus cry up God's law to drown the late cries of *heresy* and *apostasy*. I appeal to matter of fact and your own observations. Consider the religious world, and say, if ANTINOMIANISM is not in general a motto better adapted to the state of professing congregations, societies, families, and individuals, than HOLINESS UNTO THE LORD, the inscription that should be even upon our "horses' bells."

II. *Begin with* CONGREGATIONS, *and cast first your eyes upon the hearers.* In general they have curious "itching ears, and will not endure sound doctrine." Many of them are armed with the "breastplate of a righteousness" which they have vainly imputed to themselves: they have on the showy "helmet of a *presumptuous* hope," and hold fast the impenetrable shield of strong prejudice. With these they "quench the fiery darts of" convincing truth, and stand undaunted under volleys of reproof.

They say, they "will have nothing but Christ." And who could blame them, if they would have Christ in all his offices? Christ, with all his parables and sermons, cautions and precepts, reproofs and expostulations, exhortations and threatenings? Christ, preaching to the multitudes upon a mountain, as well as honourably teaching in the temple? Christ, fasting in the wilderness, or praying in Gethsemane; as well as Christ making the multitude sit down upon the grass to receive "loaves and fishes," or promising "thrones" to his disciples? Christ, "constraining them to get into a ship, and toil in rowing all night with a contrary wind"; as well as Christ "coming in the morning," and causing "the ship to be immediately at the land whither they went?" Christ upon Mount Calvary, as well as Christ upon Mount Tabor? In a word, who would find fault with them if they would have Christ with his poverty and self denial, his reproach and cross, his Spirit and graces, his prophets and apostles, his plain apparel and mean followers?

But alas! it is not so. They will have *what* they please of Christ, and that too *as* they please. If he come accompanied by legal Moses and honest Elijah, who talk of the crucifixion of the body, and "decease" of the flesh, they can do very well without him. If he preach "free grace, free will, faithfulness, or heavenly mindedness," some turn to the right, some wheel about to the left, others go directly back, and all agree to say or think, "This is a hard saying, who can hear it?"

They admire him in one chapter, and know not what to make of him in another. Some of his words they extol to the sky, and others they seem to be ashamed of. If he asserts his authority as a Lawgiver, they are ready to treat him with as little ceremony as they do Moses. If he say,

"Keep my commandments: I am a king"; like the Jews of old, they rise against the awful declaration; or they "crown him" as *a Surety,* the better to "set him at naught" as *a Monarch.* And if he add, to his ministers, "I am the prophet that was to come; go in my name, and teach all nations to observe all things whatsoever I have commanded you"; they complain, "This is *the law;* give us *the Gospel;* we can relish nothing but *the. Gospel!"*

They have no idea of "eating the paschal lamb" whole, "his head with his legs, and the purtenance thereof"; nor do they take care of "not breaking his bones"; they do not like him roast with fire neither; but "raw or sodden with water" out of their own "broken cisterns." If you present him to them as the type of the "Lamb of God that taketh away the sin of the world, and maketh an end of it"; their hearts heave, they say, "Pray have me excused" from thus feeding upon him: and though it is said, "Ye shall let nothing of it remain until the morning, you shall eat in haste," they postpone, they beg leave to keep it till the article of death: and if, in the meantime, you talk to them of "bitter herbs," they marvel at your Jewish, legal taste, and complain that you spoil the Gospel feast.

They do not consider we must "give every one his portion of meat," or proper medicine, "in due season"; and that sweet things are not always wholesome. They forget we must "leave all" Antinomian refinements "to follow Christ," who sometimes says to decent Pharisees, "How can you escape the damnation of hell?" And to a beloved disciple that shuns the cross, "Satan, thou savourest not the things of God, but the things of men." They will have nothing but the atonement. Nor do they choose to remember, that St. Paul, who "did not shun to declare the whole counsel of God," preached Christ to Felix, by "reasoning of temperance, righteousness, and judgment to come."

Hence it is that some preachers must choose comfortable subjects to please their hearers; just as those who make an entertainment for nice persons are obliged to study what will suit their difficult taste. A multitude of important scriptures may be produced, on which no minister, who is unwilling to lose his reputation as "an evangelical preacher," must dare to speak in some pulpits, unless it be to explain away or enervate their meaning. Take some instances:

The good old Calvinists, (Archbishop Leighton for one,) questioned whether a man was truly converted who did not sincerely "go on to perfection," and heartily endeavoured to "perfect holiness in the fear of God." But now, if we only quote such passages with an emphasis, and enforce their meaning with some degree of earnestness, the truth of our conversion is suspected: we even pass for enemies to Christ's righteousness.

If we have courage to handle such scriptures as these, "To do good and to distribute forget not, for with such sacrifices God is well pleased. Show me thy faith by thy works. Was not Rahab justified by works? By works was Abraham's faith made perfect," etc., the bare giving out of our text prejudices our Antinomian hearers against us, and robs us of their candid attention, unless they expect a charity sermon; for on such an occasion they will yet allow us, at the close of our discourse, to speak honourably of good works: just as those who run to the opposite extreme, will yet, on some particular days, such as Christmas and Good Friday, permit us to make honourable mention of Jesus Christ.

The evil would be tolerable if we were only obliged to select smooth texts in order to gratify an Antinomian audience; but, alas! it is grown so desperate, that unless we "adulterate the sincere milk of the word," many reject it as poison. It is a doubt whether we could preach in some celebrated pulpits on "the good man, who is merciful and lendeth, who hath dispersed abroad and given to the poor, and whose righteousness remaineth for ever"; or on "breaking off our sins by righteousness, and our iniquities by showing mercy to the poor"; or on "the righteousness which exceeds that of the scribes and Pharisees"; or on "the robes washed and made white in the blood of the Lamb," without giving general disgust; unless, to keep in the good grace of our Nicolaitan hearers, we were to dissent from all sober commentators, and offer the greatest violence to the context, our own conscience, and common sense, by saying, that *the righteousness* and *robes*, mentioned in those passages, are Christ's *imputed*, and not our *performed* obedience.

This Antinomian cavilling of hearers against preachers is deplorable; and the effects of it will be dreadful. If the Lord do not put a stop to this growing evil, we shall soon see every where, what we see in too many places, self-conceited, unhumbled men, rising against the truths and ministers of God; men who "are not *meek* doers of the law," but *insolent* judges, preposterously trying that law by which they shall soon be tried; men who, instead of sitting as criminals before all the messengers of their Judge, with arrogancy invade the Judge's tribunal, and arraign even his most venerable ambassadors— men, who should "fall on their faces before all, and give glory to God by confessing that he is with his ministers," of every denomination, "of a truth"; but who, far from doing it, boldly condemn the word that condemns them, snatch the two-edged sword from the mouth of every faithful messenger, blunt the edge of it, and audaciously thrust at him in their turn—men, who, when they see a servant of God in their pulpit, suppose he stands at their bar; try him with as much insolence as Korah, Dathan, and Abiram tried Moses; cast him with less kindness than Pilate did Jesus; force a fool's coat of their own making upon him; and then, from "the seat of the scornful," pronounce the decisive sentence: "He is legal, dark, blind, unconverted; an enemy to free grace. He is a rank Papist, a Jesuit, a false prophet, or a wolf in sheep's clothing."

III. *But whence springs this almost general Antinomianism of our congregations?* Shall I conceal the sore because it festers in my own breast? Shall I be partial? No, in the name of Him who is "no respecter of persons," I will confess my sin, and that of many of my brethren. Though I am the least, and (I write it with tears of shame) the most unworthy of them all, I will follow the dictates of my conscience, and use the authority of a minister of Christ. If Balaam, a *false* prophet, took in good part the reproof of his ass, I should wrong my honoured brethren and fathers, the *true* prophets of the Lord, if I feared their resenting some well-meant reproofs, which I first level at myself, and for which I heartily wish there was no occasion.

Is not the Antinomianism of hearers fomented by that of preachers? Does it not become us to take the greatest part of the blame upon ourselves, according to the old adage, "Like priest, like people?" Is it surprising that some of us should have an Antinomian audience? Do we not make or keep it so? When did we preach such a practical sermon as that of our Lord on the mount, or write such close letters as the epistles of St. John? Alas! I doubt it is but seldom. Not living so near to God ourselves as we should, we are afraid to come near to the consciences of our people. The Jews said to our Lord, "In so saying thou reproachest us"; but now the case is altered, and our auditors might say to many of us, "In so saying you would reproach yourselves."

Some prefer popularity to plain dealing. We love to see a crowd of worldly-minded hearers, rather than "a little flock, a peculiar people zealous of good works." We dare not shake our congregations to purpose, lest our *five thousand should,* in three years' time, be reduced to *a hundred and twenty.*

Luther's advice to Melancthon, *Scandaliza fortiter,* "So preach that those who do not fall out with their sins may fall out with thee," is more and more unfashionable. Under pretence of drawing our hearers by love, some of us softly rock the cradle of carnal security in which they sleep. For "fear of grieving the dear children of God," we let "buyers and sellers, sheep and oxen," yea, goats and lions, fill "the temple" undisturbed. And because "the bread must not be kept from the hungry children," we let those who are wanton make shameful waste of it, and even allow "dogs," which we should "beware of," and noisy parrots that can speak *shibboleth,* to do the same. We forget that God's children "are led by his Spirit," who is "the Comforter" himself; that they are all afraid of being deceived, all "jealous for the Lord of Hosts"; and therefore prefer a preacher who "searches Jerusalem with candles," and cannot suffer God's house to be made a "den of thieves," to a workman who "whitewashes *the. noisome* sepulchres," he should open, and "daubs over with untempered mortar the *bulging* walls" he should demolish.

The old Puritans strongly insisted upon *personal holiness,* and the first Methodists upon the *new birth;* but these doctrines seem to grow out of date. The Gospel is cast into another mould. People, it seems, may now be "in Christ," without being "new creatures," and "new creatures" without casting "old things" away. They may be God's children without God's image; and "born of the Spirit" without "the fruits of the Spirit." If our unregenerate hearers get orthodox ideas about the way of salvation in their heads, evangelic phrases concerning Jesus' love in their mouths, and a warm zeal for our party and favourite forms in their hearts; without any more ado, we help them to rank themselves among the children of God. But, alas! this self adoption into the family of Christ

will no more pass in heaven than self imputation of
Christ's righteousness. The work of the Spirit will stand
there, and that alone. Again:

Some of us often give our congregations particular accounts of *the covenant* between the persons of the blessed
Trinity, and speak of it as confidently as if the King of
kings had admitted us members of his privy council; but
how seldom do we do justice to the Scriptures, where the
covenant is mentioned in a *practical* manner! How rarely
do the ministers, who are fond of preaching upon the
covenant between God and David, dwell upon such scriptures as these? "Because they continued not in my covenant, I regarded them not; because they have trans-
gressed the law, changed the ordinances, and broken the
everlasting covenant, therefore hath the curse devoured
the earth, and they that dwell therein are desolate: therefore the inhabitants of the earth are burned, and few men
left. I say to the wicked, What hast thou to do to take my
covenant in thy mouth? They kept not the covenant of
God, and refused to walk in his law"; they would not be
evangelically legal, "therefore a fire was kindled in Jacob,
the wrath of God came upon them, he slew the fattest of
them, and smote down the chosen, *the elect* of Israel!"

We frequently keep back from our hearers the very
portions that honest Nathan or blunt John the Baptist
would have particularly enforced. The taste of many is
perverted; they "loathe the manna of the word," not because it is *light,* but *heavy* food. They must have "savoury
meat, such as their soul loveth"; and we "*hunt* for veni-
son," we minister to their spiritual luxury, and feast with
them on our doctrinal refinements. Hence "many are
weak and sickly among us." Some that might be "fat and
well-liking, cry out, *My leanness! My leanness!*" And
"many sleep" in a spiritual grave, the easy prey of corruption and sin.

How few Calebs, how few Joshuas are found among the many spies who bring a report of the good land! The cry is seldom, "Let us go up and possess it," unless the good land be the map of the Gospel dawn by Dr. Crisp. On the contrary, the difficulties attending the noble conquest are magnified to the highest degree. "The sons of Anak are tall and strong, and their cities are fenced up to heaven." "All our corruptions are gigantic. The castle where they dwell shall always remain a den of thieves. It is an impregnable citadel, strongly garrisoned by Apollyon's forces: we shall never love God here with all our souls: we shall always have desperately wicked hearts."

How few of our celebrated pulpits are there, where more has not been said *at times* for sin than against it. With what an air of positiveness and assurance has that Barabbas, that murderer of Christ and souls, been pleaded for! "It will humble us, make us watchful, stir up our diligence, quicken our graces, endear Christ," etc. That is, in plain English, pride will beget humility; sloth will spur us on to diligence; rust will brighten our armour; and unbelief, the very soul of every sinful temper, is to do the work of faith! Sin must not only be always lurking about the walls and gates of the town of Man's Soul, (If I may once more allude to Bunyan's *Holy War*,) but it shall dwell in it, in the King's palace, "in the inner chamber," the inmost recesses of the heart; there is no turning it out. Jesus, who cleansed the lepers with a word or a touch, cannot, with all the force of his Spirit and virtue of his blood, expel this leprosy. It is too inveterate. Death, that foul monster, the offspring of sin, shall have the important honour of killing his father. He, he alone is to give the great, the last, the decisive blow. This is confidently asserted by those who cry, *Nothing but Christ!* They allow him to lop off the branches; but death, the great saviour death, is to destroy the root of sin. In the meantime "the temple of God shall have agreement with idols, and Christ concord with Belial: the Lamb" of God shall "lie down with the roaring lion" in our hearts.

Nor does the preaching of this internal slavery, this bondage of spiritual corruption, shock our hearers. No: this mixture of light and darkness passes for Gospel in our days. And what is more astonishing still, by making much ado about "finished salvation," we can even put it off as "the only pure, genuine, and comfortable Gospel": while the smoothness of our doctrine will atone for our most glaring inconsistencies.

We have so whetted the Antinomian appetite of our hearers, that they swallow down almost any thing. We may tell them St. Paul was, at one and the same time, "carnal, sold under sin," crying, "Who shall deliver me from this body of death?" and triumphing that he did "not walk after the flesh, but after the Spirit, rejoicing in the testimony of a good conscience," and glorying that "the law of the Spirit of life in Christ Jesus had made him free from the law of sin and death!" This suits their experience; therefore they readily take our word, and it passes for "the word of God." It is a mercy that we have not yet attempted to prove, by the same argument, that lying and cursing are quite consistent with apostolic faith; for St. Paul speaks of his "lie," and St. James says, "With our tongues curse we men."

We may make them believe, that though adultery and murder are damning sins in poor blind Turks and heathens, yet they are only the spots of God's children in enlightened Jews and favoured Christians: that God is the most partial of all judges; some being accursed to the pit of hell for breaking the law in the most trifling points; while others, who actually break it in the most flagrant instances, are richly "blessed with all heavenly benedictions": and that, while God beholds "no iniquity in Jacob, no perverseness in Israel," he sees nothing but odious sins in Ishmael, and devilish wickedness in Esau; although the

Lord assures us, "The wickedness of the wicked shall be
upon him," and that "though hand join in hand the wicked
shall not go unpunished," were he as great in Jacob as
Korah, and as famous as Zimri in Israel.

We may tell our hearers, one hour, that "the love of
Christ *sweetly* constrains" all believers to walk, yea, to
"run the way of God's commandments," and that they cannot help obeying its forcible dictates: and we may persuade them, the next hour, that "how to perform what
is good they find not; that they fall continually into sin;
for that which they do they allow not, and what they
would, that do they not; but what they hate, that do they."
And that these inconsistencies may not shock their common sense, or alarm their consciences, we again touch the
sweet-sounding string of "finished salvation": we intimate
we have the key of evangelical knowledge, reflect on those
who expect deliverance from sin in this life, and "build
up" our congregations in a most comfortable, I wish I
could say, "most holy faith."

In short, we have so used our people to strange doctrines, and preposterous assertions, that, if we were to intimate, God himself sets us a pattern of Antinomianism,
by disregarding his own most holy and lovely law, which
inculcates perfect love—if we were even to hint that he
bears a secret grudge, or an immortal enmity to those
very souls whom he commands us to "love as Christ has
loved us"; that he feeds them only for the great day of
slaughter, and has determined, (so inveterate is his
hatred!) "before the foundation of the world" to "fit"
them as "vessels of wrath," that he might eternally fill
them with his fiery vengeance, merely to show what a
great and sovereign God he is; I doubt whether some
would not be highly pleased, and say we had "preached
a sound and sweet discourse." This would probably be the
case, if we address them in such a manner as to make
them believe they are *elect;* not, indeed, of those ancient,

legal, and wrestling "elect, who cry to God day and night to be avenged of their spiritual adversary," but of those modern, indolent elect, who have found out a short way to heaven, and maintain, "We are absolutely to do nothing in order to salvation."

With joy I confess, however, that glorious and rousing truths are frequently delivered in the demonstration of the Spirit and of power. But, alas! the blow is seldom followed. You have seen fond mothers violently correcting their children one instant, and the next dandling them upon their knees; and, by foolishly kissing away their tears, spoiling the correction they had given. Just so it is with several of us: we preach a close discourse, and seem determined to drive the buyers and sellers out of the temple. Our Antinomian hearers begin to awake and look about them: some are even ready to cry out, "Men and brethren, what shall we do?" but, alas! we sound a retreat when we should shout for a second battle. By an unaccountable weakness, before we conclude, we soothe them up, and make a way for their escape; or, which is not much better, the next time we preach, by setting up Dr. Crisp's doctrine as much as ever, we industriously repair the breach we had made in the Antinomian Babel.

And suppose some of us preach against Antinomianism, is not our practice contrary to our preaching? We are under a dangerous mistake if we think ourselves clear from Antinomianism merely because we thunder against Antinomian principles: for as some, who zealously maintain such principles, by the happiest inconsistency in the world, pay nevertheless, in their practice, a proper regard to the law they revile; so not a few, who profess the deepest respect for it, are so unhappily inconsistent as to transgress it without ceremony. The God of holiness says, "Go and WORK in my vineyard"; the inconsistent Antinomian answers, "I will not be bound by any law; I scorn the ties of duty": but nevertheless "he repents and goes." The inconsistent legalist replies, "It is my bounden duty to obey; *I go, Lord*": nevertheless "he does not go." Which of the two is the greater Antinomian? The latter, no doubt: his practical Antinomianism is much more odious to God and man than the speculative error of the former.

The Lord God help us to avoid both! Whether the hellish wolf comes barefaced, or "in sheep's clothing"; or, what is a still more dangerous disguise, in *Lamb's* clothing; in the clothes of the Shepherd, covered from head to foot with a righteousness which he has "imputed" to himself, and sings the siren song of "finished Salvation."

IV. *I shall close these reflections upon the Antinomianism of preachers, by presenting you with sketches of two very opposite ways of preaching.* The first is an extract from Bishop Hopkins' twenty-fourth sermon, entitled, *Practical Christianity,* upon those words of St. Paul, "Work out your own salvation with fear and trembling," etc. This testimony will weigh so much the more with you, as he was a *sound Calvinist,* and a truly converted man.

"To work out our salvation," says the godly prelate, "is to persevere in the ways of obedience until, through them, that salvation which is begun here on earth be perfected in heaven. This work implies three things: (1) Pains and labour. Salvation is that which must be wrought out; it is that which will make the soul pant and breathe, yea, run down with sweat to obtain it. (2) It implies constancy and diligence. A Christian that would 'work out his salvation' must be always employed about it. It is a web, into which we must weave the whole thread of our lives. That man who works at salvation only by some passionate fits, and then, within awhile, undoes it all again by foul apostasy and notorious sins, will never work salvation *out*. (3) It promises success; though it be hard work, it shall not be long work; continue working, it shall be wrought out; what before was your work, shall be your reward; and this salvation, that was so painful in working, shall be most blessed in the enjoyment.

"Say not, 'We have no strength to work with.' What God commands us to do he will assist us in doing. We are impotent, but God is omnipotent. Work, therefore; for this omnipotent God 'works in you both to will and to do.'

"The proposition I shall lay down from the text is this: 'That it is the duty of every true Christian to work out his own salvation with fear and trembling': or, 'that every Christian, yea, every man, ought to work for his living, even for an eternal life.'

Wherefore is it that we are commanded to 'strive that we may enter in at the strait gate? So to run that we may obtain?' So to *wrestle* that we may be 'able to stand?' So 'to fight, that we may lay hold on eternal life?' Can you strive and run, and wrestle and fight, and all this by doing nothing?

"Wherefore is it that men are justly damned? Is it not because they will not do what they are able to do? And whence have they this ability? Is it not from the grace of God's Spirit? What is it that men expect? Must God drive them to heaven by force and violence, whether they will or not?

"If man will, he may work out his salvation. I speak not this to assert the power of man to work out salvation without the aid of special grace to incline his will. Where there is special grace given to make the will willing to convert, there is nothing more required to make him able, because conversion chiefly consists in the act of the will itself; only to make him willing is required special grace; which they, that favour the undue liberty of the will, deny. Our impotency lies in the stubbornness of our wills. The greatest sinner may work out his own salvation if he will. If he be but willing, he has that already that may make him able. God puts no new powers in the soul when he converts it.

"Are there any so desperately profane as not to have prayed unto God in their whole life? Why now, to what end have you prayed? Was it not for salvation? And did you work for salvation, and at the same time believe you could not work? Thou art inexcusable, O man, whoever thou art, that wilt not work: it is in vain to plead thou wantest power! God will confute thee out of thy own mouth.

"Would a master, when he commands his servant to work, take this as a sufficient excuse for his sloth and idleness, that he has no power to work till God acts and moves him?

"OBJECTION. Thus to press men to working is derogatory to Christ's merits, by which alone we are saved, and not by our works. Christ has done all for us, and wrought out our salvation by himself. Shall we piece out his work by our obedience, when all we have now to do is to believe on him?"

"ANSWER. There is the sweetest harmony between the merits of Christ and our 'working out of our salvation.' To make it evident, I shall show what Christ has done for us, and what he expects we should do for ourselves. He has merited grace, and purchased eternal happiness. And why did Christ merit grace? Was it not that we might act it in obedience? If he merited grace that we might obey, is it sense to object, that our obedience is derogatory to his merit? If one end of his doing all that he did for us was to enable us to do for ourselves, will any man say, 'Now I am bound to do nothing, because Christ has done all?' How lost are such men both to reason and religion, who undertake so to argue! No: salvation was purchased and grace procured, that, by the acting and exercise of that grace, we might attain to that salvation. It is not by way of merit or purchase that we exhort men to work out their salvation. Those are guilty of practical blasphemy against the priestly office of Christ who think to merit it by their own works.

"As Christ has done two things for us, so he requires two things from us. (1) That we should put forth all the strength of nature in labouring after grace: and (2) That we should put forth the power of grace in labouring for the salvation purchased for us. (1) Let every sinner know it is his work to repent and return, that he may live. You cannot sit down and say, 'What need is there of my working? Christ has already done all my work for me to my hands.' No: Christ has done his own work, the work of a *Saviour* and a *Surety;* but he never did the work of a *sinner.*

V. *To speak the melancholy truth, how few individuals are free from practical Antinomianism!* Setting aside their attendance on the ministry of the word, where is the material difference between several of our genteel believers and other people? Do we not see the sumptuous furniture in their appartments, and fashionable elegance in their dress? What sums of money do they frequently lay out in costly superfluities to adorn their persons, houses, and gardens!

Wise heathens, by the help of a little philosophy, saw the impropriety of having any useless brittle vessels about them: they broke them on purpose that they might be consistent with the profession they made of *seeking wisdom.* But we, who profess to have "found CHRIST the Wisdom of God," purchase such vessels and toys at a high rate; and instead of hiding them for shame, as Rachel did her teraphim for fear, we "write our *motto* over against the candlestick upon the plaster of the wall," and any man that fears the God of Daniel may, upon studying the Chinese characters, make out ANTINOMIANISM.

Our Lord, whose garment does not appear to have been cut in the height of the fashion, as it was made without seam, informs us that they who wear "soft clothing" and splendid apparel "are in kings' houses." But had he lived in our days, he might have found them in God's houses; in our fashionable churches or chapels. There you may find people professing to believe the Bible, who so conform to this present world, as to wear gold, pearls, and precious stones, when no distinction of office or state obliges them to it; in direct opposition to the words of two apostles: "Let not their adorning," says St. Peter, "be that outward adorning of plaiting the hair, and of wearing of gold, or of putting on of apparel." "Let them adorn themselves in modest apparel," adds St. Paul, "not with curled hair, or gold, or pearls, or costly array."

Multitudes of professors, far from being convinced of their sin in this respect, ridicule Mr. Wesley for bearing his testimony against it. The opposition he dares make to that growing branch of vanity, affords matter of pious mirth to a thousand Antinomians. Isaiah could openly reprove the "haughty daughters of Zion, who walked with stretched-forth necks, wanton eyes, and tinkling feet." He could expose "the bravery of their fashionable ornaments, their round tires like the moon, their chains, bracelets, headbands, rings, and earrings." But some of our humble Christian ladies will not bear a reproof from Mr. Wesley on the head of dress. They even laugh at him, as *a pitiful legalist:* and yet, O the inconsistency of the Antinomian spirit! they call Isaiah *the evangelical prophet!*

Finery is often attended with an expensive table, at least with such delicacies as our purse can reach. St. Paul "kept his body under, and was in fastings often"; and our Lord gives us directions about the proper manner of fasting. But the apostle did not *know* the easy way to heaven taught by Dr. Crisp; and our Lord did not *approve* of it, or he would have saved himself the trouble of his directions. In general, we look upon fasting, much as we do upon penitential flagellation. Both equally raise our pity. We leave them both to Popish devotees. Some of our good old

Church people will yet fast on Good Friday; but our fashionable believers begin to cast away that last scrap of self denial. Their faith, which should produce, animate, and regulate works of mortification, goes a shorter way to work—it explodes them all.

"But perhaps 'we wrestle not with flesh and blood,' because we are entirely taken up with 'wrestling against principalities, powers, and spiritual wickedness in high places.'"

Alas! I fear this is not the case. Few of us know what it is "to cry out of the deep," to pray and believe, till in the name of Jesus we force our way beyond flesh and blood, come within the reach of the eternal world, conflict in an agony with the powers of darkness, vanquish Apollyon in all his attacks, and continue wrestling till the day of eternity break upon us, and the God of Jacob "bless us with all spiritual benedictions in heavenly places." John Bunyan's pilgrim, the old Puritans, and the first Quakers, had such engagements, and gained such victories; but they soon got over the hedge of internal activity, into the smooth easy path of Laodicean formality. Most of us, called Methodists, have already followed them; and when we are in that snare, Satan scorns to conflict with us; puny flesh and blood are more than a match for us. We fall asleep under their bewitching power, and begin to dream strange dreams. "Our salvation is finished, we have got above legality, we live without frames and feelings, we have attained Christian liberty, we are perfect in Christ, we have nothing to do, our covenant is sure," etc. True! But unhappily it is a covenant with the flesh. Satan, who is too wise to break it by rousing us in the spirit, leaves us to our delusions; and we think ourselves in the kingdom of God, when we are only in a fool's paradise.

"At midnight, I will rise and praise thee," said once a pious Jew; but we pious Christians, who enjoy both health and strength, are imprisoned within our bed curtains long after the sun has "called *the diligent* to their labour." When "the fear of the Lord" was in us "the beginning of wisdom," we durst "not so confer with flesh and blood." We had then a little faith; and, so far as it went, it showed itself by our works. Then we could without hesitation and from our hearts pray, "Stir up, we beseech thee, O Lord, the wills of thy faithful people, that they, plenteously bringing forth the fruit of good works, may by thee be plenteously rewarded, through Jesus Christ our Lord." (*Collect for the last Sunday in Trinity.*) We believed there was some truth in these words of our Lord: "Except a man forsake all that he hath, deny himself, and take up his cross daily, he cannot be my disciple. He that will save his life shall lose it, and he that will lose his life for my sake shall find it. If thine eye offend thee, pluck it out: it is better for thee to enter into life with one eye, than having two eyes to be cast into hell fire. Strive to enter in at the strait gate; for I say unto you, that many shall seek to enter in, and shall not be able"; because they will seek to enter in at the *wide*, rather than the *strait gate;* the Antinomian or Pharisaic, rather than the evangelically legal gate of salvation. But now "we know better," say some of us, "we have got over our scruples and legality." We can "conform to this present world"; cleave to instead of "forsaking all we have," and even grasp what we have not. What a strange way this of "growing in grace, and in the knowledge of Christ crucified!"

Daniel informs us, that he "made his petition *three times*," and David, that he offered up his "praises *seven* times a day." Once also, like them, we had fixed hours for private prayer and self examination, for reading the Scriptures, and meditating upon them perhaps upon our knees; but we thought this was legality too; and under the specious pretence of going beyond forms, and learning "to pray always," we first threw away our forms, and,

soon after, our endeavours to watch unto prayer. Now we
scarcely ever, for any length of time, solemnly bend the
knee before "our Father who sees in secret." And, instead
of leaning on Christ's bosom in all the means of grace, we
take our graceless rest on the bosom of that painted Jezebel, *formality*.

If we are backward in performing that leading work
of PIETY, secret prayer, is it a wonder if, in general, we are
averse to every work of MERCY that costs us something, beside a little of our superfluous money? And would to God
some did not even grudge this, when it is pressed out of
their purses, by the importunate address of those who beg
for the poor! However, we give yet at the door of a
church, or at the communion; whether with indifference
or joy, whether out of custom, shame, or love, we seldom
examine. But that important branch of St. James' "pure
and undefiled religion before God, even the Father," which
consists "in visiting the fatherless and widows in their
afflictions," is, with many, almost as much out of date as a
pilgrimage to our Lady of Loretto.

O ye forsaken of poverty, and ancient daughters of
sorrow, who pine away in your desolate garrets or cellars,
without fire in winter, destitute of food, physic, or nurse
in sickness! Raise a moment your emaciated bodies,
wrapped up in thread-bare blankets, if you are possessed
of any such covering, and tell me, tell the world, how
many of our gay professors of religion have sought and
found you out in your deplorable circumstances! How
many are come to visit, in you, and to worship, with you,
"the Man of sorrows" who once lay on the cold ground in
a bloody sweat! When did they "make your bed in your
sickness?" When have they kindly inquired into all your
wants, sympathized in all your temptations, supported
your drooping heads in a fainting fit, revived your sinking
spirits with suitable cordials, gently wiped your cold
sweats, or mixed them with their tears of pity?

Alas! you sometimes find more compassion and assistance in your extremity from those who never "name the name of Christ," than from our easy, Antinomian, Laodicean *believers*. Their wants are richly supplied; that is enough: they do not inquire into yours, and *you* are ashamed or afraid to trouble them with the dismal story. Nor indeed would some of them understand you if you did. Their uninterrupted abundance makes them as incapable of feeling for you, as the warm inhabitants of Ethiopia are to feel for the frozen Icelanders.

While the table of some believers, (so called,) is alternately loaded with a variety of delicate meats and rich wines, what have *ye* to sustain sinking nature? Alas! one can soon see your all of food and physic. A pitcher of water stands by your bed side upon a stool, the only piece of furniture left in your wretched apartment. The Lord God bless the poor widow that brought it you, with her *two mites!* Heaven reward a thousand-fold the loving creature, that not only shares with you, but freely bestows upon you "all her living, even all that she has," when *they* forgot to inquire after you, and to send you something out of their luxurious abundance! "The Son of man, *once* forsaken by all the disciples, and comforted by an angel, make her bed in the time of sickness!" and a waiting band of celestial spirits "carry" her charitable soul "into Lazarus' bosom" in the awful hour of dissolution! I had rather be in her case, though she should not confidently profess the faith, than in *yours*, O ye caressed believers, who let your affluence overflow to those that have more need to learn frugality in the school of scarceness, than to receive bounties which feed their sensuality, and indulge their pride.

And ye women professing godliness, who enjoy the comforts of health and abundance, in whose "streets there is no complaining, no decay, whose daughters are as the polished corners of the temple!" when did *you* ever want visitors? Alas! ye have too many, for the good they do you, or that you do them. Does not your conversation, which begins with the love of Jesus, terminate in religious scandal; as naturally as your soul, which once "began in the spirit, ends now in the flesh?" O that your visitors were as ready to attend work houses, jails, infirmaries, and hospitals, as they are to wait upon you! O that at least, like the Dorcases, the Phebes, and Priscillas of old, you would teach them cheerfully to work for the poor, to be the free servants of the Church, and tender nurses of the sick! O that they saw in you all, now the holy women, "the widows who were widows indeed," formerly "entertained strangers, washed the saints' feet, instructed the younger women, and continued night and day in prayer!" But alas! "the love of many," once warm as the smoking flax, "is waxed cold," instead of taking fire, and flaming. They who once began "to seek the profit of many," now seek "their own" ease, or interest; their own honour, or indulgence.

Almost all, when they come to the foot of the hill Difficulty, take their leave of Jesus as a guide, because he leads on through spiritual death to the regeneration. Some, disliking that "door," like "thieves and robbers, climb up" an easier way. And others, leaving the highway of the *cross*, under the fair pretence that blind Papists walk therein, make for themselves and others broad and downward roads, to ascend the steep hill of Zion.

Those easy paths are innumerable, like the people that walk in them. O that "my eyes, like David's, did run down like water, because men," professing godliness, "keep not God's law," and are even offended at it! "Their mouth talketh of vanity; they dissemble with their double heart, and their right hand is a right hand of *sloth, or positive* iniquity." O that I had the tenderness of St. Paul, "to tell you, even weeping, of those who mind earthly things"; those "who have sinned and have not repented"; those who, while they boast they "are made free by the Son" of God are "brought under the power of *many* things"; whom foolish desires, absurd fears, undue attachments, imported superfluities, and disagreeable habits, keep in the most ridiculous bondage!

"O that my head were waters, and my eyes fountains of tears," to deplore with Jeremiah, "the slain of the daughter of God's people, who live in pleasure, and are dead while they live!" And to lament over spiritual Pharisees of every sort; those who say, "Stand by, I am holier than thou"; and those who fix the names of *poor creature! blind!* and *carnal!* upon every publican they see in the temple; and boldly placing themselves among *the elect,* "thank God they are not as other men," and in particular as *the reprobates!*

Who can number "the adulterers and adulteresses, who know not that the friendship of the world is enmity against God? The concealed idolaters, who have their "chambers of imagery within, and set up their idols in their hearts?" The envious Cains, who carry murder in their breasts? The profane Esaus, who give up their birthright for a sensual gratification; and covetous Judases, who "sell the truth" which they should *buy,* and part with Christ "for filthy lucre's sake?" The sons of God, who look at the fair daughters of men, and take to themselves wives of all whom they choose? The gay Dinahs, who "visit the daughters of the land," and come home polluted in body or in soul. The filthy Onans, "who defile the temple of God." "The prophets of Bethel," who deceive the "prophets of Judah," entice them out of the way of self denial, and bring the roaring lion and death upon them. The fickle Marcuses, who depart when they should "go to the work." The self-made prophets, who "run before they are sent," and scatter instead of "profiting the people." The spiritual Absaloms, who rise against their fathers in the Gospel, and in order to reign without them, raise a rebellion against them. The furious Zedekiahs, who "make themselves horns of iron to push" the true servants of the Lord, because they will not "prophesy smooth things and deceit," as they do?

VI. *Time would fail to describe the innumerable branches of Antinomianism, with all the fruits they bear.* It may be compared to the astonishing tree which Nebuchadnezzar saw in his mysterious dream: "A strong tree set in the midst of the *church;* the height thereof reaches unto heaven, and the sight thereof unto the ends of the earth. Its leaves are fair, and its fruit much." Thousands sleep under its fatal shadow, and myriads feed upon its pernicious fruit. At a distance it looks like "the tree of life planted in the midst of paradise"; but it only proves "the tree of knowledge of good and evil." The woman, (the Antinomian Church,) is deceived by the appearance. "She sees that it is good for food, pleasant to the eye, and desirable to make one wise." She eats to the full, and flushed with fond hopes of heaven, nay, fancying herself as God, she presents of the poisonous fruit that intoxicates her, to the nobler part of the Church, the obedient members of the second Adam.

O ye sons of God, and daughters of Abraham, who, in compliance with the insinuation of this deceived Eve, have already stretched forth your hands to receive her fatal present, instantly draw them back, for eternal "death is in the *fruit!*" Flee from the tree on which she banquets to the tree of life, the despised cross of Jesus; and there feed on "him crucified," till you are "crucified with him"; till the body of sin is destroyed," and you feel eternal life abundantly circulating through all your sanctifying powers.

And ye uncorrupted, self-denying followers of Jesus, whom love and duty still compel to bear your cross after him, join to pray that "the Watcher and his holy ones may come down from heaven, and cry aloud, Hew down the tree of *Antinomianism;* cut off its branches, shake off its leaves, scatter its fruit, and let not even the stump of its roots be left in the earth! Your prayer is heard:

> *He comes! he comes! the Judge severe!*
> *The seventh trumpet speaks him near.*

Behold, he appears in his glory, "with ten thousand of his saints, to execute judgment upon all. The thrones are cast down; the Ancient of days doth sit, whose garment is white as snow, and the hair of his head like pure wool; his throne is like the fiery flame, and his wheels as burning fire. A fiery stream issues, and comes forth from before him: thousand thousands minister unto him, and ten thousand times ten thousand stand before him. The trumpet sounds: the sea gives up the dead which are in it, death and hades deliver up the dead which are in them." The just are separated from the unjust; and while the "earth and the heaven flee away from the face of him that sits on the great *resplendent* throne, and there is found no place for them, the judgment is set, the books are opened, and the dead, small and great, are judged, every one according to their works."

Fear not, ye righteous. Ye are "in the hand of the Lord, and there shall no torment touch you. In the sight of the unwise ye seemed to die," they laughed at your dying daily: "but ye are in peace, and your joy is full of immortality." Having been a little chastised, you shall be greatly rewarded; for God proved you, and found you worthy for himself. And now that "the time of your visitation is come," judge the nations, and reign with your Lord for ever; for, "such as are faithful in love shall abide with him; grace and mercy are to his saints, and he careth for his elect: he sets his sheep on his right hand," and stretching it toward them with ravishing looks of benignity and love, he finally justifies *by works* those whom he freely justifies *by faith*. How sublime and solemn is the sentence!

" 'Come, ye blessed of my Father! inherit the kingdom prepared for you from the foundation of the world. For I was hungry, and ye gave me meat; I was thirsty, and ye gave me drink; I was a stranger, and ye took me in; naked and ye clothed me; I was sick, and ye visited me; I was in prison, and ye came to me!' And do not ask, with astonishment, WHEN you gave me all these tokens of your love: for whatever you did out of regard to me, my law, and my people, you did it 'in my name'; and whatever you did 'in my name' to the least of my creatures, and in particular 'to the least of these my brethren, you did it unto me!' "

As if he said, "Think not that I am biassed by lawless partiality. No: I am 'the Author of eternal salvation to them that obeyed me,' and made a right use of my sanctifying blood. Such are 'the blessed of my Father'; and such are ye. 'Your faith unfeigned' produced unfeigned love: you 'loved not in word only, but in deed and in truth': witness the works of mercy that adorned your lives, or the fruits of the Spirit that now replenish your souls. 'You, of all the families of the earth, have I known' with approbation. Ye have not 'denied me in works'; or, if ye have, bitter repentance, and purifying, renovating faith followed your denial; and by "keeping that faith, ye continued in my covenant, and endured unto the end.'

"Thou seest it, righteous Father, for to thee the books are always open. Thou readest 'my laws in their minds,' and beholdest my loving precepts 'written in their hearts': I therefore 'confess them before thee'; and before you, my angels, who have seen them agonize, and 'follow me through the regeneration.' I take the new heavens and the new earth to witness, that 'I am to them a God, and they are to me a people. They walked WORTHY of God who called them to his kingdom and glory; *therefore* they are worthy of me.'

"I have confessed your PERSONS, O ye 'just men made perfect!' Ye precious jewels of my mediatorial crown; let me next reward your works. In the days of my flesh I declared, that 'a cup of water given in my name,' (and my name ye know is Mercy, Goodness, and Love,) 'should in no wise lose its reward'; and that 'whosoever should forsake' earthly friends or property for righteousness' sake, should have 'a hundred fold, and everlasting life.' The pillars of heaven have given way; but my promise stands firm as the basis of my throne. Triumph in my faithfulness, as you have in my forgiving love. I bestow, on all, crowns of blissful immortality; 'I appoint unto each a kingdom' which shall not be destroyed. Be 'kings and priests unto God for ever.' Prepare to follow me to the realms of glory, and there 'whatsoever is right (διχαιον) that shall ye receive'; in *just* proportion to the various degrees of perfection, with which you have obeyed my law and improved your talents."

Thus are the persons of the righteous accepted, and their works "praised in the gate" of heaven, and "rewarded in the kingdom of their Father." Thus they receive crowns of life and glory; but it is only to cast them, to all eternity, with unutterable transports, grateful, humble love, at the feet of him who was crowned with piercing thorns, and hung bleeding upon the cross, to purchase their thrones.

While they shout, "Salvation to God and the Lamb!" the Judge turns to the left hand, where trembling myriads stand waiting for their fearful doom. O how does confusion cover their faces, and guilty horror rack their breasts, while he says, with the firmness of the eternal Lawgiver, and the majesty of the Lord of lords: "Depart from me, ye cursed, into everlasting fire, prepared for the devil and his angels! For I was hungry, and ye gave me no meat;

I was thirsty, and ye gave me no drink; I was a stranger, and ye took me not in; naked, and ye clothed me not; sick and in prison, and ye visited me not!"

Some are not yet *speechless;* they only falter. With the trembling insolence of Adam, not yet driven out of paradise, they even dare to plead their desperate cause. While stubborn sons of Belial say, "Lord, thy Father is merciful: and if thou didst die for *all,* why not for *us?"* While the obstinate Pharisees plead the good they did in their own name to supersede the Redeemer's merit, methinks I hear a bold Antinomian address thus the Lord of glory:

" 'Lord, when saw we thee hungry, or athirst, or a stranger, or naked, or sick, or in prison, and did not minister to thee?' Had we seen thee, dear Lord, in any distress, how gladly would we have relieved thy wants! Numbers can witness how well we spoke of thee and thy righteousness: it was all our boast. Bring it out in this important hour. Hide not the Gospel of thy free grace. We always delighted in pure doctrine, in *salvation without any condition; especially without the condition of* WORKS. Stand, gracious Lord, stand by us, and the preachers of thy free grace, who *made us hope thou wouldest confirm their word.*

"While they taught us to call thee, *Lord! Lord!* they assured us that love would *constrain* us to do good works; but finding no inward constraint to entertain strangers, visit the sick, and relieve prisoners, we did it not; supposing we were not called thereto. They continually told us, *'human righteousness was mere filth before thee; and we could not appear, but to our everlasting shame, in any righteousness but thine in the day of judgment.'* As to works, we were afraid of doing them, lest we should have 'worked out' abomination instead of 'our salvation.'

"And indeed, Lord, what need was there of our 'working it out'? For they perpetually assured us, it was *fin-*

ished; saying, *If we did any thing toward it, we worked for life, fell from grace like the bewitched Galatians, spoiled thy perfect work, and exposed ourselves to the destruction which awaits yonder trembling Pharisees.*

"They likewise assured us, *that all depended on* THY *decrees; and if we could but firmly believe our election, it was a sure sign we were interested in thy salvation.* We did so; and now, Lord, for the sake of a few dung works we have omitted, let not our hope perish! Let not electing and everlasting love fail! Visit our offences with a rod, but take not thy loving kindness altogether from us; and break not David's covenant, 'ordered in all things and sure,' of which we have so often made our boast.

"May it please thee also to consider, that if we did not love and assist some of those whom thou callest *thy brethren,* it was because they appeared to us so exceeding legal; so strongly set against free grace, that we judged them to be obstinate Pharisees, and dangerous reprobates. We therefore thought, that, in hating and opposing them, we did thee service, and walked in thy steps. For thou hast said, 'It is enough if the servant is as his Lord': and supposing 'thou didst hate them,' as thou dost Satan; *we* thought we need not be more righteous than thou, by loving them more than thou didst.

"O suffer us to speak on, and tell thee, we were champions for thy free grace. Like true Protestants, we could have burned against the doctrine of a *second justification by works.* Let then 'grace' justify us 'freely without works.' Shut those books, filled with the account of our deeds, open the arms of thy mercy, and receive us just as we are.

"If *free grace* cannot justify us alone, let *faith* do it, together with free grace. We do *believe* finished salvation, Lord; we can join in the most evangelical creeds, and are ready to confess the virtue of thy atoning blood. But if thou sayest, we have 'trampled it under foot, and made it a common thing,' grant us our last request, and it is enough.

"Cut out the immaculate garment of 'thy righteousness' into robes that may fit us all, and put them upon us by *imputation:* so shall our nakedness be gloriously covered. We confess we have not dealt our bread to the hungry; but impute to us thy feeding five thousand people with loaves and fishes. We have seldom given drink to the thirsty, and often 'put our bottle' to those who were not athirst; but impute to us thy turning water into wine, to refresh the guests at the marriage feast in Cana; and thy loud call, 'in the last day of the feast at Jerusalem: *If any man thirst, let him come to me and drink!'* We never supposed it was our duty to 'be given to hospitality': but impute to us thy loving invitations to strangers, thy kind assurances of receiving 'all that come to thee'; thy comfortable promises of 'casting out none,' and of feeding them even with thy 'flesh and blood.' We did not clothe the naked as we had opportunity and ability; but impute to us thy patient parting with thy seamless garment for the benefit of thy murderers. We did not visit sick beds and prisons, we were afraid of fevers, and especially of the jail distemper; but compassionately impute to us thy visiting Jairus' daughter, and Peter's wife's mother, who lay sick of a fever; and put to our account thy visiting putrefying Lazarus in the offensive prison of the grave.

"Thy imputed righteousness, Lord, can alone answer all the demands of thy law and Gospel. We did not dare to *fast;* we should have been called *legal* and *Papists* if we had; but thy forty days' fasting in the wilderness, and thy continual abstinence, imputed to us, will be self denial enough to justify us ten times over. We did not 'take up our cross'; but impute to us thy 'carrying THINE'; and even fainting under the oppressive load. We did not 'mortify the deeds of the flesh, that we might live': this would have been evidently *working for life;* but impute to us the crucifixion of *thy* body, instead of our 'crucifying our flesh, with its affections and lusts.' We hated private prayer; but impute to us thy love of that duty, and the prayer thou didst offer upon a mountain all night. We have been rather hard to forgive; but that defect will be abundantly made up if thou impute to us thy forgiving of the dying thief: and, if that will not do, add, we beseech thee, the merit of that good saying of thine, 'Forgive, and you shall be forgiven.' We have cheated the king of his customs; but no matter; only impute to us thy exact paying of the tribute money, together with thy good advice, 'Render unto Caesar the things which are Caesar's.'

"It is true, we have brought up our children in vanity, and thou never hadst any to bring up. May not thy mercy find out an expedient, and impute to us, instead of it, thy obedience to thy parents? And if we have received the sacrament unworthily, and thou canst not cover that sin with thy worthy *receiving,* indulge us with the imputation of thy worthy *institution* of it, and that will do yet better.

"In short, Lord, own us *freely* as thy children. Impute to us thy perfect righteousness. Cast it as a cloak upon us to cover our filthy souls and polluted bodies. *We will have no righteousness but thine.* Make no mention, we beseech thee, of *our* righteousness and personal holiness; they are but 'filthy rags,' which thy purity forbids thee to take into heaven; therefore accept us without, and we shall shout, *Free grace! Imputed righteousness!* and *finished salvation!* to eternity."

While the bold Antinomian offers, or prepares to offer, this most impious plea, the Lord, who "is of purer eyes than to behold iniquity," casts a flaming look upon all the obstinate violators of his law. It pierces their conscience, rouses all its drowsy powers, and restores their memory to its original perfection. Not one wish passed their heart, or thought their brain, but is instantly brought to their remembrance. "The books are opened" in their own breast, and every character has a voice which answers to the voice of "the Lion of the tribe of Judah."

"Shall I pervert judgment," says he, "and justify the wicked for a bribe? the bribe of your abominable praise? 'Think you,' by your base flatteries 'to escape the righteous judgment of God?' Is not my 'wrath revealed from heaven against all ungodliness, and unrighteousness of men, who hold the truth in unrighteousness?' Much more against you, 'ye vessels of wrath'; who hold an impious absurdity in matchless insolence.

"Said I not to Cain himself at the beginning, 'If thou doest well, shalt thou not be accepted?' Personal holiness, which ye scorned, is 'the wedding garment' I now look for. 'I swear in my wrath,' that without it, 'none shall taste of my *heavenly* supper. Ye have rejected my word' of commandment, 'and I reject you from being kings. Ye cried unto me and I delivered you. Yet have ye forsaken me and served other gods; therefore I will deliver you no more. Go and cry unto the gods whom ye have chosen. I wound the hairy scalp of such as have gone on still in their wickedness. Whosoever hath sinned against me *to the last*, him do I blot out of my book.' And this have you done, 'ye serpents, ye generation of vipers, awake to everlasting shame! Will ye set the briers and thorns against me in battle,' and make them pass 'for roses of Sharon and lilies of the valley? I will go through them *with a look*, and consume them together. The day is come that burneth like an oven; all that have DONE wickedly are stubble, and *must* be burned up root and branch. Upon such I rain snares, fire and brimstone, storm and tempest: this is the portion of their cup. Drink the dregs of it. Ye hypocrites, DEPART! and wring them out in everlasting burnings.'

"Said I not, 'He that does good is of God; but he that does evil is not of God? Be faithful unto death, and I will give you the crown of life; for he that overcometh, *and he only*, shall be clothed in white raiment, and I will not blot out his name out of the book of life?' And shall I keep *your* name in that book for having 'continued in doing evil?' Shall I give *you* the crown of life for having been *unfaithful* unto death, and clothe *you* with the bright robes of my glory, because you *defiled* your *garments* to the last? Delusive hope! Because 'your mind was not to do good,' be ye rather 'clothed with cursing, like as with a garment! Let it come into your bowels like water, and like oil into your bones!' "

VII. If "*these shall go into eternal punishment*"; if such will be the dreadful end of all the impenitent Nicolaitans; if our churches and chapels swarm with them; if they crowd our communion tables; if they are found in most of our houses, and too many of our pulpits; if the seeds of their fatal disorder are in all our breasts; if they produce Antinomianism around us in all its forms; if we see bold Antinomians in *principle*, barefaced Antinomians in *practice*, and sly *Pharisaical Antinomians*, who speak well of the law, to break it with greater advantage: should not every one "examine himself whether he be in the faith," and whether he have a *holy Christ* in his heart, as well as a *sweet Jesus* upon his tongue; lest he should one day swell the tribe of Antinomian reprobates? Does it not become every minister of Christ to drop his prejudices, and consider whether he ought not to imitate the old watchman, who, fifteen months ago, gave a "legal alarm" to all the watchmen that are in connection with him? And should we not do the Church excellent service, if, agreeing to lift up our voices together against the common enemy, we gave God no rest in prayer, and our hearers in preaching, till we all "did our first works," and "our latter end," like Job's, "exceeded our beginning"?

May the Lord God help us to sail safely through these opposite rocks, keeping at an equal distance from both, by taking Christ for our pilot, and the Scripture for our compass! So shall we enter full sail the double haven of present and eternal rest. Once we were in immediate danger of splitting upon "works without faith": now we are threatened with destruction from faith "without works." May the merciful Keeper of Israel save us from both, by *a living faith,* legally *productive* of all good works, or by *good works,* evangelically springing from a living faith!

Should the Divine blessing upon these sheets, bring one single reader a step toward that good old way, or only confirm one single believer in it, I shall be "rewarded a hundred-fold" for this little "labour of love"; and I shall be even content to see it represented as the invidious labour of malice; for what is my reputation to the profit of one blood-bought soul!

Beseeching you, dear sir, for whom these letters are first intended, to set me right where I am wrong; and not to despise what may recommend itself in them to reason and conscience, on account of the blunt and Helvetic manner in which they are written, I remain with sincere respect, honoured and reverend sir, your affectionate and obedient servant in the practical Gospel of Christ.

J. FLETCHER

THIRD CHECK TO ANTINOMIANISM
TO THE AUTHOR OF PIETAS OXONIENSIS

I. *I thank you, sir, for doing Mr. Wesley the justice in your first letter of acknowledging, that "man's faithfulness is an expression which may be used in a sober, Gospel sense of the words."* It is just in such a sense we use it; nor have you advanced any proof to the contrary.

We never supposed that "the faithfulness of God, and the stability of the covenant of grace, are affected by the unfaithfulness of man." Our Lord, we are persuaded, keeps his covenant when he *spews a lukewarm,* unfaithful Laodicean *out of his mouth,* as well as when he says to the good and faithful servant, "Enter thou into the joy of thy Lord." For the same covenant of grace which says, "He that believeth shall be saved—he that abideth in me bringeth forth much fruit," says also, "He that believeth not shall be damned—every branch in me that beareth not fruit, is cast forth and burned."

Thanks be to Divine grace, we make our boast of *God's faithfulness* as well as you, though we take care not to charge him, even indirectly, with our own unfaithfulness. But from the words which you quote, "My covenant shall stand fast with his seed," etc., we see no more reason to conclude that the obstinately unfaithful seed of Christ, such as Hymeneus, Philetus, and those who to the last "tread under foot the blood of the covenant wherewith they were sanctified," shall not be cast off; than to assert that many individuals of David's royal family, such as Absalom and Amnon, were not cut off on account of their flagrant and obstinate wickedness.

We beseech you, therefore, for the sake of a thousand careless Antinomians, to remember that the apostle says to every believer, "Thou standest by faith; behold there-

fore the goodness of God *toward thee*, if thou continue in
his goodness; otherwise thou also shalt be cut off." We entreat you to consider, that even those who admire the
point of your epigram, "Whenever we say one thing, we
mean quite another," will not be pleased if you apply it
to St. Paul, as you have done to Mr. Wesley. And when
we see God's covenant with David grossly abused by
Antinomians, we beg leave to put them in mind of God's
covenant with the house of Eli. "Thus saith the Lord God
of Israel, I chose thy father out of all the tribes of Israel
to be my priest; [but thou art unfaithful] thou honourest
thy sons above me. I said indeed, *that thy house, and the
house of thy father, should walk before me for ever:* but
now be it far from me; for them that honour me, I will
honour; and they that despise me, shall be lightly esteemed. Behold, the days come, that I will cut off thine
arm, and the arm of thy house; and I will raise me up a
faithful priest, that shall do according to that which is in
my heart" (I Sam. 2).

II. *Your second Letter respects working for life. You
make the best of a bad subject, and really some of your
arguments are so plausible, that I do not wonder so many
men should commence Calvinists, rather than be at the
trouble of detecting their fallacy.* I am sorry, dear sir, I
cannot do it without dwelling upon *Calvinism*. My design
was to oppose *Antinomianism alone:* but the vigorous
stand which you make for it upon Calvinian ground,
obliges me to encounter you there, or to give up the truth
which I am called to defend. I have long dreaded the
alternative of displeasing my friends or wounding my conscience; but I must yield to the injunctions of the latter,
and appeal to the candour of the former. If impetuous
rivers of Geneva Calvinism have so long been permitted
to flow through England, and even deluge Scotland, have
not I some reason to hope that a rivulet of Geneva anti-
Calvinism will be suffered to glide through some of Great

Britain's plains; especially if its little murmur harmonizes with the clearest dictates of reason, and loudest declarations of Scripture?

Before I weigh your arguments against *working for life,* permit me to point out the capital mistake upon which they turn. You suppose, that *free preventing grace* does not visit all men; and that all those in whom it has not prevailed, are as totally dead to the things of God, as a dead body is to the things of this life: and from this unscriptural supposition you very reasonably conclude, that we can no more turn to God than corpses can turn themselves in their graves; no more *work for life,* than putrid carcasses can help themselves to a resurrection.

This main pillar of your doctrine will appear to you built upon the sand, if you read the Scriptures in the light of that mercy which is over all God's works. There you will discover the various dispensations of the everlasting Gospel; your contracted views of Divine love will open into the most extensive prospects; and your exulting soul will range through the boundless fields of that grace which is both richly free *in* all, and abundantly free *for* all.

Let us rejoice with reverence while we read such scriptures as these: "The Son of man is come to save that which is lost, and to call sinners to repentance. This is a true saying, and worthy of all acceptation—worthy of all men to be received—that Christ Jesus came into the world to save sinners. To this end he both died and rose again, that he might be the Lord of the dead and living. He came not to condemn the world, but that the world through him might be saved, and that at the name of Jesus every knee should bow, and every tongue confess that he is Lord."

"Bound every heart, and every bosom burn," while we meditate on these ravishing declarations: "God so loved the world, that he gave his only begotten Son, that whosoever believeth on him should not perish, but have

everlasting life. He was made under the law, to redeem
them that were under the law," that is, all mankind; unless it can be proved that some men never came under the
curse of the law. He is the Friend of *sinners*, the Physician of the sick, and the Saviour of the *world:* "He died,
the just for the unjust; he is the propitiation, not for our
sins only, but for the sins of the whole world. One died
for all, because all were dead. As in Adam all die, even
so in Christ," [during the day of their visitation,] all are
blessed [with quickening grace, and therefore in the last
day] "all shall be made alive," to give an account of their
blessing or talent. "He is the Saviour of all men, especially of them that believe": and the news of his birth are
"tidings of great joy to all people. As by the offence of one
judgment came upon all men, even so by the righteousness of one, the free gift came upon all men; for Christ by
the grace of God tasted death for every man; he is the
Lamb of God who taketh away the sin of the world:
therefore God commandeth all men every where to repent—to look unto him and be saved."

Do we not take choice jewels from Christ's crown,
when we explain away these bright testimonies given by
his free grace? "It pleased the Father by him to reconcile
all things to himself. The kindness and pity of God our
Saviour toward man has appeared. I will draw all men
unto me. God was in him reconciling the world unto himself." Hence he says to the most obstinate of his opposers,
"These things have I spoken unto you, that ye might be
saved. If I had not come and spoken unto them, they had
not had sin, [in rejecting me,] but now they have no cloak
for their sin," no excuse for their unbelief.

Once indeed, when the apostles were on the brink of
the most dreadful trial, their compassionate Master said,
"I pray for them, I pray not for the world." As if he had
said, Their immediate danger makes me pray as if there
were but these eleven men in the world, "Holy Father,

keep them." But having given them this seasonable testimony of a just preference, he adds, "Neither pray I for these alone, but for them who shall believe, that they all may be one," may be united in brotherly love. And he adds, "that the world may believe, and may know that thou hast sent me."

If our Lord's not praying, for a moment, on a particular occasion, for the world, implies that the world is absolutely reprobated, we should be glad of an answer to the two following queries: (1) Why did he pray the next day for Pilate and Herod, Annas and Caiaphas, the priests and Pharisees, the Jewish mob, and Roman soldiers; in a word, for the countless multitude of his revilers and murderers? Were they all elect, or was this ejaculation no prayer, "Father, forgive them, for they know not what they do?" (2) Why did he commission St. Paul to say, "I exhort, first of all, that supplications, prayers, and intercessions be made for all men; for this is acceptable in the sight of God our Saviour, who will have all men to be saved, and come to the knowledge of the truth. For there is one God, and one Mediator between God and men, the man Christ Jesus; who gave himself a ransom for all?"

Without losing time in proving that none but artful and designing men use the word *all* to mean the *less number!* and that *all,* in some of the above-mentioned passages, must absolutely mean *all mankind,* as being directly opposed to *all* that are *condemned* and "die in Adam"; and without stopping to oppose the new Calvinian creation of "a whole world of elect"; upon the preceding scriptures I raise the following doctrine of free grace: If *Christ tasted death for every man,* there is undoubtedly a Gospel for every man, even for those who perish by rejecting it.

St. Paul says, that "God shall judge the secrets of men, according to his Gospel." St. Peter asks, "What shall be the end of those who obey not the Gospel of God?" and the apostle answers, "Christ revealed in flaming fire, will take vengeance upon them who obey not the Gospel," that is, all the ungodly who "receive the grace of God in vain, or turn it into lasciviousness." They do not perish because the Gospel is a lie with respect to them, but "because they receive not the love of the truth, that they might be saved." God, to punish their rejecting the truth, permits that they should believe a lie; that they all might be damned, who, *to the last hour of their day of grace,* believe not the truth, but had pleasure in unrighteousness."

The latitude of our Lord's commission to his ministers demonstrates the truth of this doctrine: "Go into all the world, and teach all nations, baptizing them in the name of the Father, and of the Son, and of the Holy Ghost." Hence those gracious and general invitations, "Ho, every one that thirsteth, [after happiness,] come ye to the waters; if any man thirst, [after pleasure,] let him come to me and drink. Come unto me, all ye that labour, [for want of rest,] and I will give it to you. Whosoever will, let him come and take the water of life freely. Ye adulterers, draw nigh unto God, and he will draw nigh unto you. Behold, I stand at the door and knock; if any man open, I will come in and sup with him. Go out into the highways and hedges, preach the Gospel to every creature; and lo, I am with you to the end of the world."

If you compare all the preceding scriptures, I flatter myself, Hon. sir, you will perceive, that as the redemption of Christ is general, so there is a general Gospel, which is more or less clearly revealed to all, according to the clearer or more obscure dispensation which they are outwardly under.

This doctrine may appear strange to those who call nothing *Gospel* but the last dispensation of it. Such should remember that as a little seed, sown in the spring, is one with the large plant into which it expands in summer; so the Gospel, in its least appearance, is one with the Gospel grown up to full maturity. Our Lord, considering it both as sown in man's heart, and sown in the world, speaks of it under the name of "the kingdom of heaven," compares it to corn, and considers first the *seed,* then the *blade,* next the *ear,* and last of all *the full corn in the ear.*

1. The Gospel was sown in the world as a *little but general seed,* when God began to quicken mankind in Adam by the precious promise of a Saviour; and when he said to Noah, the second general parent of men, "With thee will I establish my covenant"; blessing him and his sons after the deluge.

2. The Gospel appeared as *corn in the blade,* when God renewed the promise of the Messiah to Abraham, with this addition, that though the Redeemer should be born of his elect family, Divine grace and mercy were too free to be confined within the narrow bounds of a peculiar election: therefore, "in his seed," that is, in Christ the Sun of righteousness, "all the families of the earth should be blessed"; as they are all cheered with the genial influence of the natural sun, whether he shines above or below their horizon, whether he particularly enlightens the one or the other hemisphere.

3. The Gospel word grew much in the days of Moses, Samuel, and Isaiah; "for the Gospel," says St. Paul, "was preached unto them as well as unto us," though not so explicitly. But when John the Baptist, a greater prophet than any of them, began to preach the Gospel of repentance, and point sinners to "the Lamb of God that taketh away the sins of the world," then *the ear* crowned *the blade,* which had long been at a stand, and even seemed to be blasted.

4. The great Luminary of the Church shining warm upon the earth, his direct beams caused a rapid growth. The Favonian breathings and sighs which attended his preaching and prayers, the genial dews which distilled on Gethsemane during his agony, the fruitful showers which descended on Calvary, while the blackest storm of Divine

wrath rent the rocks around, and the transcendent radiance of our Sun, rising after this dreadful eclipse to his meridian glory; all concurred to minister fertile influences to the *Plant of Renown.* And on the day of pentecost, when power came from on high, when the fire of the Holy Ghost seconded the virtue of the Redeemer's blood, the *full corn* was seen *in the* mystical *ear;* the most perfect of the Gospel dispensations came to maturity; and Christians began to ring "forth fruit unto" the "perfection" of their own economy.

As some good men overlook the gradual display of the manifold Gospel grace of God, so others, I fear, mistake the essence of the Gospel itself. Few say, with St. Paul, "The Gospel *of which* I am not ashamed, is the power of God unto salvation, to every one that believeth—with the heart unto righteousness," according to the light of his dispensation. And many are afraid of his catholic doctrine, when he sums up the general everlasting Gospel in these words: "God *was* not the God of the Jews only, but of the Gentiles also; because that which may be known of God," under their dispensation, "is manifest in them, God having showed it unto them. For the grace of God, which bringeth salvation," or rather η χαρις η σωτηριος, *the grace* emphatically *saving,* "hath appeared unto all men; teaching us to deny all ungodliness and worldly lusts, and to live soberly, justly, and godly, in this present world."

"But how does this saving grace teach us?" By proposing to us the saving truths of our dispensation, and helping our unbelief, that we may cordially embrace them; for "without faith it is impossible to please God." Even the heathens who "come to God, must believe that he is, and that he is the rewarder of them that diligently seek him; for there is no difference between the Jew and the Greek, the same Lord over all being rich unto all them that call upon him."

Here the apostle starts the great Calvinian objection: "But how shall they believe, and call on him. of whom they have not heard?" etc. And having observed that the Jews had heard, though few had believed, he says, "So then faith cometh by hearing, and hearing by the word of God," which is nigh, even in the mouth and in the heart of all who receive the truth revealed under their dispensation. Then resuming his answer to the Calvinian objection, he cries out, "Have not they" (Jews and Greeks) all "heard" preachers, who invite them to believe that God is good and powerful, and consequently that he is the rewarder of those who diligently seek him? "Yes, verily," replies he, "their sound went into all the earth, and their words unto the end of the world."

If you ask, "Who are those general heralds of free grace, whose sound goes from pole to pole?" The Scripture answers with becoming dignity: "The heavens declare the glory of God, and the firmament showeth his handy work. Day unto day uttereth speech, and night unto night showeth knowledge. There is no speech or language [no country or kingdom] where their voice is not heard. Their [instructing] line went through the earth, [their vast parish,] and their words to the ends of the world,". their immense diocese. For "the invisible things of God, [that is, his greatness and wisdom, his goodness and mercy,] his eternal power and Godhead, are clearly seen, being understood by the things that are made, [and preserved,] so that [the very heathens, who do not obey their striking speech,] are without excuse; because that when they knew God, they glorified him not as God, neither were thankful."

This is the Gospel alphabet, if I may be allowed the expression. The apostle, like a wise instructer, proceeded upon the plan of this free grace, when he addressed himself to the heathens: "We preach unto you," said he to the Lycaonians, "that ye should turn from these vanities to serve the living God, who made heaven and earth, and the sea, and all things therein; who, *even when he* suffered all nations to walk in their own ways, left not himself without witness"; that is, without preachers, according to that saying of our Lord to his disciples, *Ye shall be my witnesses, and teach all nations.* And these witnesses were *the good* which God did, "the rain he gave us from heaven, and fruitful seasons, and the food and gladness with which he filled our hearts."

St. Paul preached the same Gospel to the Athenians, wisely coming down to the level of their inferior dispensation: "The God that made the world, dwells not," like a statue, "in temples made with hands, nor hath he need of any thing; seeing he giveth to all life, and breath, and all things. He hath made of one blood all nations of men, to dwell on all the face of the earth," not that they might live like atheists, and perish like reprobates, but "that they might seek the Lord, if haply they might feel after him, and find him." Nor is this an impossibility, as "he is not far from everyone of us! for in him we live, and move, and have our being, as certain of our own poets have taught," justly asserting that "we are the offspring of God." Hence he proceeds to declare that "God calls all men every where to repent," intimating that upon their turning to him, he will receive them as his dear children, and bless them as his beloved offspring.

These, and the like scriptures, forced Calvin himself into a happy inconsistency with Calvinism: "The Lord," said he, in an epistle prefixed to the French New Testament, "never left himself without a witness, even toward them unto whom he has not sent any knowledge of his word. Forasmuch as all creatures, from the firmament to the center of the earth, might be witnesses and messengers of his glory unto all men, to draw them to seek him; and indeed there is no need to seek him very far, for every one might find him in his own self."

And no doubt some have; for although "the world knew not God" by the wisdom that is "earthly, sensual, and devilish"; yet many have savingly known him by his general witness, that is, "the wonderful works that he doth for the children of men; for that which may be known of God," in the lowest economy of Gospel grace, "Is manifest in them," as well as shown unto them.

"What! Is there something of God inwardly manifest in, as well as outwardly shown to, all men?" Undoubtedly: the grace of God is as the wind, "which bloweth where it listeth"; and it listeth to blow with more or less force successively all over the earth. You can as soon meet with a man that never felt the wind, or heard the sound thereof, as with one that never felt the Divine breathing, or heard the still small voice, which we call *the grace of God*, and which bids us turn from sin to righteousness. To suppose the Lord gives us a thousand tokens of "his eternal power and Godhead," without giving us a capacity to consider, and grace to improve them, is not less absurd than to imagine, that when he bestowed upon Adam all the trees of paradise for food, he gave him no eyes to see, no hands to gather, and no mouth to eat their delicious fruits.

We readily grant, that Adam, and we in him, lost all by the fall; but Christ, "the Lamb slain from the foundation of the world, Christ, the repairer of the breach," mightier to save than Adam to destroy, solemnly gave himself to Adam, and to us in him, by the free everlasting Gospel which he preached in paradise. And when he preached it, he undoubtedly gave Adam, and us in him, a capacity to receive it, that is, a power to believe and repent. If he had not, he might as well have preached to stocks and stones, to beasts and devils. It is offering an insult to "the only wise God," to suppose that he gave mankind the light, without giving them eyes to behold it;

or, which is the same, to suppose that he gave them the Gospel, without giving them power to believe it.

As it is with Adam, so it is undoubtedly with all his posterity. By what argument or scripture will you prove, that God excluded part of Adam (or what is the same thing, part of his offspring, which was then part of his very person) from the promise and gift which he freely made him of "the seed of the woman, and the bruiser of the serpent's head?" Is it reasonable to deny the gift, because multitudes of infidels reject it, and thousands of Antinomians abuse it? May not a bounty be really given by a charitable person, though it is despised by a proud, or squandered away by a loose, beggar?

Waiving the case of infants and idiots, was there ever a sinner under no obligation to repent and believe in a merciful God? O ye opposers of free grace, search the universe with Calvin's candle, and among your reprobated millions, find out the person that never had a merciful God: and show us the unfortunate creature whom a sovereign God bound over to absolute despair of his mercy from the womb. If there be no such person in the world—if all men are bound to repent and believe in a merciful God, there is an end of Calvinism. And unprejudiced men can require no stronger proof that all are redeemed from the curse of the Adamic law, which admitted of no repentance; and that the covenant of grace, which admits of, and makes provision for it, freely extends to all mankind.

"Out of Christ's fullness all have received grace, a little leaven" of saving power, an inward monitor, a Divine reprover, a ray of *true* heavenly *light,* which manifests, first moral, and then spiritual good and evil. St. John "bears witness of that light," and declares it was the spiritual "life of men, the true light which enlightens" not only every man that comes into the Church, but "every man that cometh into the world," without excepting those who are yet in darkness. For "the light shineth in darkness, *even when* the darkness comprehends it not." The Baptist bore also "witness of that light, that all men through *it*," not through *him*, "might believe," φως, "*light*," being the last antecedent, and agreeing perfectly with δια αυτχ.

Hence appears the sufficiency of that Divine light to make all men believe in Christ "the light of the world"; according to Christ's own words to the Jews, "While ye have the light, believe in the light, that ye may be the children of light. Walk while ye have the light, lest darkness come upon you," even that total night of nature, "when no man can work."

Those who resist this internal light, generally reject the external Gospel, or receive it only in the letter and history. And too many such there have been in all ages; for Christ "was in the world, *even when* the world knew him not": therefore he was "manifest in the flesh." The same sun which had shined as the dawn, arose "with healing in his wings"; and came to deliver the truth which was held in unrighteousness, and to help the light which was not comprehended by the darkness. But alas! when "he came to his own," even then "his own received him not." Why? Because they were *reprobates?* No: but because they were *moral agents.*

"This is the condemnation," says he himself, "that light came into the world, but men" shut their eyes against it. "They loved darkness rather than light, because their works were evil." They would go on in the sins which the light reproved, and therefore they opposed it till it was quenched, that is, till it totally withdrew from their hearts. To the same purpose our Lord says, "The heart of this people is waxed gross, their ears are dull of hearing, and their eyes have they closed" against the light, "lest they should see with their eyes, and understand with their hearts, and should be converted, and I should heal them." The same unerring Teacher informs us, that "the devil cometh" to the way-side hearers, and "taketh away the word out of their hearts, lest they should believe and be saved." And "if our Gospel be hid," says St. Paul, "it is hid to them that believe not, and are lost, whose minds the god of this world hath blinded, lest the glorious Gospel of Christ should shine unto them."

From these scriptures it is evident that Calvin was mistaken, or that the devil is a fool. For if a man is now totally blind, why should the devil bestir himself *to blind him?* And why should he fear "lest the Gospel should shine to them that are lost," if there be absolutely no Gospel for them, or they have no eyes to see, no capacity to receive it?

Whether sinners know their Gospel day or not, they have one. Read the history of Cain, who is supposed to be the first reprobate; and see how graciously the Lord expostulated with him. Consider the old world: St. Peter, speaking of them, says, "The Gospel was preached to them also that are dead; for Christ went by the Spirit and preached even to those who were disobedient, when once the long suffering of God waited one hundred and twenty years in the days of Noah." Nor did the Lord wait with an intention of having them completely fattened for the day of slaughter; far be the unbecoming thought from those who worship the God of love! Instead of entertaining it, let us "account that the long suffering of our Lord is salvation," that is, a beginning of salvation; and a sure pledge of it, if we know and redeem the accepted time: for "the Lord is long suffering to us-ward, and not willing that any should perish, but that all should come to repentance."

Nor does God's long suffering extend to the elect only. It embraces also those "who treasure up unto themselves wrath against the day of wrath, by despising the riches of *Divine* goodness, and forbearance, and long suffering, not knowing that the goodness of God leads them to repentance." Of this the Jews are a remarkable instance: "What could God have done more to his *Jewish* vineyard? He gathered the stones out of it, and planted it with the choicest vine; and yet when he looked that it should have brought forth grapes, it brought forth wild grapes; when he sent his servants to receive the fruits, they were abused and sent away empty." Hence it is evident that the Jews had a day in which they could have brought forth fruit, or the *wise God* could no more "have looked for it" than a wise man expects to see the pine apple grow upon the hawthorn.

Nay, the most obstinate, Pharisaic, and bloody of the Jews had a day, in which our Lord in person "would have gathered them" with as much tenderness as a hen gathers her brood under her wings." And when he saw their free agency absolutely set against his loving kindness, he wept over them, and deplored their not having "known the things belonging unto their peace, before they were hid from their eyes."

Our gracious God freely gives one or more talents of grace to every man: nor was ever any man "cast into outer darkness, where shall be weeping and gnashing of teeth," but for the not using his talent aright, as our Lord sufficiently declares, Matt. 25:30. Alluding to that important parable, I would observe, that the Christian has *five talents,* the Jew *two,* and the heathen *one.* If he that has *two talents* lays them out to advantage, he shall "receive a reward," as well as he that has *five:* and the *one talent* is as capable of a proportionable improvement as the *two* or the *five.* The equality of God's ways does not consist in giving just the same number of gracious talents to all; but, FIRST, in not desiring "to gather where he has not strewed," or, "to reap" above a proportion of his *seed;* and, SECONDLY, in graciously dispensing rewards according to the number of talents improved, and the degrees of that improvement; and in justly inflicting punishments according to the number of talents buried, and the aggravations attending men's unfaithfulness. "For unto whomsoever much is given, of him shall much be required; and to whom men have committed much, of him they will ask the more."

We frequently speak of God's secret decrees, the knowledge of which is as useless as it is uncertain, but seldom consider that solemn decree so often revealed in the Gospel: "To him that has grace *to purpose,* more shall be given; and from him that has not," that has buried his talent, and therefore in one sense has it not, "shall be taken away even that which he hath" to no purpose: according to our Lord's awful command, "Take the talent from him" that hath buried it, "and give it to him that hath ten," for the good and faithful servant shall have abundance. He who says, "Whatsoever a man soweth, that shall he also reap," is too just to look for an increase from those on whom he bestows no talent; and as he calls for repentance and faith, and for a daily increase of both, he has certainly bestowed upon us the seed of both, for he "gives seed to the sower," and does not desire "to reap where he hath not sown."

Methinks my honoured opponent cries out with amazement, "What! have all men power to repent and believe?" And in the meantime a Benedictine monk comes up to vouch, that this doctrine is rank Pelagianism. But permit me to observe, that if Pelagius had acknowledged, as we do, the total fall of man, and ascribed, with us, to the free grace of God in Jesus Christ, all the power we have to repent and believe, none of the fathers would have been so injudicious and uncharitable as to rank him among heretics. We maintain, that although "without Christ we can do nothing," yet so long as the "day of salvation" lasts, all men, the chief of sinners not excepted, can, through his free preventing grace, "cease to do evil, and learn to do well," and use those means which will infallibly end in the repentance and faith peculiar to the dispensation they are under, whether it be that of the heathens, Jews, or Christians.

If the author of *Pietas Oxoniensis,* and father Walsh, deny this, they might as well charge Christ with the absurdity "of tasting death for every man" in order to keep most men from the very possibility of being benefitted by his death. They might as well assert, that although "the free gift came upon all men," yet it never came upon a vast majority of them; and openly maintain, that Christ deserves to be called the *destroyer,* rather than the *Saviour* of the world. For if the greatest part of mankind may be considered as *the world,* if repentance and faith are absolutely impossible to them, and Jesus came to denounce destruction to all who do not repent and believe, let every thinking man say whether he might not be called with greater propriety the *destroyer* than the *Saviour* of the world; and whether preaching the Christian Gospel is not like reading the warrant of inevitable damnation to millions of wretched creatures. But upon the scheme of what you call the "Wesleyan orthodoxy," Christ is really "the Saviour of all men, but especially of those that believe": for he indulges all with a day of salvation; and if none but believers make a proper use of it, the fault is not in his partiality, but in their own obstinacy.

In what a pitiful light does your scheme place our Lord! Why did he "marvel at the unbelief" of the Jews, as if they could no more believe than a stone can swim? And say not, "he marvelled *as a man*"; for the assertion absolutely unmans him. What man ever wondered that an ass does not bray with the nightingale's melodious voice? Nay, what child ever marvelled that the ox does not fly above the clouds with the soaring eagle?

The same observation holds with regard to repentance. "Then he began," says St. Matthew, "to upbraid the cities wherein most of his mighty works were done, because they repented not." Merciful Saviour, forgive us! We have insulted thy meek wisdom, by representing thee as cruelly upbraiding the lame for not running, the blind for not seeing, and the dumb for not speaking!

But this is not all: if Capernaum could not have repented at our Lord's preaching, as well as Nineveh at the preaching of Jonas, how do we reflect upon his mild equity, and adorable goodness, when we represent him as pronouncing woe upon woe over the impenitent city, and threatening to sink it into a deeper hell than Sodom, "because it repented not!" and how ill does it become us to exclaim against Deists for robbing Christ of his *divinity*, when we ourselves divest him of common *humanity*.

Suppose a schoolmaster said to his English scholars, "Except you instantly speak Greek you shall all be severely whipped," you would wonder at the injustice of the school tyrant. But would not the wretch be merciful in comparison of a Saviour, (so called,) who is supposed to say to myriads of men, that can no more repent than ice can burn, "Except ye repent, yet shall all perish?" I confess, then, when I see real Protestants calling this doctrine *the pure Gospel*, and extolling it as *free grace*, I no more wonder that real Papists should call their bloody inquisition *the. house of mercy*, and their burning of those whom they call heretics an *auto de fe*; (an act of faith.)

OBJECTION. "At this rate our salvation or damnation turns upon the good or bad use which we make of the manifold grace of God: and we are in this world in a state of probation, and not merely upon our passage to the rewards, which everlasting love, or to the punishments, which everlasting hatred, has freely allotted us, from the foundation of the world."

ANSWER. Undoubtedly; for what man of sense, (I except those who through hurry and mistake have put on the veil of prejudice,) could show his face in a pulpit, to exhort a multitude of reprobates to avoid a damnation absolutely unavoidable; and invite a little flock of elect, to lose no time in making sure an election surer than the pillars of heaven?

Again: who but a tyrant will make the life of his subjects turn upon a thing that is not at all at their option? When Nero was determined to put people to death, had he not humanity and honesty enough not to tantalize them with insulting offers of life? To whom did he ever say, "If thou pluckest one star from heaven thou shalt not die; but if thou failest in the attempt, the most dreadful and lingering torments shall punish thy obstinacy?" And shall I—shall my Christian brethren, represent the King of saints as guilty of (what my pen refuses to write) that which Nero himself was too merciful to contrive?

OBJECTION. "You do not state the case fairly. If *all have sinned in Adam,* and *the wages of sin is death,* God did the reprobates no wrong when he condemned them to eternal torments, before they knew their right hand from their left; yea, before the foundation of the world."

ANSWER. The plausibility of this objection, heightened by voluntary humility, has misled thousands of pious souls: God give them understanding to weigh the following reflections:

1. If an unconditional, absolute decree of damnation passed upon the reprobates *before* the foundation of the world, it is absurd to account for the justice of such a decree, by appealing to a sin committed *after* the foundation of the world.

2. If Adam sinned necessarily according to the *secret will and purpose* of God, as you intimate in your fourth letter, many do not see how he, much more his posterity,

could justly be condemned to eternal torments for doing an iniquity which "God's hand and counsel determined before to be done."

3. As we sinned only *seminally* in Adam, if God had not intended our redemption, his goodness would have engaged him to destroy us *seminally,* by crushing the capital offender who contained us all: so there would have been a just proportion between the sin and punishment; for as we sinned in Adam without the least consciousness of guilt, so in him we should have been punished without the least consciousness of pain. This observation may be illustrated by an example: If I catch a mischievous animal, a viper for instance, I have undoubtedly a right to kill her, and destroy her dangerous brood, if she is big with young. But if, instead of despatching her as soon as I can, I feed her on purpose to get many broods from her, and torment to death millions of her offspring, I can hardly pass for the good man who regards the life of a beast. Leaving to you the application of this simile, I ask, Do we honour God when we break the equal beams of his perfections? when we blacken his *goodness* and *mercy,* in order to make his *justice* and *greatness* shine with exorbitant luster? If "a God all mercy is a God unjust," may we not say, according to the rule of proportion, that "a God all justice is a God unkind," and can never be he whose "mercy is over all his works?"

4. But the moment we allow, that the blessing of the second Adam is as general as the curse of the first; that God "sets" again "life and death" before every individual; and that he mercifully restores to all a capacity of choosing life, yea, and of having it one day more abundantly than Adam himself had before the fall; we see his goodness and justice shine with equal radiance, when he spares guilty Adam to propagate the fallen race, that they may share the blessings of a better covenant. For,

according to the Adamic law, "judgment was by one sin to condemnation; but the free gift of the Gospel is of many offences to justification. For if through the offence of one the many be dead, much more the grace of God, and the gift by grace, which is by one man, Jesus Christ, hath abounded unto the many."

5. Rational and scriptural as the preceding observations are, we could spare them, and answer your objection thus: You think God may justly decree that millions of his unborn creatures shall be "vessels of wrath" to all eternity, overflowing with the vengeance due to Adam's preordained sin; but you are not nearer the mark: for, granting that he could do it as a just, good, and merciful God; yet he cannot do it as the God of "faithfulness and truth." His word and oath are gone forth together; hear both: "What mean ye, that ye use this proverb, *The fathers have eaten sour grapes, and the children's teeth are set on edge?* as I live, says the Lord God, ye shall not have occasion any more to use this proverb. The soul that sinneth *personally* shall die *eternally:* every one shall die for his own *avoidable* iniquity. Every man that eateth sour grapes," when he might have eaten the sweet, "his teeth shall justly be set on edge." When God has thus made oath of his equity and impartiality before mankind, it is rather bold to charge him with contriving Calvin's election, and setting up the Protestant great image, before which a considerable part of the Church continually falls down and worships.

O ye honest Shadrachs, who gaze upon it with admiration, see how some Calvinian doctors deify it, *decreta Dei sunt ipse Deus,* "The decrees of God are God himself." See Elisha Coles advancing at the head of thousands of his admirers, and hear how he exhorts them to worship: "Let us make election our all; our *bread, water, munition of rocks,* and whatever else we can suppose ourselves to want"—that is, Let us make *the great image* our God. Ye candid Meshachs, ye considerate Abednegos, follow not this mistaken multitude. Before you cry with them, "Great is the Diana of the Calvinists!" walk once around the celebrated image, and, I am persuaded, that if you can make out FREE GRACE written in running hand upon her smiling face, you will see FREE WRATH written in black capitals upon her deformed back: and then, far from being angry at the liberty I take to expose her, you will wish speed to the "little stone" which I level at her "iron-clay feet."

Think not, honoured sir, that I say about *free wrath* what I cannot possibly prove: for you help me yourself to a striking demonstration. I suppose you are still upon your travels: you come to the borders of a great empire; and the first thing that strikes you is a man in an easy carriage, going with folded arms to take possession of an immense estate, freely given him by the king of the country. As he flies along, you just make out the motto of the royal chariot, in which he doses, FREE REWARD. Soon after you meet five of the king's carts, containing twenty wretches loaded with irons; and the motto of every cart is, FREE PUNISHMENT. You inquire into the meaning of this extraordinary procession, and the sheriff, attending the execution, answers: "Know, curious stranger, that our monarch is *absolute;* and to show that *sovereignty* is the prerogative of his imperial crown, and that he is no *respecter of persons,* he distributes every day *free rewards* and *free punishments* to a certain number of his subjects." "What! without any regard to merit or demerit, by mere caprice!" "Not altogether so; for he *pitches upon the worst of men, and chief of sinners, and upon such to choose* for the subjects of his rewards. (Elisha Coles, page 62.) And that his punishments may do as much honour to *free* sovereign *wrath* as his bounty does to *free* sovereign *grace,* he pitches upon those that shall be executed before they are born." "What! have these poor creatures in chains done no harm?" "O yes!" says the sheriff, "the king contrived that their parents should let them fall and break their legs, before they had any knowledge: when they came to years of discretion he commanded them to run a race with broken legs; and, because they cannot do it, I am going to see them quartered. Some of them, besides this, have been obliged to fulfil the king's *secret will, and bring about his purposes;* and they shall be burned in yonder deep valley, called *Tophet,* for their trouble." You are shocked at the sheriff's account, and begin to expostulate with him about the freeness of the *wrath* which burns a man for doing the king's will; but all the answer you can get from him is, that which you give me in your fourth letter, (page 23,) where speaking of a poor reprobate, you say, "Such a one is indeed accomplishing" the king's, you say, "God's decree, but he carries a dreadful mark in his forehead, that such a decree is, that he shall be punished with everlasting destruction from the presence of the lord" of the country. You cry out, "God deliver me from the hands of a monarch who *punishes with everlasting destruction* such as accomplish his decree!" And while the magistrate intimates that your exclamation is *a dreadful mark,* if not *in your forehead,* at least upon your *tongue,* that you yourself shall be apprehended against the next execution, and made a public instance of the king's free wrath, your blood runs cold, you bid the postilion turn the horses; they gallop for your life, and the moment you get out of the dreary land you bless God for your narrow escape.

May reason and Scripture draw your soul with equal speed from the dismal fields of Coles' *sovereignty* to the smiling plains of primitive Christianity! Here you have God's *election,* without Calvin's *reprobation.* Here Christ chooses the Jews without rejecting the Gentiles; and elects Peter, James, and John, to the enjoyment of peculiar privileges, without reprobating Matthew, Thomas, and Simon. Here nobody is damned for not doing impossibilities, or for doing what he could not possibly help. Here all that are saved enjoy rewards, through the merits of Christ, according to the degrees of evangelical obedience which the Lord enables, not forces, them to perform. Here *free wrath* never appeared: all our damnation is of ourselves, when we "neglect such great salvation," by obstinately refusing to "work it out with fear and trembling." But this is not all: here *free grace* does not rejoice over *stocks,* but over *men,* who gladly confess that their salvation is all of God, who for Christ's sake rectifies their free agency, helps their infirmities, and "works in them both to will and to do of his good pleasure." And from the tenor of the Scripture, as well as from the consent of all nations, and the dictates of conscience, it appears, that part of God's "good pleasure" toward man is, that he shall remain invested with the awful power of choosing life or death, that his will shall never be forced, and, consequently, that overbearing, irresistible grace, shall be banished to the land of Coles' *sovereignty,* together with free, absolute, unavoidable wrath.

Now, honoured sir, permit me to ask, Why does this doctrine alarm good men? Why are those divines deemed *heretics,* who dare not divest God of his essential love, Emmanuel of his compassionate humanity, and man of his connatural free agency? What are Dominicus and Calvin when weighed in the balance against Moses and Jesus Christ? Hear the great prophet of the Jews: "I call heaven and earth to record this day against you, that I have set before you life and death, blessing and cursing, *heaven and hell;* therefore choose life that ye may live." And "he that hath ears," not yet absolutely stopped by prejudice, "let him hear" what the great Prophet of the

Christians says upon the important question: "I am come that they might have life; all things are now ready—but ye will not come unto me that ye might have life. I would have gathered you, and ye would not. Because I have called and ye refused, I will laugh when your destruction cometh. For that they did not choose the fear of the Lord, therefore shall they eat," not "the fruit" of my decree, or of Adam's sin, but "of their own *perverse* way: they shall be filled with their own doings."

If these words of Moses and Jesus Christ are overlooked, should not, at least, the experience of near six thousand years teach the world, that God does not force rational beings, and that, when he tries their loyalty, he does not obey for them, but gives them sufficient grace to obey for themselves? Had not all the angels sufficient grace to obey? If some "kept not their first estate," was it not through their own unfaithfulness? What evil has our Creator done us, or what service have devils rendered us, that we should fix the blot of Calvinian reprobation upon the former, to excuse the rebellion of the latter? Did not Adam and Eve stand some time, by means of God's sufficient grace; and might they not have stood for ever? Have not unconverted men sufficient grace to forsake or complain of some evil; to perform, or attempt some good? Had not David sufficient grace to avoid the crimes into which he plunged? Have not believers sufficient power to do more good than they do? And does not the Scripture address sinners, (Simon Magus not excepted,) as having sufficient grace to pray for more grace, if they have not yet sinned the sin unto death?

In opposition to the above-stated doctrine of *grace,* *free* FOR *all,* as well as *free* IN *all,* our Calvinian brethren assert, that God binds his free grace, and keeps it from visiting millions of sinners, whom they call *reprobates.* They teach that man is not in a state of probation, that his lot is absolutely cast; a certain little number of souls being immovably fixed in God's favour, in the midst of all their abominations; and a certain vast number under his eternal wrath, in the midst of the most sincere endeavours to secure his favour. And their teachers maintain, that the names of the former were "written in the book of life," without any respect to foreseen repentance, faith, and obedience; while the names of the latter were put in the book of death, (so I call *the decree of reprobation,*) merely for the sin of Adam, without any regard to personal impenitency, unbelief, and disobedience. And this *narrow grace* and *free wrath* they recommend to the world under the engaging name of FREE GRACE.

This doctrine, dear sir, we are in conscience bound to oppose; not only because it is the reverse of the other, which is both Scriptural and rational; but because it is inseparably connected with doctrinal Antinomianism, as your fourth letter abundantly demonstrates: and, above all, because it appears to us that it fixes a blot upon all the Divine perfections. Please, honoured sir, to consider the following queries:

What becomes of God's *goodness,* if the tokens of it, which he gives to millions, be only intended to enhance their ruin, or cast a deceitful veil over his everlasting wrath? What becomes of his *mercy,* which is "over all his works," if millions were for ever excluded from the least interest in it, by an absolute decree that constitutes them "vessels of wrath" from all eternity? What becomes of his *justice,* if he sentences myriads upon myriads to everlasting fire, "because they have not believed on the name of his only-begotten Son?" when, if they had believed that he was their Jesus, their Saviour, they would have believed a monstrous lie, and claimed what they have no more right to than I have to the crown of England. What becomes of his *veracity,* and the *oath he swears,* that "he willeth not the death of a sinner," if he never affords most sinners sufficient means of escaping eternal death? If he sends his ambassadors to every creature, declaring that "all things are now ready" for their salvation, when nothing but "Tophet is prepared of old" for the inevitable destruction of a vast majority of them? What becomes of his *holiness,* if, in order to condemn the reprobates with some show of justice, and secure the end of his decree of reprobation, which is, that *millions shall absolutely be damned,* he absolutely fixes *the means* of their damnation, that is, their sins and wickedness? What becomes of his *wisdom,* if he seriously expostulates with souls as dead as corpses, and gravely urges to repentance and faith persons that can no more repent and believe than fishes can speak and sing? What becomes of his *long suffering,* if he waits to have an opportunity of sending the reprobates into a deeper hell, and not to give them a longer time to "save themselves from this perverse generation?" What of his *equity,* if there was mercy for Adam and Eve, who, *personally* breaking the hedge of duty, wantonly rushed out of paradise into this howling wilderness? And yet there is no mercy for millions of their unfortunate children, who were born in a state of sin and misery, without any *personal* choice, and consequently without any *personal* sin. And what becomes of his *omniscience,* if he cannot foreknow future contingencies? If to foretell without a mistake that such a thing shall happen, he must do it himself? Was not Nero as wise in this respect? Could not he foretell that Phebe should not continue a virgin, when he was bent upon ravishing her; that Seneca should not die a natural death, when he had determined to have him murdered; and that Crispus should fall into a pit, if he obliged him to run a race at midnight in a place full of pits? And what old woman in the kingdom cannot precisely foretell that a silly tale shall be told at such an hour if she is resolved to tell it herself, or at any rate to engage a child to do it for her?

Again: what becomes of God's *loving kindnesses,* "which have been ever of old" toward the children of men? And what of his *impartiality,* if most men, absolutely reprobated for the sin of Adam, are never placed in a state of personal trial and probation? Does not God use them far less kindly than devils, who were tried every one for himself, and remain in their diabolical state, because they brought it upon themselves by a *personal* choice? Astonishing! That the Son of God should have been flesh of the flesh, and bone of the bone of millions of men, whom, upon the Calvinian scheme, he never indulged so far as he did devils! What a hardhearted relation to myriads of his fellow men does Calvin represent our Lord! Suppose Satan had become our *kinsman* by incarnation, and had by that means got "the right of redemption," would he not have acted like himself, if he had not only left the majority of them in the depths of the fall, but enhanced their misery by the sight of his partiality to the little flock of the elect?

Once more: what becomes of *fair dealing,* if God every where represent sin as the dreadful evil which causes damnation, and yet the most horrid sins "work for good" to some, and, as you intimate, *accomplish their salvation through Christ?* And what of *honesty,* if the God of truth himself promises, that "all the families of the earth shall be blessed in Christ?" when he has cursed a vast majority of them with a decree of absolute reprobation, which excludes them from obtaining an interest in them, even from the foundation of the world.

Nay, what becomes of his *sovereignty* itself, if it be torn from the mild and gracious attributes by which it is tempered? If it be held forth in such a light as renders it more terrible to millions, than the sovereignty of Nebuchadnezzar, in the plain of Dura, appeared to Daniel's companions, when "the forms of his visage was changed against them," and he decreed that they should be "cast into the burning fiery furnace"; for they might have saved their bodily lives by bowing to the golden image, which was a thing in their power; but poor reprobates can escape at no rate. The horrible decree is gone forth; they must, in spite of their best endeavors, *dwell* body and soul *with everlasting burnings.*

And let none say, that we wrong the Calvinian decree of reprobation, when we call it *a horrible decree;* for Calvin himself is honest enough to call it so. *Unde factum est, tot gentes, una cum liberis eorum infantibus æternæ morti involveret lapsus Adæ absque remedio, nisi quia Deo ita visum est?* DECRETUM QUIDEM HORRIBILE, *fateor; inficiari tamen nemo poterit, quin præsciverit Deus quem exitum habiturus esset homo, antequam ipsum conderet, et ideo præsciverit, quia decreto suo sic ordinaret.* That is, "How comes it to pass that so many nations, together with their infant children, are by the fall of Adam involved in eternal death without remedy, unless it is because God would have it so? A HORRIBLE DECREE, I confess! Nevertheless, nobody can deny that God foreknew what would be man's end before he created him, and that he foreknew it, because he had ordered it by his decree." (*Calvin's Institutes,* book iii, chap. 23, sec. 7.)

This is some of the contempt which Calvinism pours upon God's perfections. These are some of the blots which it fixes upon his word. But the moment man is considered as a candidate for heaven, a probationer for a blissful immortality; the moment you allow him what *free grace* bestows upon him, that is, "a day of salvation," with "a talent" of living light and rectified free agency to enable him to *work for life* faithfully promised, as well as *from life* freely imparted; the moment, I say, you allow this, all the Divine perfections shine with unsullied lustre. And, as reason and majesty returned to Nebuchadnezzar after his shameful degradation, so consistency and native dignity are restored to the abused oracles of God.

Having thus shown the inconsistency of Calvinism, and the reasonableness of what you call the Wesleyan, and what we esteem the Christian orthodoxy, (so far at least as it respects the gracious power and opportunity that man, as redeemed and prevented by Christ, has to *work for life,* or to "work out his own salvation,") it is but just I should consider some of the most plausible objections which are urged against our doctrine.

FIRST OBJECTION. "Your Wesleyan scheme pours more contempt upon the Divine perfections than ours. What becomes of God's *wisdom,* if he gave his Son to die for all mankind, when he foreknew that most men would never be benefited by his death?"

ANSWER. (1) God foreknew just the contrary. All men, even those who perish, are benefited by Christ's death: for all enjoy, through him, a "day of salvation," and a thousand blessings both spiritual and temporal. And, if all do not enjoy heaven for ever, they may still thank God for his gracious offer, and take the blame upon themselves for their obstinate refusal of it. (2) God, by reinstating all mankind in a state of probation, for ever shuts the mouths of those who choose "death in the error of their ways," and clears himself of their blood before men and angels. If he cannot eternally benefit unbelievers, he eternally vindicates his own adorable perfections. He can say to the most obstinate of all the reprobates, " 'O Israel, thou hast destroyed thyself, In me was thy help; but thou wouldst not come unto me that thou mightest have life.' Thy destruction is not from *my decree, but thine own determining.*"

SECOND OBJECTION. "If God wills all men to be saved, and yet many are damned, is he not disappointed? And does not this disappointment argue that he wants either wisdom to contrive the means of some men's salvation, or power to execute his gracious designs?"

ANSWER. (1) God's purpose is, that all men should have sufficient grace to believe according to their dispensation; that "he who believeth shall be saved, and he who believeth not shall be damned." God cannot, therefore, be disappointed, even when man's free agency throws in the weight of final unbelief, and turns the scale of probation for death. (2) Although Christ is the author of "a day of salvation" to all, yet he "is the author of *eternal salvation*" to none but to such as "obey him, by working out their own salvation" while it is day.

If you say, that "suppose God wills the salvation of *all*, and none can be saved but *the obedient*, he should make all obey." I reply, So he does, by a variety of gracious means, which persuade, but do not force them. For he says himself, "What could I have done more to my vineyard than I have done?" "O, but he should *force* all by the sovereign power of irresistable grace." You might as well say that he should renounce his wisdom, and defeat his own purpose. For if his wisdom places men in a state of probation; the moment he forces them, he takes them out of that state, and overturns his own counsel; he destroys the work of his hands; he unmans man, and saves him, not as a rational creature, but as a stock or a stone. Add to this, that *forced obedience* is a contradiction in terms; It is but another word for *disobedience*, at least in the account of him who says, "My son, give me thy heart"; obey me with an unconstrained, free, and cheerful will. In a word, this many "are willingly ignorant of," that when God says, "he wills all men to be saved," he wills them to be saved as *men*, according to his own method of salvation laid down in the abovementioned scriptures, and not in their own way of wilful disobedience, or after Calvin's scheme of irresistible grace.

THIRD OBJECTION. "You may speak against *irresistible* grace, but we are persuaded that nothing short of it is sufficient to make us believe. For St. John informs us, that the Jews, toward whom it was not exerted, *could* not believe."

ANSWER. (1) Joseph said to his mistress, "How can I do this great wickedness?" But this does not prove that he was not able to comply with her request, if he had been so minded. The truth was, that some of the Pharisees had "buried their talent," and therefore could not improve it; while others had so provoked God, that he had "taken it from them"; they had "sinned unto death." But most of them obstinately held that evil which was an insurmountable hinderance to faith; and to them our Lord said, "How can ye believe who receive honour one of another?" (2) I wonder that modern Predestinarians should make so much of this scripture, when Augustine their father solves the seeming difficulty with the utmost readiness: "If you ask me," says he, "why the Jews *could* not believe? I quickly answer, Because they *would* not. For God foresaw their evil will, and foretold it by the prophet; and if he blinded their eyes, their own wills deserved this also." They obstinately said, "We *will* not see," and God justly said at last, "Ye *shall* not see."

FOURTH OBJECTION. "You frequently mention the parable of the *talents,* but take care to say nothing of the parable of the *dry bones,* which shows not only the absurdity of supposing that men can work for life, but the propriety of expostulating with souls as void of all spiritual life as the dry bones to which Ezekiel prophesied."

ANSWER. (1) If you read that parable without comment, you will see that it is not descriptive of the spiritual state of souls, but of the political condition of the Jews during their captivity in Babylon. They were scattered throughout Chaldea, as dry bones in a valley; nor was there any human probability of their being collected to form again a political body. Therefore God, to cheer their desponding hearts, favoured Ezekiel with the vision of the resurrection of the dry bones. (2) This vision proves just the reverse of what some imagine: for the dry bones are thus described by the Lord himself: "These bones are the whole house of Israel. Behold, they say," (this was the language of their despairing minds,) "our bones are dried, our hope is lost, we are cut off for our parts." Here these Israelites, (compared to dry bones,) even before Ezekiel prophesied, and the Spirit entered into them, knew their misery and complained of it, saying, "Our bones are dried up." How far then were they from being as insensible as corpses? (3) The prophecy to the dry bones did not consist in threatenings and exhortations; it was only of the declarative kind. Nor was the promise of their resurrection fulfilled in the Calvinian way, that is, *irresistibly.* For although God had said, "I will open your graves," that is, your prisons, "and will bring you out of them into your own land," we find that multitudes, when their graves were opened, chose to continue in them. For when Nehemiah and Ezra breathed, under God, courage into the dry bones, the Jewish captives dispersed throughout Chaldea, many preferred the land of their captivity to their own land, and refused to return: so that, after all, their political resurrection turned upon their own choice.

FIFTH OBJECTION. "We do not altogether go by the parable of the dry bones, when we affirm there is no absurdity in preaching to souls as dead as corpses. We have the example of our Lord as well as that of Ezekiel. Did he not say to Lazarus, when he was dead and buried, *Come forth?*"

ANSWER. If Christ had called Lazarus out of the grave without giving him power to come forth, his friends would have had some reason to suspect that he was "beside himself." How much more, if they had heard him call a thousand corpses out of their graves, denouncing to all, that if they did not rise they should be "cast into a lake of fire," and eaten up "by a worm that dieth not!" It is a matter of fact, that Christ never commanded but one dead man to come out of the grave; and the instant he gave him the command, he gave him also power to obey it. Hence we conclude, that as the Lord "commands all men every where to repent," he gives them all power so to do. But some Calvinists argue just the reverse. "Christ," say they, "called *one* corpse without using any entreaty, threatening, or promise; and he gave it power to obey: therefore when he calls *a hundred* dead souls, and enforces his call with the greatest variety of expostulations, threatenings, and promises, he gives power to obey only to *two* or *three.*" What an inference is this! How worthy of the cause which it supports!

In how contemptible a light does our Lord appear, if he says to souls as dead as Lazarus in the grave, "All the day long have I stretched out my hands unto you. Turn ye, why will ye die? Let the wicked forsake his way, and I will have mercy upon him: but if he will not turn, I will whet my sword, I have bent my bow and made it ready; I have also prepared for him the instruments of death."

But suppose the resurrection of Lazarus, and that of the dry bones, did not overthrow Calvinism, would it be reasonable to lay so much stress upon them? Is a dead soul in every respect like a dead body; and is *moral* death absolutely like *natural* death? Can a parabolical vision, wrested from its obvious meaning, supersede the plainest declarations of Christ, who personally addresses sinners as free agents? Should not metaphors, comparisons, and parables, be suffered to walk erect like reasonable men? Is it right to make them *go upon all four,* like the stupid ox? What loads of heterodoxy have degraded parables brought into the Church? And how successfully has error carried on her trade, by dealing in *figurative expressions,* taken in a *literal sense!*

"This is my body," says Christ. "Therefore bread is flesh," says the Papist, "and transubstantiation is true." "These dry bones are the house of Israel," says the Lord. "Therefore Calvinism is true," says my objector, "and we can do no more toward our conversion, than dry bones toward their resurrection." "Lost sinners" are represented in the Gospel as a "lost piece of silver." "Therefore," says the author of *Pietas Oxoniensis,* "they can no more seek God, than the piece could seek the woman who had lost it." "Christ is the Son of God," says St. Peter. "Therefore," says Arius, "he is not co-eternal with the Father, for I am not so old as my parents." And I, who have a right to be as wise as any of them, hearing our Lord say, that "the seven Churches are seven candlesticks," prove by it that the seven Churches can no more repent than three pair and a half of candlesticks, or, if you please, seven pair of snuffers! And shall we pretend to overthrow the general tenor of the Scripture by such conclusions as these? Shall not, rather, unprejudiced persons of every denomination agree to turn such arguments out of the Christian Church, with as much indignation as Christ turned the oxen out of the Jewish temple?

Permit me, honoured sir, to give you two or three instances more of an undue stretching of some particular words for the support of some Calvinian errors. According to the oriental style, a follower of wisdom is called "a son of wisdom"; and one that deviates from her paths, "a son of folly." By the same mode of speech, a wicked man, considered as wicked, is called "Satan, a son of

Belial, a child of the wicked one, and a child of the devil."
On the other hand, a man who turns from the devil's
works, and does the works of God, by believing in him,
is called "a child or a son of God." Hence the passing
from the ways of Satan to the ways of God was naturally
called *conversion* and *a new birth,* as implying a turning
from sin, a passing into the family of God, and being
numbered among the godly.

Hence some divines, who, like Nicodemus, carnalize
the expressions of *new birth, child of God,* and *son of
God,* assert, that if men who once walked in God's ways
turn back, even into adultery, murder, and incest, they
are still God's *dear people* and *pleasant children,* in the
Gospel sense of the words. They ask, "Can a man be a
child of God today, and a child of the devil tomorrow?
Can he be born this week, and unborn the next?" And
with these questions they as much think they have
overthrown the doctrine of holiness, and one half of the
Bible, as honest Nicodemus supposed he had demolished
the doctrine of regeneration, and stopped our Lord's
mouth, when he said, "Can a man enter a second time
into his mother's womb and be born?"

The questions of our brethren would be easily answered, if, setting aside the oriental mode of speech, they
simply asked, "May one who has 'ceased to do evil, and
learned to do well *today,* cease to do well, and learn to
do evil' *tomorrow?*" To this we could directly reply, If
the dying thief, the Philippian jailer, and multitudes of
Jews, in one day went over from the *sons of folly* to the
sons of wisdom, where is the absurdity of saying, they
could measure the same way back again in one day; and
draw back into the horrid womb of sin as easily as Satan
drew back into rebellion, Adam into disobedience, David
into adultery, Solomon into idolatry, Judas into treason,
and Ananias and Sapphira into covetousness? When
Peter had shown himself a blessed son of heavenly wis-

dom, by confessing Jesus Christ, did he even stay till the
next day to become a son of folly, by following the "wisdom which is earthly, sensual, and devilish?" Was not
our Lord directly obliged to rebuke him with the utmost
severity, by saying, "Get thee behind me, Satan?"

Multitudes, who live in open sin, build their hopes of
heaven upon a similar mistake; I mean, upon the unscriptural idea which they fix to the Scriptural word *sheep.*
"Once I heard the Shepherd's voice," says one of these
Laodicean souls; I *followed him,* and therefore I was one
one of his *sheep;* and now, though I follow the voice *of
a stranger,* who leads me into all manner of sins, into
adultery and murder, I am undoubtedly a sheep still:
for it was never heard that a sheep became a goat." Such
persons do not observe, that our Lord calls "sheep" *those
who hear his voice,* and "goats" *those who follow that of
the tempter.* Nor do they consider that if Saul, a grievous wolf, "breathing slaughter" against Christ's sheep,
and "making havoc" of his little flock, could in a short
time be changed both into sheep and a shepherd; David,
a harmless sheep, could, in as short a time, commence
a goat with Bathsheba, and prove a wolf in sheep's
clothing to her husband.

Pardon me, honoured sir, if, to make my mistaken
brethren ashamed of their argument, I dedicate to them
the following soliloquy, wherein I reason upon their own
plan:—

"Those very Jews whom the Baptist and our Lord
called 'a brood of vipers and serpents,' were soon after
compared to 'chickens,' which Christ wanted 'to gather
as a hen does her brood.' What a wonderful change was
here! The *vipers* became *chickens!* Now, as it was never
heard that chickens became vipers, I conclude that those
Jews, even when they came about our Lord like 'fat
bulls of Bashan,' like 'ramping and roaring lions,' were
true chickens still. And indeed, why should not they

have been as true chickens as David was a true sheep when he murdered Uriah? I abhor the doctrine which maintains that a man may be a chick or a sheep today, and a viper or a goat tomorrow.

"But I am a little embarrassed. If none go to hell but *goats*, and none to heaven but *sheep*, where shall the *chickens* go? Where 'the wolves in sheep's clothing?' And in what *limbus* of heaven or hell shall we put that '*fox* Herod,' the *dogs* who 'return to their vomit,' and the *swine*, before whom we must 'not cast our pearls?' Are they all species of goats, or some particular kind of sheep?

"My difficulties increase! The Church is called *a dove*, and Ephraim *a silly dove*. Shall the *silly dove* be admitted among the sheep? Her case seems rather doubtful. The hair of the spouse in the Canticles is likewise said to be like 'a flock of goats,' and Christ's shepherds are represented as 'feeding kids, or young goats, beside their tents.' I wonder if those *young goats* became young sheep, or if they were all doomed to continue reprobates! But what puzzles me most is, that the Babylonians are in the same verse compared to 'lambs, rams, and goats.' Were they mongrel elect, or mongrel reprobates, or some of Elisha Coles' *spiritual monsters?*"

I make this ridiculous soliloquy, to show the absurdity and danger of resting weighty doctrines upon so sandy a foundation as the particular sense which some good men give to a few Scriptural expressions, stretched and abused on the rack of my countryman, Calvin; especially such expressions as these, "A child of God, a sheep, a goat," and, above all, "the dead in sin."

Upon this last expression you seem, honoured sir, chiefly to rest the merit of your cause, with respect to *working for life*. Witness the following words: "That *we are to work for life* is an assertion most exceedingly self contradictory, if it be a truth that man is 'dead in trespasses and sins.' " Had you given yourself the trouble of reading, with any degree of attention, the forty-second page of the Vindication, you would have seen your difficulty proposed and solved: witness the following words, which conclude the solution: "In this Scriptural view of free grace, what room is there for the ridiculous cavil, that Mr. Wesley wants the *dead to work for life?*" Had I been in your place, I confess, honoured sir, I could not have produced that cavil again, without attempting at least to wipe off the ridicule put upon it. I should think truth has better weapons with which to defend herself than *a veil.* I grant that the reverend divine, whose second you are, has publicly *cast a veil* over all my arguments under the name of *mistakes:* but could you possibly think that his veil was thick enough to cover them from the eyes of unprejudiced readers, and palliate your answering, or seeming to answer me, without taking notice of my arguments? But if you cast a veil over them, I shall now endeavour to do yours justice, and clear the matter a little farther.

(A) *Availing yourself of St. Paul's words to the Ephesians and Colossians, "You hath he quickened, who were dead in trespasses and sins;* and you, being dead in your sins, hath he quickened together with him"; you dwell upon the absurdity of "expecting living action from a dead corpse," or living works from a dead soul.

1. I wonder at the partiality of some persons. If we assert, that "strong believers are *dead* TO sin," they tell us very properly that such are not so dead, but they may commit sin if they please, or if they are off their watch. But if we say, that "many who are *dead* IN sin, are not so dead, but in the strength imparted, together with the Light that enlightens every man, they may leave off some of their sins if they please," we are exclaimed against as using metaphysical distinctions, and *dead* must absolutely mean *impotent as a corpse.*

2. The word *dead,* etc., is frequently used in the
Scriptures to denote a particular degree of helplessness
and inactivity, very short of the total helplessness of a
corpse. We read of the *deadness* of Sarah's womb, and of
Abraham's body being *dead;* and he must be a strong
Calvinist indeed, who, from such expressions, peremp-
torily asserts, that Sarah's *dead* womb was as unfit for
conception, and Abraham's *dead* body for generation, as
if they both had been "dead corpses." Christ writes to
the Church of Sardis, "I know thy works; thou hast a
name to live, and art dead." But it is evident, that *dead*
as they were, something remained alive in them, though
like the smoking flax, it was "ready to die." Witness the
words that follow: "Be watchful, and strengthen the
things which remain, that are ready to die." Now, sir, if
the dead Sardians could *work for life,* by "strengthening the things" belonging to the Christian "which remained" in them; is it modest to decide *e cathedra,* that
the dead Ephesians and Colossians could not as well
work for life, by "strengthening the things that remained
and were ready to die," under *their own* dispensation?
Is it not evident that a beam of "the Light of the world"
still shone in their hearts, or that the Spirit still strove
with them? If they had absolutely quenched him, would
he have helped them to believe? And if they had not,
was not there something of "the Light which enlightens
every man" remaining in them; with which they both
could, and did work for life, as well as the dead Sardians?

3. The absurdity of always measuring the meaning
of the word *dead,* by the idea of *a dead corpse,* appears
from several other scriptures. St. Paul, speaking of one
who grows wanton against Christ, says, "She that liveth
in pleasure is dead while she liveth." Now, if this means
that she is entirely devoid of every degree of spiritual
life, what becomes of Calvinism? Suppose all that live in
pleasure are as dead to God as corpses, what became of

the everlasting life of Lot, when he lived in pleasure with his daughters? of David with Bathsheba, and Solomon with his idolatrous wives? When the same apostle observes to the Romans, that their "body was dead because of sin," did he really mean they were already *dead* corpses? And when he adds, "Sin revived and I died," did Calvinian death really pass upon him? Dead as he was, could not he complain like the dry bones, and ask, "Who shall deliver me from this body of death?" Again: when our Lord says to Martha, "He that believeth in me, though he were dead, yet shall he live," does he not intimate, that there is a work consistent with the degree of death of which he speaks? A believing *out of death* into life? A doing the work of God *for life,* yea, for eternal life?

4. From these and the like scriptures, it is evident, that there are different degrees of spiritual death, which you perpetually confound. (1) Total death, or a full departure of the Holy Spirit. This passed upon Adam, and all mankind in him, when he lost God's moral image, fell into selfish nature, and was buried in sin, guilt, shame, and horror. (2) Death freely visited with a seed of life in our fallen representative, and of course in all his posterity, during the day of their visitation. (3) Death oppressing this living seed, and holding it "in unrighteousness," which was the death of the Ephesians and Colossians. (4) Death prevailing again over the living seed, after it had been powerfully quickened, and burying it in sin and wickedness. This was the death of David during his apostasy, and is still that of all who once believed, but now live in Laodicean ease or Sardian pleasure. And, (5) The death of confirmed apostates, who, by absolutely quenching "the Spirit of life in Christ Jesus," the second Adam, are fallen into the miserable state of nature and total helplessness, in which the first Adam was when God preached to him the Gospel of his

quickening grace. These are said by St. Jude to be *twice dead;* dead by Adam's total apostasy from God, and dead by their own personal and final apostasy from "the Light of the world."

(B) *The foundation of the Crispian Babel is literally laid in confusion.* When you have confounded all the degrees of spiritual death, we may naturally expect to see you confound all the degrees of spiritual life, which our Lord meant when he said, "I am come that they may have life, and that they may have it more abundantly." "All that are quickened," do you say, "are pardoned and justified!" As if a man could not be quickened to see his sins and reform, before he is quickened so to believe in Christ as to receive the pardon and justification mentioned Col. 2:13, and Rom. 5:1.

If you read the Scriptures without prejudice, you will see that there are several degrees of spiritual life, or quickening power. (1) The living "Light which shines in the darkness" of every man during the day of his visitation. (2) The life of the returning sinner, whether he has always lived in open sin, as the publican, or once walked in the ways of God, as David. (3) The life of the heathen, who, like Cornelius, "fears God and works righteousness" according to his light, and is accepted in his dispensation. (4) The life of the pious Jew, who, like Samuel, fears God from his youth. This degree of life is far superior to the preceding, being cherished by the traditions of the patriarchs, the books of the Old Testament, the sacraments, priests, prophets, temples, Sabbaths, sacrifices, and other means of grace, belonging to the Jewish economy. (5) The life of the feeble Christian, or disciple of John, who is "baptized with water unto repentance for the remission of sins," and believing in "the Lamb of God," immediately pointed out to him, enjoys the blessings of the primitive Christians before the day of pentecost. And, (6) The still more abundant life, the life of the adult or perfect Christian, imparted to him when the love of God, or power from on high, is plentifully shed abroad in his believing soul, on the day that Christ "baptizes him with the Holy Ghost and with fire, to sanctify him wholly, and seal him unto the day of redemption."

(C) *When you have overlooked all the degrees of spiritual death and life, what wonder is it that you should confound all the degrees of acceptance and Divine favour, with which God blesses the children of men!* Permit me, honoured sir, to bring also this article of the Christian faith out of the Calvinian tower of Babel, where it has too long been detained.

1. I have already proved, that in consequence of the love of benevolence and pity, with which "God loved the world," and through the "propitiation *which Christ made* for the sins of the whole world, the free gift of an accepted time, and a day of salvation, came upon all men." In this sense they are all *accepted,* and sent "to work in the vineyard of their respective dispensations. This degree of acceptance, with the seed of light, life, and power that accompanies it, is certainly previous to any work; and, in virtue of it, infants and complete idiots go to heaven, for "of such is the kingdom of God." As they are not capable of burying or improving their talent of inferior acceptance, they are admitted with it to an inferior degree of glory.

2. While many abandoned heathens, and those who follow their abominable ways, bury their talents to the last, and lose it, together with the degree of acceptance they once enjoyed in or through "the Beloved"; some, by improving it, are accepted in a higher manner, and, like Cornelius, receive tokens of increasing favour. The love of pity and benevolence which God bore them, is now mixed with some love of complacence and delight.

3. Faithful Jews, or those who are, under their dispensation, improving a superior number of talents, are accepted in a superior manner, and as a token of it they are made "rulers over five cities," they partake of greater grace here, and greater glory hereafter.

4. John the Baptist and his disciples—I mean Christians who have not yet been "baptized with the Holy Ghost and with fire"—are yet more highly accepted: for John, and the souls who live up to the height of his dispensation, are "great in the sight *and favour* of the Lord." They exceed all those who attain only to the perfection of inferior economists.

5. But those Christians who live in the kingdom of God, which was opened to believers on the day of pentecost, whose hearts burn with his love, and flame with his glory, are accepted in a still higher degree. For our Lord informs us, that great as John himself was, "The least in the kingdom of God is greater than he"; and as a token of superior acceptance, he shall be made "ruler over ten cities"; he shall enter more deeply "into the joy *and glory* of his Lord."

Although *concurrence with grace given* is necessary, in order to these four last degrees of acceptance, none enjoys them but *in* and *through* "the Beloved": for as his blood is the meritorious spring of all our pardons, so his Spirit is the inexhaustible fountain of all our graces. Nor are we less indebted to him for power, to "be workers together with God" in the great business of our salvation, than for all the other wonders of his unmerited goodness and redeeming love.

Let nobody say, that the doctrine of these degrees of acceptance is founded upon metaphysical distinctions, and exceeds the capacity of simple Christians: for a child of ten years old understands that he may be accepted to run a race before he is accepted to receive the prize; and that a man may be accepted as a day labourer, and not as a servant; be as a steward, and not as a child; as a friend, and not as a spouse. All these degrees of acceptance are very distinct, and the confusion of them evidently belongs to the Calvinian Babel.

(D) *As we have considered three of the walls of your tower, it will not be amiss to cast a look upon the fourth, which is the utterly confounding of the four degrees that make up a glorified saint's eternal justification:*

1. That which passes upon all infants universally, and is thus described by St. Paul: "As by the offence of one, judgment came upon all men to condemnation; even so, by the righteousness of one, the free gift came upon all men, unto *present* justification *from original sin, and future* justification of life"; upon their repenting and believing in the light, *during* the day of their visitation." In consequence of this degree of justification, we may, without impeaching the veracity of God, say to every creature, "God so loved the world, that he gave his only begotten Son, to reconcile them unto himself, not imputing to them" original sin unto eternal death, and blotting out their personal transgressions in the moment "they believe with the heart unto righteousness."

2. The justification consequent upon such believing, is thus described by St. Paul: This blessing of "faith imputed for righteousness" shall be ours, "if we believe on him that was raised from the dead for our justification. We have believed in Jesus Christ, that we might be justified by the faith of Christ, and not by the works of the law. Therefore, being justified by faith, we have peace with God through our Lord Jesus Christ," etc.

3. The justification consequent upon bringing forth the fruit of a lively faith in the truths that belong to our dispensation. This justification is thus mentioned by St. James: "Rahab the harlot was justified by works. Abraham our father was justified by works. Ye see then how by works a man is justified, and not by faith only."

And, 4. Final justification, thus asserted by our Lord and St. Paul: In the day of judgment "by thy words shalt thou be justified, and by thy words shalt thou be condemned. Circumcision and uncircumcision avail nothing, but the keeping of the commandments; for the doers of the law shall be justified."

All these degrees of justification are equally merited by Christ. We do nothing in order to the *first,* because it finds us in a state of total death. Toward the *second* we believe by the power freely given us in the first, and by the additional help of Christ's word and the Spirit's agency. We work by faith in order to the *third.* And we continue believing in Christ and working together with God, as we have opportunity, in order to the *fourth.*

The preaching distinctly these four degrees of a glorified saint's justification is attended with peculiar advantages. The *first* justification engages the sinner's attention, encourages his hope, and draws his heart by love. The *second* wounds the self-righteous Pharisee, who works without believing; while it binds up the heart of the returning publican, who has no plea but "God be merciful to me a sinner!" The *third* detects the hypocrisy and blasts the vain hopes of all Antinomians, who, instead of "Showing their faith by their works, deny *in works* the Lord that bought them, and put him to an open shame." And while the *fourth* makes even a "Felix tremble," it causes believers to "pass the time of their sojourning here in *humble* fear" and cheerful watchfulness.

Though all these degrees of justification meet in glorified saints, we offer violence to Scripture if we think, with Dr. Crisp, that they are inseparable. For all the wicked who "quench the *convincing* Spirit," and are finally given up to a reprobate mind, fall from the FIRST, as well as Pharaoh. All who "receive the seed among thorns," all who "do not forgive their fellow servants," all who "begin in the Spirit and end in the flesh," and all "who draw back," and become sons or daughters of "perdition," by falling from the THIRD, lose the SECOND, as Hymeneus, Philetus, and Demas. And none partake of the FOURTH but those who "bear fruit unto perfection," according to one or another of the Divine dispensations; "some producing thirty-fold," like heathens, "some sixty-fold," like Jews, "and some a hundred-fold," like Christians.

From the whole it appears, that although we can absolutely do nothing toward our first justification, yet to say that neither faith nor works are required in order to the other three, is one of the boldest, most unscriptural, and most dangerous assertions in the world; which sets aside the best half of the Scriptures, and lets gross Antinomianism come in full tide upon the Church.

Having thus taken a view of the confusion in which Calvin and Crisp have laid the foundation of their schemes, I return to the arguments by which you support their mistakes.

1. "If you suppose," you say, "that there are any conditional works before justification, these works must either be the works of one who is in a state of nature, or in a state of grace, either condemned by the law or absolved by the Gospel."

A new sophism this! No works are previous to justification from original sin, and to the quickening "light which enlightens every man that comes into the world." And the works that a penitent does in order to the subsequent justifications, such as "ceasing to do evil, learning to do well," repenting, and persevering in obedient faith, are all done in a state of initial, progressive, or perfected grace; not under the Adamic law, which did not admit of repentance, but under the Gospel of Christ, which says, "Let the wicked forsake his way, and the unrighteous man his thoughts; and let him return unto the Lord, who will abundantly pardon his sins, cleanse him from all unrighteousness," and even "fill him with the fulness of God."

2. You proceed: "If a man in a state of nature do works in order to justification, they cannot please God, because he is in a state of utter enmity against him."

What, sir! do you think that a man *in a state of utter enmity against God* will do any thing in order to recover his favour? When Adam was in that state did he so much as once ask pardon? If he had, would he not have evidenced a desire of reconciliation, and consequently a degree of apostasy short of what you call *utter enmity?*

3. You quote Scripture: "He that does something in order to justification cannot please God, because he 'is alienated from the life of God, through the ignorance that is in him, because of the blindness of his heart.' "

An unhappy quotation this! For the apostle did not speak these words of those honest heathens, who, in obedience to "the Light of the world," did something in order to justification; but of those abandoned Pagans, who, as he observes in the next verse, "being past feeling, had given themselves over unto lasciviousness, to work all uncleanness with greediness." Thus, to prove that men have not a talent of power to "work the works of God," you produce men who have buried it, that they might "work all uncleanness" without control, yea, "with greediness."

You would have avoided this mistake if you had considered that the heathens mentioned there by St. Paul were of the stamp of those whom he describes, Rom. 1, and whom he represents as "given up" by God "to a reprobate mind, because when they knew God they glorified him not as God, and did not like to retain him in their knowledge." Here we may observe, (1) That those reprobate heathens had once some knowledge of God, and, of course, some life: for "this is eternal life," to know God. (2) That if they were given up, *because* they did not use that talent of Divine knowledge, it was not because they were eternally and unconditionally reprobated; whence I beg leave to conclude, that if eternal, unconditional reprobation is a mere chimera, so is likewise eternal, unconditional election.

You might have objected, with much more plausibility, that when the Ephesians were in the flesh they were "without hope, without Christ, and without God in the world": and if you had, I would have replied, that these words cannot be taken in their full latitude, for the following reasons, which appear to me unanswerable: (1) The Ephesians, before their conversion, were not totally *without hope,* but without a *good* hope. They probably had as presumptuous a hope as David in Uriah's bed, or Agag when he thought the bitterness of death was past. (2) They were *without Christ,* just as a man who has buried his talent is without it. But as he may dig it up and use it if he sees his folly in time, so could, and so did the Ephesians. (3) If they were in every sense *without Christ,* what becomes of the doctrine maintained in your fourth letter, that they "were for ever and for ever complete in Christ?" (4) They were not entirely *without God:* "for in him they lived, moved, and had their being." Nor were they without him as absolute reprobates; for they "knew the day of their visitation" before it was over. It remains, then, (5) That they were *without God,* as the prodigal son was without his father when "he fed swine in a far country"; and that they could and did return to their heavenly Father as well as he.

4. You go on: "He who does something in order to justification, not being grafted in Christ the true vine, cannot bring forth any good fruit; he can do nothing at all."

I beg, sir, you would produce one man who has not "sinned the sin unto death," that can absolutely do nothing, that cannot cease from one sin, and take up the practice of one duty. You will as soon find a saint in hell as such a man upon earth. Even those who in their voluntary humility say perpetually that *they can do nothing,* refute their own doctrine by their very confessions: for he who confesses his helplessness, undoubtedly does something, unless by some new rule in logic it can be demonstrated that confessing our impotence, and complaining of our misery, is *doing nothing.*

When our Lord says, "Without me ye can do nothing," does he say that *we are totally without him?* When he declares, that "no man cometh unto him unless the Father draw him," does he insinuate that the Father does *not draw all?* Or that he draws *irresistibly?* Or that those who are drawn at one time, may not *draw* back at any other? Is it right to press Scripture into the service of a system, by straining its meaning so far beyond the import of the words?

Again: though a man may not be "grafted in Christ," according to the Jewish or Christian dispensation, may he not partake of his quickening sap, according to the more general dispensation of that "saving grace which has appeared to all men?" May not the branches in which that "saving grace appears," have some connection with Christ, the heavenly vine, and bring forth fruit meet for repentance, as well as Job and his friends, Melchisedec, Plato, the wise men, Cornelius, some of his soldiers, and many more who brought forth fruits according to their dispensation? Does not the first general justification so graft all men in Him that if they bear not fruit during their "accepted time," they are justly "taken away, cast forth, and burned," as barren branches?

5. Your knowledge of the Scripture made you foresee this answer, and to obviate it, you say: "If you tell me *that I mistake, that although we must cease from evil, repent, etc., yet you are far from supposing we can perform these things in our own natural strength.* I ask

then, In whose strength are they performed? You say, *In the strength of Christ, and by the power of the Holy Ghost, according to these scriptures: 'I can do all things through Christ strengthening me, being strengthened with might in the inner man.'*"

Permit me to tell you, honoured sir, that I do not admire your quoting Scripture for me. You take care to keep out of sight the passages I have quoted, and to produce those which are foreign to the question. To show that even a sinful heathen may work *for,* as well as *from* life, I could never be so destitute of common sense as to urge the experience of St. Paul, "a father in Christ"; and that of the Ephesians, who were Christians "sealed unto the day of redemption."

To do justice to free grace, instead of the above mentioned improper scriptures, you should have produced those which I have quoted in the Vindication: Christ is "the Light of the world, which enlightens every man that cometh into the world. I am come that they might have life. Ye will not come unto me that ye might have life. The grace of God, which bringeth salvation, hath appeared unto all men. God's Spirit strives with man, *even with those who perish.* He commands all men every where to repent; nor does he desire to reap where he has not sown."

6. Such scriptures as these would have been to the purpose. But I excuse your producing others: for if these had appeared, you would have raised more dust in six lines than you could have laid in sixty pages; and every attentive reader would have detected the fallacy of your grand argument: "As soon may we expect living actions from a dead corpse; light out of darkness; sight out of blindness; love out of enmity; wisdom out of ignorance; fruit out of barrenness, etc., etc., etc., as look for any one good work or thought from a soul who is not" (in some degree) "quickened by the Holy Ghost, and who

has not yet found favour with God": so far at least as to be blessed with "a day of salvation," and to be a partaker of "the free gift, which is come upon all men."

But, I pray, who is guilty of these absurdities? Who expects living actions from a dead corpse, etc., etc.? You, or we? You, who believe that the greatest part of mankind are left as graceless as devils, as helpless as corpses; and yet gravely go and preach to them repentance and faith, threatening them with an aggravated damnation if they do not turn? or we, who believe that "Christ by the grace of God tasted death for every man"; and that his "saving, quickening grace hath appeared unto all men?" Who puts foolish speeches in the mouth of the "only wise God"? You, who make him expostulate with souls as dead as corpses, and say, "Ye will not come unto me that ye might have life?" or we, who assert, upon the testimony of the Holy Ghost, that God, by "working in us both to will and to do," puts us again in a capacity of "working out our salvation with fear and trembling?" Will not our impartial readers see that the absurdity, which you try to fix upon us, falls at your own door; and if your doctrine be true, at the door of the sanctuary itself?

7. You pursue: "It is most clear that every soul who works in the strength of Christ, and by the power of the Holy Ghost, is already a pardoned and justified soul; he already has everlasting life."

Here is some truth and some error: let us endeavour to separate them. Every soul who works in the strength of Christ's preventing grace, and by his Spirit "convincing the world of sin," is undoubtedly interested in the first degree of justification: he is justified from the guilt of original sin, and, when he believes, from the guilt of his own actual sins; but it is absurd to suppose he is justified in the day of judgment, when that day is not yet come. He hath a seed of life, or else he could not work;

but it is a doubt if this seed will take root; and in case it does, the heavenly plant of righteousness may be "choked by the cares of the world, the deceitfulness of riches, or the desire of other things, and *by that mean* become unfruitful."

As many barbarous mothers destroy the fruit of their womb, either before or after it comes to the birth, so many obstinate sinners obstruct the growth of the spiritual "seed *that* bruises the serpent's head"; and many flagrant apostates, in whose heart "Christ *was once* formed, crucify him afresh, and quench the Spirit" of his grace. Hence the many miscarriages and apostasies, for which Elisha Coles is obliged to account thus: There are "monsters in spirituals, in whom there is something begotten in their wills, by the common strivings and enlightenings of the Spirit, which attains to a kind of formality, but proves in the end a lump of dead flesh." Surely that great Calvinian divine was brought to a strait when he thus fathered *formality and dead* flesh upon the Holy Ghost!

8. I follow you: "Therefore all talk of *working for life, in order to find favour with God,* is not less absurd than if you were to suppose that a man could at the same moment be both condemned and absolved."

What, sir, may not a man be justly condemned, and yet graciously reprieved? Nay, may not the judge give him an opportunity to make the best of his reprieve, in order to get a full pardon and place at court? At Geneva, we think that the absurdity does not consist in asserting, but in denying it. "Awake and asleep!" What, sir, is it an absurdity to think that a man may be at the same moment *awake* in one respect, and *asleep* in another? Does not St. Paul say, "Let us awake out of sleep?" But this is not all; even in Geneva people can be drowsy, that is, half awake and half asleep. "Dead and alive!" I hope you will not fix the charge of absurdity upon Christ, for saying that a certain man was left "half dead," and of course *half alive;* and for exhorting the people of Sardis who were *dead,* to "strengthen the things which remained and were ready to die:" nor yet upon St. Paul, for saying that the "dead body" of Abraham begat Isaac, and for speaking of a woman who was "dead while she lived."

9. You go on to say, that "it is as absurd to talk of *working for life,* as to assert that we can be at the same time loved and hated of God."

But you forget, sir, that there are a thousand degrees of love and hatred; and that, in Scripture language, *loving less* is called *hating:* "Jacob have I loved, and Esau have I hated. Except a man hate his father, etc., he cannot be my disciple." Yea, and we can without absurdity say that we *love* the same person in one respect, and *hate* her in another. I may love a woman as a neighbor, and yet loathe her in the capacity of a wife. And what absurdity is there in asserting that while the day of grace lasts, God loves, and yet hates an impenitent sinner? He loves him as his redeemed creature, yet hates him as his rebellious creature: or, in other terms, he loves him with a love of benevolence, but has no more love of complacence for him than for the devil himself.

10. You proceed: "To talk of *working for life,* is not less absurd, than if you were to suppose that a man can be at the same moment one with Christ, by his spirit dwelling in the heart, and yet not have redemption, peace, and reconciliation by the blood of his cross."

Here is, if I mistake not, the language of Babel.

(1.) You confound the various degrees of redemption. Are not thousands of souls redeemed by the blood of Christ's cross, who are not yet redeemed by the power of his Spirit? May not every rebellious sinner out of hell say, "God redeemeth my life from destruction?" Is it not a degree of redemption to be kept out of hell, enjoying the good things of this life, and called to secure the blessings of the next? Did not Cain, Esau, Pharaoh, Saul, and Judas, the five great reprobates, as some account them, enjoy this degree of redemption for many years? Have not believers a higher degree of "redemption, even the forgiveness of sins?" And do they not wait for the highest degree of it, even "the redemption of their body," when the trump of God will sound and awake the dead? Rom. viii, 23.

(2.) As you confound all the degrees of redemption, so you do all the degrees of the "manifestation of the Spirit." He visits all, so as to strive with and reprove them, as he did mankind in the days of Noah; but this is no mark that their peace is made, and a firm reconciliation brought about: witness the deluge, which God sent upon those with whom the Spirit had striven particularly one hundred and twenty years, in the days of Noah. Again: some have "the spirit of bondage unto fear;" but this, far from being a sign that they have full reconciliation, is a Divine consciousness that they have it not. And others have had the Spirit of adoption, and after having begun in him, so grieve or quench him as to end in the flesh. But in the Calvinian Babel, these Scriptural, experimental distinctions are exploded as metaphysical, if not dreadfully heretical.

11. You proceed: "You will not assert that a soul who is 'quickened together with Christ,' and in whom the Spirit of Jesus dwells by his gracious influences, can be in a state of enmity with God."

Still the same confounding of things which should be carefully distinguished! May not a sinner "be quickened" by the seed of life, and yet "hold it in unrighteousness?" May not a backslider "crucify Christ afresh," in *the gracious influences of his Spirit?* And are not such persons *in a state of enmity with God?* But if, by a soul "quickened together with Christ, and in whom the Spirit of Jesus dwells," you mean *a believer completely baptized with the Holy Ghost and with fire,* in whom he that once visited as a Monitor now fully resides as a Comforter, you are right; the enmity ceases, the carnal mind and body of sin are destroyed, and "God is all in all" to that just man "made perfect in love."

12. You add: "If a man is not in a state of enmity, then he must be in a state of pardon and reconciliation."

What, sir! Is there no medium between these extremes? There is, as surely as the morning dawn intervenes between midnight and noonday. If the king say to some rebels, "Lay down your arms, surrender, kiss my son, and you shall be pardoned," the reconciliation on the king's part is undoubtedly begun. So far "was God in Christ reconciling the world unto himself." But can it be said that the reconciliation is begun on the part of the rebels, who have not yet laid down any of their arms? Does not the reconciliation gradually take place, as they gradually comply with the king's terms? If they are long in coming to kiss the king's son, is not their full reconciliation suspended till they have fulfilled the last of the king's terms? And though the king made the overtures of the reconciliation, is there the least absurdity in saying, that "they surrender, and kiss the son, in order to find reconciliation?" Nay, is it either sense or truth to assert, that "they are absolutely to do nothing toward it?"

13. What you say about the thirteenth article of our Church is answered beforehand. (*Vindication,* p. 37.) But what follows deserves some notice: "Whenever God puts forth quickening power upon a soul, it is in consequence of his having already taken that soul into covenant with himself, and having washed it white in the blood of the Lamb slain."

This is very true, if you speak of the covenant of grace, which God made with our first parent and representative after the fall; and of the washing of all mankind white in the blood of the Lamb from the guilt of original sin, so far as to remit the eternal punishment of it. But you are dreadfully mistaken, if you understand it of the three subsequent degrees of justification and salvation, which do not take place, but as we "work them out with fear and trembling, *as God* works in us both to will and to do of his good pleasure."

14. In the next page you ask some scriptural questions, which I shall scripturally answer: "What did the expiring thief do?" Some hours before he died he obeyed this precept, "Today if ye will hear his voice harden not your heart"; he confessed his sin and believed in Jesus.

"What did Mary Magdalene do? She forsook her lovers, and followed Jesus into Simon's house.

"What Lydia?" She "worshipped *God,* and resorted where prayer was wont to be made."

"What the Philippian jailer?" He ceased from attempting self murder, and "falling at the apostle's feet, *inquired* what he must do to be saved?"

"What the serpent-bitten Israelites?" They "looked at the brazen serpent."

"What Paul himself?" "For this cause I obtained mercy," says he, "because I did it ignorantly in unbelief," I Tim. 1:13. But this was not all; for he "continued praying three days and three nights"; and when Ananias came to him he tarried no longer, but "arose and washed away his sins, calling on the name of the Lord."

"What did the Corinthians do?" They "heard and believed," Acts 8:8.

"And what the Ephesians?" They "trusted in Christ, after that they heard the word of truth," Eph. 1:13.

15. In the next paragraph, (page 6, line 28,) you gravely propose the very objection which I have answered, (*Vindication,* page 26,) without taking the least

notice of my answer. And in the next page you advance
one of Dr. Crisp's paradoxes: "Wherever God puts forth
his power upon a soul, (and he does so whenever he
visits it even with a touch of preventing grace,) pardon
and reconciliation are already obtained by such a one. He
shall never come into condemnation."

Young penitents, beware! If you admit this tenet,
you will probably stay in the "far country," vainly
fancying you are in your "father's house," because you
have felt a desire to be there. Upon this scheme of doctrine, Lot's wife might have sat down at the gate of
Sodom, concluding, that because the angels had taken
her by the hand she was already in Zoar. A dangerous
delusion this, against which our Lord himself cautions
us by crying aloud, "Remember Lot's wife!"

I would take the liberty to expostulate with you,
honoured sir, about this paradox, if I had not some hope,
that it is rather owing to the printer's mistake than your
own. If you wrote in your manuscript, "Pardon is already obtained *for*," not *by*, such a one, we are agreed;
for "Christ made upon the cross a sufficient sacrifice and
satisfaction for the sins of the whole world." But what
he procured *for* us, is not obtained *by* us, till the Holy
Ghost makes the application by faith. "If I had a mind,"
said the Rev. Mr. Whitefield, "to hinder the progress of
the Gospel, and to establish the kingdom of darkness, I
would go about telling the people, *they might have the
Spirit of God, and yet not feel it*"; or, which is much the
same, that the pardon which Christ procured *for* them, is
already obtained *by* them, whether they enjoy a sense of
it or not.

16. In the next paragraph, page 7, (who could believe it?) you come fully into Mr. Wesley's doctrine of
"doing something in order to obtain justification." You
were reminded (*First Check*) that "St. Paul and Mr.
Wesley generally mean by *justification,* that wonderful

transaction of the Spirit of God in a returning prodigal's conscience, by which the forgiveness of his sins is proclaimed to him through the blood of sprinkling." Nevertheless, speaking of the sense of pardon, and the testifying of it to a sinner's conscience, you grant that "this knowledge of our interest in Christ," (this experienced justification,) "is certainly to be sought in the use of all appointed means; we are to seek that we may find, to ask that we may have, to knock that it may be opened unto us. In this sense," (the very sense we generally fix to the word justification,) "all the texts you have brought to prove that man is to do something in order to obtain justification, and to find favour with God, admit of an *easy solution*": that is, in plain English, easily demonstrate the truth of Mr. Wesley's proposition, which has been so loudly exclaimed against as *dreadfully heretical!*

O prejudice, thou mischievous cause of discord, why didst thou cast thy black veil in June, and the following months, over the *easy solution,* which has been found out in December? And what a pity is it, dear sir, you did not see this *solution* before you had attempted to expose our gray-headed Elisha, by the publication of that weak and trifling dialogue with the Popish friar at Paris!

17. Page 10. After showing that you confound the atonement with the application of it, the work of Christ with that of the Holy Ghost, you produce one of my arguments, (the first you have attempted to refute,) brought to prove, that we must do something in order to justification. I had asserted that we must *believe,* faith being previous to justification. You say, "*I deny the assertion!*" Do you, indeed, honoured sir? Upon what ground? "The Holy Ghost teaches," say you, "that all who believe *are* justified." And does this prove the point? The king says to a deserter, "Bow to my son, and thou shalt not be shot." "Bow to the prince," adds an officer; "all who bow to him *are* pardoned." Must the

soldier conclude from the words, "*are* pardoned," that the *pardon* is previous to the *bow*? Again: you are sick, and your physician says, "Take this medicine; all who take it *are* cured." "Very well!" answers your nurse, "you need not then distress and perplex my master, by making him take your remedy. The taking of it cannot possibly be previous to his recovery; for you say, All who take it *are* cured." This is just such another argument as that of my honoured friend. O sir, how tottering is that system, which even such a writer as yourself cannot prop up, without putting so forced a construction upon the apostle's words, "All that believe *are* justified?"

Now we have seen upon what scriptural ground you maintain, that believing cannot be previous to justification, permit me, honoured sir, to quote some of the many scriptures which induce us to believe just the reverse: "Believe in the Lord Jesus Christ, and thou shalt be saved"; that is, in the lowest sense of the word, thou shalt be justified: for God justifies the ungodly that believe in Jesus. "We have believed in Jesus Christ, that we might be justified by the faith of Christ—whom he hath set forth to be a propitiation through faith in his blood, for the remission of sins that are past. As Moses lifted up the serpent, even so must the Son of man be lifted up, that whosoever believeth in him should not perish"; should be pardoned, etc. "Faith shall be imputed to us for righteousness, if we believe on him who raised up Jesus. Being therefore justified by faith, we have peace with God. Without faith it is impossible to please God. He that believeth not," far from being justified, as is insinuated, "shall be damned; the wrath of God abideth on him; he is condemned already," John 3: 18. Light cannot be more opposite to darkness, than this doctrine of Christ to that which my honoured friend thinks it his duty to patronize.

18. When you have ineffectually endeavoured to defend your sentiment from Scripture, you attempt to do it from reason. "Faith," say you, "can no more subsist without its object than there can be a marriage without a husband."

This is as proper an argument as you could advance, had you intended to disprove the doctrine you seem studious to defend; for it is evident that a woman must be married before she can have a husband. So sure then as marriage is previous to having a husband, faith is previous to receiving Christ: for we receive him by faith, John 1:12. However, from this extraordinary argument, you conclude that "the doctrine of believing before justification is not less contrary to reason than it is to Scripture"; but I flatter myself that my judicious readers will draw a conclusion diametrically opposite.

19. A quotation from St. Augustine appears next, and secures the ruin of your scheme. For if faith be compared to a *lantern,* and Christ to *the light in the lantern,* common sense tells us we must have the lantern before we can receive the candle which is to give us light. Or, in other words, we must have faith before we can receive Christ: for you very justly observe, that "faith receiveth Christ, who is the true Light."

20. St. Augustine's lantern makes way for the witticism with which you conclude your second epistle. "No letters," says my honoured friend, "were sent through the various provinces against old Mordecai, for supposing that the woman, Luke 15, lights a candle, etc., in order to find her lost piece; but because he insists upon it, that the piece lights the candle, sweeps the house, and searches diligently in order to find the woman."

Permit me to ask, whether your wit here has not for a moment got the start of your judgment? I introduced *the woman seeking the piece she had lost,* merely to show that it is neither a heresy nor an absurdity to

"seek something in order to find it"; and that instance
proved my point, full as well as if I had fixed upon Saul
seeking his father's asses, or Joseph seeking his brethren
in Dothan.

If it be as great an absurdity to say, that sinners are
"to seek the Lord," as it is to say, that "a piece seeks
the woman that has lost it"; let me tell you, that Mr.
Wesley has the good fortune to be countenanced in his
folly, *First,* by yourself, who tell us, page 7, that the
knowledge of Christ, and our interest in him, "is certainly to be sought in the use of all the appointed means."
And, *Secondly,* by Isaiah, who says, "Seek ye the Lord
while he may be found." By St. Paul, who tells the
Athenians, that "all nations of men are to seek the Lord."
And by Christ himself who says, "They that seek me
early shall find me: seek that you may find," etc.

I leave you to judge whether it was worth your while
to impeach Mr. Wesley's good sense, not only by reflect-
ing upon your own, but by inevitably involving Isaiah,
St. Paul, and our Lord himself, in the ridicule cast upon
my vindicated friend! For the same sinner, who is represented by *the lost piece,* is, a few verses before, represented by *the lost son;* and, you know, Jesus Christ tells
us that he came from far to seek his father's pardon and
assistance.

III. (A) *"David's sin displeased the Lord,"* but not
"his person." This is what you must mean, if you oppose
Mr. Wesley's proposition. I like your shifting the terms;
it is a sign that you are a little ashamed the world should
see the good doctor's scheme without some covering. *Eru-
buisti, salva res est.* (1) Your intimation, that the Lord
was not displeased at David's *person,* bears hard upon
the equity and veracity of God. David commits adultery
and murder in Jerusalem, and Claudius in Rome. God
sees them, and says, agreeably to your scheme, "They
are both guilty of the same crimes, and both impenitent;

but David is a Jew, an elect, a sheep, and therefore, though he sins against *ten* times more light than the other, I am not at all displeased at him. But Claudius is a heathen, a reprobate, a goat, and my anger smokes against him; he shall surely die." If this is God's method, how can he make the following appeal? "O house of Israel, are not my ways equal? Are not your ways unequal! The soul that sinneth it shall die: wherefore, turn ye, why will ye die, O house of Israel?" See Ezek. 18, and Second Check, pp. 109, 110.

(2) Your distinction is overthrown by Scripture: for we read, Gen. 38:10, that "the thing which Onan did displeased the Lord." "True," might you say, upon your scheme, "this is the very thing I assert. This mode of speech shows that God was angry at Onan's *sin,* and not at his *person.*" But this would be a great mistake, honoured sir; for the sacred historian adds immediately, *Wherefore God slew him also.* He showed his heavy displeasure at his *person,* by punishing him with death, as well as his brother Er, who *was wicked in the sight of the Lord.*

(3) But if you will not believe Mr. Wesley when he declares, that God is displeased at the *persons* of the righteous, the moment they do those *things* which displease him, believe at least the oracles of God. "God's anger was kindled against Moses," Exod. 4:14. "The Lord was very angry against Aaron," Deut. 9:20; and with all Israel: witness those awful words, "Let me alone, that I may consume them in a moment!" Isaiah, whom you allow to be an elect, says, "Thou wast angry with me." God himself says, Isaiah 47:6, "I was angry with my people": and David, who frequently deprecates God's wrath in his penitential Psalms, observes, that "his anger smokes against the sheep of his pasture," when they go astray, Psalms 74:1.

(4) The New Testament inculcates this doctrine as well as the Old. St. Paul having reminded the believers of Ephesus, that "no whoremonger, or covetous person, hath an inheritance in the kingdom of Christ and of God," subjoins this seasonable caution, "Let no man deceive you"; no, not those good men, Dr. Crisp and the author of *Pietas Oxoniensis:* "for because of these things the wrath of God cometh upon the children of disobedience." "Impossible!" say those orthodox Protestants; "you may be 'children of disobedience,' not only unto 'whoredom and covetousness,' but unto adultery and murder, without fearing that 'the wrath of God will come upon you for these things.' No, no, you will be 'pleasant children still.' " See *Vindication,* pp. 59, 60.

(B) *You proceed: "Shall I believe, that, because Davide was ungrateful, God, whose gifts and callings are without repentance, was unfaithful?"* And shall I believe that God is not as *faithful* when he accomplishes his threatenings, as when he fulfils his promises? You reply, *"God's gifts and callings are without repentance."* And does this prove that God's warnings are without meaning, and his threatenings without truth? St. Paul spoke those words of the election of the Jews; and, it is certain, God does not repent that he formerly *called* them, and *gave* them the land of Canaan; any more than he repents his having now *rejected* them, and *taken from them* the good land which he gave their fathers: for as he had once sufficient reasons to do the one, so he has now to do the other.

But if you will make this passage mean, that the Divine favour and blessings can never be forfeited through any fall into sin, I beg you will answer these queries. Had not God *given* all angels a place in his favour and glory? and did not many of them lose it by their fall? Was not innocent Adam interested in the Divine favour and image? and did he not lose both, together with paradise, when he fell into sin? Did not King Saul forfeit the crown which God had *given* him, and the throne to which he had *called* him? Were not Judas' *calling* and apostleship forfeited by his unfaithfulness, as well as one of the twelve *thrones* which Christ had promised him? What will you say of the unprofitable servant from whom his lord took the talent unimproved? Lost he not a blessing *given,* and *his calling to occupy* with it? And can you assert that the man who took his fellow servant by the throat did not lose *the forgiveness of a debt of ten thousand talents*? Or that those apostates, who "tread under foot the blood of the covenant wherewith they were sanctified," do not forfeit their sanctification by *doing despite to the Spirit of grace?* Is it right thus to set the author of the Epistle to the Romans against the author of the Epistle to the Hebrews?

(C) *Your bringing in "backsliding Ephraim, the pleasant child," as a witness of the truth of your doctrine, is a most unhappy proof.* "Rejoice not, O Israel, as other people," says the Lord, Hosea 9:1, "for thou hast gone a whoring from thy God." This whoring Israel is called Ephraim, verse 13. *Ephraim,* the pleasant child, *is planted as a pleasant plant.* Notwithstanding, "Ephraim shall bring forth his children for the murderer. All their wickedness is in Gilgal: for there I *hated* them. For the wickedness of their doings I will drive them out of mine house: *I will love them no more."* Hence the prophet observes immediately after, "Ephraim is smitten; my God will cast them away because they did not hearken unto him."

(D) *However, my honoured friend still affirms, that "David, notwithstanding his horrible backslidings, did not lose the character of the man after God's own heart."* But you will permit me to believe the contrary.

1. Upon the testimony of the psalmist himself, who says, in your favourite Psalm, "Thou hast cast off and ab-

horred, thou hast been very wroth with thine anointed; thou hast made void the covenant of thy servant; thou hast profaned his crown by casting it to the ground," Psalms 89: 38.

2. Where is David called *the man after God's own heart,* while he continued an impenitent adulterer? How much more guarded is the Scripture than your Letters? "David did that which was right in the eyes of the Lord, and turned not aside, SAVE only in the matter of Uriah," I Kings 15: 5. Here you see the immoral parenthesis of ten months spent in adultery and murder, expressly pointed at, and excepted by the Holy Ghost.

3. David himself, far from thinking that sin could never separate between God and *a just man* who *draws* back into wickedness, speaks thus in the last charge which he gave to Solomon: "And thou, Solomon, my son, know the God of thy father, and serve him with a perfect heart. If thou seek him, he will be found of thee; but if thou forsake him, he will cast thee off for ever," I Chron. 28: 9. Hence it appears that the God of *Solomon's father* is very different from the picture which Dr. Crisp draws of *David's God!* The former can be so displeased at an impenitent backslider, as to *cast him off for ever;* while the latter accounts him *a pleasant child still.* But let us come to matter of fact.

4. Displeasure, anger, or wrath in God, is not that disturbing, boisterous passion so natural to fallen man; but an invariable disapprobation of sin, and a steady design to punish the sinner. Now God severely manifested his righteous displeasure at David's person, when he punished him by not restraining any longer the ambition of his rebellious son. How remarkably did his dreadful punishments answer his heinous crimes! He wanted the fruit of his adultery to live, but inflexible justice destroys it. "The crown of *righteousness* was fallen from his head," and his royal crown is "profaned

and cast to the ground." He had not turned out "the way faring man," the hellish tempter; and he is turned out of his own palace and kingdom. He flees beyond Jordan for his life; and, as he flees, Shimei throws stones at him; volleys of curses accompany the stones; and the most cutting challenges follow the curses: "Come out, thou bloody man," said he, "thou man of Belíal! The Lord hath delivered thy kingdom into the hand of Absalom thy son; and behold, thou art taken in thy mischief, because thou art a bloody man." To which David could answer nothing, but " *'Let him curse; for the Lord,'* by not restraining his wickedness, *hath* permissively *'said unto him, Curse David.'* I see the impartial justice of a sin-avenging God, through the cruel abuse of this raging man." This was not all. He had *secretly* committed adultery with Uriah's wife, and his son *publicly* commits incest with his wives. And, to complete the horror of his punishment, he leaves the most dreadful curse upon his posterity. "Thou hast slain Uriah with the sword of the children of Ammon," says the Lord, "now therefore the sword shall never depart from thy house," and thy own children shall murder one another. What a terrible punishment was this! And how strong must be the prejudice of those who maintain that God was not displeased at David's *person!*

(E) *Pass we now to an argument which you seem to consider as one of the main pillars of your doctrine:* "If *one believer sin by an unclean thought,"* say you, *"and another by an unclean act, does the former continue in a state of grace, and the other forfeit his sonship? Take heed lest you should be forced to go to Rome for an answer to this query."*

Without going even to the convent of the Benedictine monks in Paris, I answer, It is evident from Scripture that an adulterous thought, delighted in, is adultery. He that entertains such a thought is an adulterer, one who is absolutely unfit for the presence of a holy God. "Be not deceived," says St. Paul, "neither fornicators nor adulterers shall inherit the kingdom of God." Therefore adultery of heart certainly excludes an impenitent backslider out of heaven; though it will not sink him into so deep a hell, as if he had drawn another into the commission of his intended crime. You add:

"But if David had only had an angry thought, he had still been a murderer in the sight of God." Not so: for there is a righteous anger, which is a virtue and not a sin; or else how could Christ "have looked round about on the Pharisee with anger," and continued sinless? You mean, probably, that if David had only *hated* Uriah in his heart, he would have been a murderer. If so, your observation is very just, for, "he that hateth his brother," says St. John, "is a murderer; and you know," adds he, "that no murderer," though he were a royal psalmist, "hath eternal life abiding in him."

But what do you get by these arguments? Nothing at all. You only make it easier to prove that your doctrine is erroneous. For if David would have forfeited heaven by "looking on Uriah's wife, to lust after her in his heart," or by intending in his breast to murder her husband; how much more did he forfeit it when mental sin fully ripened into outward enormities! "Ye are of your father the devil, whose works ye do," said Christ to some of the chosen nation. And if adultery and murder are works of the devil, it follows from those words of our Lord, that while David continued impenitent, he was *not* "a man after God's own heart," as my honoured opponent too charitably supposes; but *a man after the own heart of him* "who abode not in the truth, and was a murderer from the beginning."

(F) *But you add, "Sin did not reign in him as a king, it only for a time usurped as a tyrant."* Nay, sir, sin is a tyrant wherever he reigns, and he reigns wherever he usurps. "Where will you draw the line" between the *reign* and *tyranny* of sin? Are not both included under the word *dominion?* "Sin," says St. Paul, "shall not have DOMINION over you that are under grace." Had I made such a distinction as this, some Protestants would deservedly have called it *metaphysical;* but as it comes from the orthodox author of *Pietas Oxoniensis,* it will probably pass for *evangelical.*

Very different, however, is St. Peter's orthodoxy. "Of whom a man is overcome," says he, "of the same is he brought into bondage. For if after they have escaped the pollution of the world through the knowledge of the Lord Jesus Christ, they are again entangled therein and overcome, the latter end is worse with them than the beginning." Nevertheless, even such apostates, so long as the day of their visitation lasteth, may again repent and believe; for, as you justly observe, they have still "an Advocate with the Father, Jesus Christ the righteous."

(G) *You try to prove your point by Scripture.* "*There is,*" *say you,* "*no condemnation to them who are in Christ.*" True: but it is while they "walk not after the flesh, but after the Spirit"; a clause which you prudently keep out of sight. And, surely, David walked after the flesh, when in the act of adultery and murder. You proceed: "Who shall lay any thing to the charge of God's elect?" Nobody, if God's elect are penitent believers, "who walk not after the flesh"; but if they are impenitent adulterers and hypocritical murderers—Jews and Gentiles, law and Gospel, prophets and apostles, God and their own conscience, ALL will agree to lay their crimes to their charge. You urge, that "Christ, by one offering, hath for ever perfected them that are sanctified." True! But not those who are *unsanctified:* and, certainly, such are all adulterers and murderers. These ought rather to be ranked with those who "tread under foot

the blood of the covenant wherewith they WERE sanctified."

It is said, however, "Ye," believing, loving, fruitful
Colossians, see chap. 1: 4, 6, "are complete in him." It is
so; but not, *ye impenitent backsliders, ye unclean de-
filers of another's bed.* Such are "complete" in *evil,* not
in *good,* in Belial, not in Christ. Alas, for the prostitution
of the sacred and pure word of God! Can it also be
pressed into the service of profaneness and impurity?
To rescue at least one sentence from such manifest abuse,
I might observe, the original may with the greatest propriety be rendered, *filled with* (or *by*) *him,* instead of
"complete in him"; and I think the context fixes this
sense upon it. The apostle is cautioning the Colossians
against vain philosophers, whose doctrine was empty and
deceitful. Now, that he may do this the more effectually,
he points out a more excellent Teacher, whose character
and qualifications he describes when he says, "In him
dwelleth the fulness, ωληρωμα, of the Godhead." He immediately adds, ωεπληρωμενοι εν αυτώ (a verb of the
same etymology with the noun, and undoubtedly of a
similar import.) "ye are filled *with* (or *by*) him." As if
he had said, "Christ is filled with the Godhead of the
Father, and ye with the Spirit of Christ, the Spirit of
wisdom, righteousness, and strength. *Plenitudo Christi,*
says the learned and pious Bengelius on the passage,
redundat in ecclesiam, "The fulness of God dwelleth in
the Mediator, and overflows upon his Church." The very
sense our translators have given the very same two
words in Eph. 3: 19. Why they rendered them differently
here is hard to say.

(H) *You go on: "No falls or backslidings in God's
children can ever bring them again under condemnation, because the law of the Spirit of life in Christ Jesus
hath made them free from the law of sin and death."* A
most dangerous proposition, exposed, (*First Check,* p.

59,) and contrary to the very Scripture by which you try to support it. (1) To the context, where those to whom "there is no condemnation," are said to be persons "who walk not after the flesh," and are therefore very different from impenitent adulterers and murderers, who bring forth the most execrable fruits of the flesh. (2) To the text itself: for if "the law, *or power* of the Spirit of life in Christ Jesus, hath made *the believer* free from the law *or power* of sin," how can he be represented as the same "servant of sin"; as "sold under sin"; sold under adultery and murder for ten months! But you are at a loss for an answer.

(I) *"We are very apt,"* say you, *"to set up mountainous distinctions concerning the various degrees of sin, especially of sins after conversion."* This, together with your placing "an angry thought" upon a level with deliberate murder, seems to insinuate, that you make very little difference between an atrocious crime and a sin of surprise; so that, upon your scheme, a bloody murderer may plead that he is not more guilty than a man who has felt a motion of impatience; and the latter may be hurried out of his wits, as if he had committed murder. To remove this mistake, I need only observe, that if all are Papists who make a material difference between various sins, or between the same sins variously aggravated, my worthy opponent is as sound a Papist as myself: for when he acts as a magistrate, he does not promiscuously pass the same sentence upon every one. He commits one to prison, and dismisses another with a gentle reprimand. Our Lord himself sets you the example. Pharisees shall receive "the GREATER damnation," and it shall be "more tolerable for Sodom than for Chorazin in the day of judgment." Whence we may justly infer, that the sin of some is more "mountainous" than that of others.

But as you have made choice of David's case, permit me to argue from his experience. He was once, you know, violently angry with Nabal; but as he seasonably restrained his anger, and meekly confessed his sin, God forgave him without "breaking his bones." Not so when the unrestrained evil of his heart, in the matter of Uriah, produced the external fruits of treachery and murder. For *then* the Lord inflicted upon him all the dreadful punishments which we have already considered. "Hear the rod," therefore, and learn what *vast* difference the Lord makes between sins, whether committed after, or before conversion.

(J) *What follows is a sweet and smooth Antinomian pill, so much the more dangerous as it is gilt with gold taken from the sanctuary, from the golden altar itself.* Hence it is that multitudes swallow it down as *rich grace,* without the least scruple or suspicion. Lord, dart a beam of thy wisdom into the mind of thy servant, that I may separate the precious from the vile, and expose the dangerous ingredient without depreciating the gold that covers it!

1. "What is all sin," do you say, "before the infinitely precious atoning blood of Jesus?" Nothing at all, when that blood is humbly apprehended by penitent believers, who depart from all iniquity. But when it is "accounted a common thing, and trodden under foot" by impenitent apostates; or wantonly pleaded in defence of sin, by loose Nicolaitans or lukewarm Laodiceans, it does not answer its gracious design. On the contrary, "How shall we escape," says St. Paul, "if we thus neglect such great salvation?" And "of how much sorer punishment *than others* shall they be thought worthy, who do such despite to the Spirit of grace?" See Hebrews 2:5; 10:29. You go on:

"If Christ has fulfilled the whole law and borne the curse, then all debts and claims against his people, be they more or be they less, be they small or be they great, be they before or be they after conversion, are for ever and for ever cancelled. All trespasses are forgiven them. They are justified from all things. They already have everlasting life." What! before they repent and believe? A bold assertion this! which sets Jesus against Christ— our Priest against our Prophet. For Christ himself teaches us, that many for whom his "fatlings are killed, and all things are now ready," through an obstinate refusal of his *sincere* (I hope nobody will say *hypocritical*) invitation, "shall never taste of his supper." And as if this were not enough to arm us against your doctrine, he commissioned an apostle to assure his Church, that some who have *tasted* of his Gospel supper, that is, who "have been enlightened, have tasted the heavenly gift, the good word of God, and the powers of the world to come, do crucify to themselves the Son of God afresh," and, by that means, so totally fall away, that "it is impossible to renew them again to repentance." A clear proof this that those who "once *truly* repented" and were even "made partakers of the Holy Ghost," may "quench the Spirit, and sin against the Holy Ghost"; may not only fall, but fall finally, Heb. 6: 4.

2. Your doctrine sets also our High Priest against our heavenly King, who declares, that if he who was once his faithful servant, "begins to beat his fellow servants," much more to murder them, he will, as Judge of all, command him to be "bound hand and foot, and delivered to the tormentors." See Second Check, p. 71.

3. Your doctrine drags after it all the absurdities of eternal, absolute justification. It sets aside the use of repentance and faith, in order to pardon and acceptance. It represents the sins of the elect as forgiven, not only before they are confessed, but even before they are committed; a notion which that strong Calvinist, Dr. Owen himself, could not but oppose. It supposes, that all the

penitents who have believed that they were once "children of wrath," and that God was displeased at them when they lived in sin, have believed a lie. It makes the preaching of the Gospel one of the most absurd, wicked, and barbarous things in the world. For what can be more absurd than to say, "Repent ye, and believe the Gospel. He that believeth not shall be damned," if a certain number can never repent or believe, and a certain number can never be damned? And what can be more wicked than to distress elect sinners, by bidding them "flee from the wrath to come," if there is absolutely no *wrath*, neither past, present, nor *to come*, for them; if all their sins, "be they more or less, be they small or great, are for ever and for ever cancelled?" As for the reprobates, how *barbarous* is it to bid them flee, if adamantine chains, eternal decrees of past wrath perpetually bind them down, that they may never escape the repeated, eternal strokes of "the wrath to come!"

4. But what shocks me most in your scheme, is the reproach which it unavoidably fixes upon Christ. It says, The elect "are justified from all things," even before they believe. In all their sins "God views them 'without spot, wrinkle, or any such thing.' They stand always complete in the everlasting righteousness of the Redeemer." "*Black in themselves,* they are comely through his comeliness": so that when they commit adultery and murder, He, "who is of purer eyes than to behold iniquity," can, nevertheless, address them with "Thou art *all fair,* my love, my undefiled, there is no spot in thee."

What a prostitution of the word of God is here! We blame a wild youth for dropping some bold innuendos about Jupiter, in a play composed by a poor heathen. But I acquit thee of indecency, O Terence, if a vindicator of Christian piety has a right to represent our holy and righteous God as saying to a bloody adulterer, *in flagranti delicto,* "Thou art all FAIR, my love, my undefiled, there is no spot in thee." And are these the fat pastures and limpid waters where Gospel preachers "feed the sheep?" Where then! O where are the "barren pastures and muddled waters" in which barefaced Antinomians feed the goats? Is not this "taking the children's bread to cast it to the dogs?" I had almost asked, Is it not "the abomination of desolation standing in the holy place?" See ye not the Lord, O ye mistaken Christians, looking down from the habitation of his holiness? And do ye not hear him thunder this expostulation from heaven? *How long will ye blaspheme mine honour, and have such pleasure in deceit! Know ye not that I have chosen to myself the man that is godly; and that him who delighteth in iniquity doth my soul abhor?*

5. And plead not that you have quoted Scripture in defence of your point. If the Church says, in a mystical song, "*I am black* in the eyes of the world, *because* the *sun* of affliction and persecution *hath looked upon me,* while I *kept the vineyards;* but *I am comely* in the sight of God, whose Spirit enables me with unwearied patience *to bear the burden and heat of the day*"; you have absolutely no right, either from divinity or criticism, to make those words mean as they do upon your scheme, "*I am black* by the atrocious crimes which I actually commit, black by the horrors of adultery and murder; but no matter; *I am comely* by the purity and chastity of my Saviour. My sins, be they small or be they great, are for ever and for ever cancelled; I am justified from all things." Again: if God says to a soul actually "washed, walking with him as Enoch, and walking in white as the few names in Sardis, who had not defiled their garments," *Thou art all fair, my undefiled;* is it right to take those gracious words, and apply them to every lukewarm Laodicean we meet with; and to every apostate, who not only "defiles his garment, but wallows in the mire like the sow that was washed?"

6. Another great, and, if I am not mistaken, insurmountable difficulty attends your scheme. You tell us that "a believer's person stands absolved and always complete in the everlasting righteousness of the Redeemer." But I ask, Was he absolved *before* he was a believer? If you answer, "No, he was absolved the moment he began to believe," it follows, that he *does something,* that is, he *believes* toward his absolution. And thus your main pillars, "that faith is not previous to justification, that there is no wrath in God for the elect, and that all claims against his people before or after conversion are for ever cancelled," are not only broken, but ground to powder. Add to this, that if the believer be justified in consequence of his faith, it is evident that his justification, while he is on earth, can stand no longer than his faith, and that if he "make shipwreck of faith and a good conscience, as Hymeneus, he must again come into condemnation." But supposing, that to avoid these inconsistencies, you boldly say, "He was justified from the time 'the Lamb was slain, that is, from the beginning of the world';" you point blank contradict Christ, who says, that "he who believeth not is condemned already." Thus, either the veracity of our Lord, or the truth of your doctrine, must go to the bottom. A sad dilemma this, for those who confound *Crispianity* with CHRISTIANITY.

(K) *You reply, "As soon shall Satan pluck Christ's crown from his head as his purchase from his hand."* Here is a great truth, making way for a palpable error, and a dreadful insinuation.

Let us FIRST, see the great truth. It is most certain, that nobody shall ever be able to pluck Christ's sheep, that is, penitent believers, who "hear his voice and follow him," John 10:27, out of his protecting, almighty hand. But if the minds of those penitent believers are "corrupted from the simplicity that is in Christ: if they wax wanton against him, turn after Satan, end in the flesh, and draw back to perdition"; if, "growing fat with kicking," like Jeshurun, they "neigh," like high-fed horses, "after their neighbours' wives," we demand proof that they belong to the fold of Christ, and are not rather *goats* and wolves in sheep's clothing, who cannot, without conversion, enter into the kingdom of heaven.

SECONDLY: The palpable error is, that none of those for whom Christ died can be cast away and destroyed; that no "virgin's lamp can go out"; no promising harvest be "choked with thorns"; no "branch in Christ cut off" for unfruitfulness; no pardon forfeited, and no "name blotted out of God's book": that no "salt can lose its savour, nobody receive the grace of God in vain, bury his talent, neglect such great salvation, trifle away a day of visitation, look back after setting his hand to the plough, and grieve the Spirit" till he is quenched, and strives no more." This error, so conducive to the Laodicean case, is expressly opposed by St. Peter, who informs us, that some "deny the Lord that bought them, and bring upon themselves swift destruction." Christ himself, far from desiring to keep his lukewarm purchase "in his hand," declares he will "spew it out of his mouth," Rev. 3: 16.

Pass we on, THIRDLY, to the "dreadful insinuation." While you perpetually try to comfort *a few elect,* some of whom, for aught I know, comfort themselves already with their neighbours' wives, yea, and the wives of their fathers; please to tell us how we shall comfort *millions of reprobates,* who, for what you know, try "to save themselves from this adulterous generation?" Do ye not hear how Satan, upon a supposition of the truth of your doctrine, triumphs over those unhappy victims of what some call God's sovereignty? While that old murderer shakes his bloody hand over the myriads devoted to endless torments, methinks I hear him say to his fellow executioners of Divine vengeance, "As soon shall Christ's crown be plucked from his head as this his free gift from my hand. Let yonder little flock of the elect commit adultery and incest without any possibility of missing heaven. I object no more. See what crowds of reprobates may pray, and reform, and strive without any possibility of escaping hell. Let those gay elect shout, *Everlasting love! Eternal justification!* and *Finished salvation!* I consent! See, ye fiends, see the immense prey that awaits us, and roar with me, beforehand, *Everlasting wrath! Eternal reprobation!* and *Finished damnation!*"

(L) *"Our twelfth article maintains, that good works necessarily spring out of a lively faith, insomuch that by them a lively faith may be as evidently known as a tree discerned by its fruits."* "This," you say, "I most firmly believe": and nevertheless, to prove just the contrary— to show that when David committed adultery and murder, he had "a lively faith, and was in a state of justification and sanctification," you quote a verse of a hymn, composed by the Rev. C. Wesley, which only confirms what I say of *undervaluing, Vindication,* p. 55. But you mistake him, if you suppose that, when "not one bud of grace appears to ourselves, many may not appear to others"; and if you apply to outward enormities greedily committed, what the poet means of inward motions of sin cordially lamented and steadily opposed. Nevertheless, as some expressions in this hymn are not properly guarded, the pious author will forgive me, if I transcribe part of a letter which I lately received from him:

"I was once on the brink of Antinomianism by unwarily reading Crisp and Saltmarsh. Just then, warm in my first love, I was in the utmost danger, when Providence threw in my way BAXTER'S treatise, entitled, *A Hundred Errors of Dr. Crisp Demonstrated.* My brother was sooner apprehensive of the dangerous abuse which would be made of our unguarded hymns and expressions than I was. Now I also see and feel we must all sink, unless we call St. James to our assistance. Yet let us still insist as much, or more than ever, on St. Paul's justification. What God has joined together let no man put asunder. The great Chillingsworth saw clearly the danger of separating St. James from St. Paul. He used to wish, that whenever a chapter of St. Paul's justification was read, another of St. James might be read at the same time."

(M) *When my honoured correspondent has endeavoured to prove, by the above-mentioned scriptures, arguments, and quotations, that an impenitent adulterer and murderer, instead of being under God's displeasure, is "a pleasant child still"; to complete his work, he proceeds to show the good that falls into sin do to believers.* Never did the pious author of *Pietas Oxoniensis* employ his pen in a work less conducive to piety!

"God," says he, "often brings about his purposes by those very means, which to the human eye would certainly defeat them. He has always the same thing in view, his own glory and the salvation of his elect by Jesus Christ. This Adam was accomplishing when he put the whole world under the curse." Hail, Adam, under the fatal tree! Pluck and eat abundantly, for "thou accomplishest the salvation of the elect!" O the inconsistency of your doctrine! If we insist upon "doing the will of God," in order to "enter his kingdom," we are boldly exclaimed against as proudly sharing the glory of our redemption with Christ. But here Adam is represented as his partner in the work of salvation, and a share of his glory positively assigned to the fall, that is, to his disobedience to the Divine will. St. Paul asserts, that "by one man [Adam] came death, and sin the sting of death; and so death [with his sting] passed upon all men." But you inform us, that Adam by his sin "accomplished the salvation of the elect." If this is not plucking a jewel from Christ's crown, to adorn the most improper head in the world, next to that of Satan, I am very much mistaken.

But if God "brought about his purpose" concerning "the salvation of the elect" by the fall of Adam; tell us, I pray, who brought about the purpose concerning *the damnation of the reprobates?* Had the Lord "always this thing in view" also? On the brink of what a dreadful abyss hath your doctrine brought me? Sir, my mind recoils; I fly from the God whose unprovoked wrath rose before the beginning of the world against millions of his unformed, and therefore guiltless creatures! He that "tasted death for every man" bids me fly! and he points me from Dr. Crisp to God, "whose mercy is over all his works," till they personally forfeit it by obstinately trampling upon his richest grace.

(N) *As if it was not enough to have represented our salvation in part "accomplished" by the transgression of our first parents, you bring in "Herod and Pontius Pilate," and observe, to the honour of the good which sin does to the elect, that those unrighteous judges did whatsoever God's hand and counsel determined before to be done!* If you quote this passage to insinuate that God predetermined their sin, you reflect upon the Divine holiness, and apologize for the murderers of our Lord as you have for the murderer of Uriah.

I grant that when God saw, in the light of his infinite foreknowledge, that Pilate and Caiaphas would absolutely choose injustice and cruelty, he "determined" that they should have the awful opportunity of exercising them against his Anointed. As a skilful pilot, without predetermining, and raising a contrary wind, foresees it will rise, and predetermines so to manage the rudder and sails of his ship, as to make it answer a good purpose; so God overruled the foreseen wickedness of those men, and made it subservient to his merciful justice in offering up the true Paschal Lamb. But, as it would be very absurd to ascribe to the "contrary wind" the praise due to the "pilot's skill"; so it is very unevangelical to ascribe to the sin of Pilate, or of Joseph's brethren, the good which God drew from some of its extraordinary circumstances.

(O) *"The Lord has promised to make 'all things work for good to those that love him'; and if all things, then their very sins and corruptions are included in the royal promise."* A siren song this! which you unhappily try to support by Scripture. But, (1) if "this is the love of God, that we keep his commandments," how will you prove that David *loved God* when he left his own wife for that of Uriah? Does not our Lord declare, that those who will not "forsake husband, wife, children, and all things for his sake, are not worthy of him," either as believers or lovers? And are those "worthy of him" who break his commandment, and take their neighbours' wives? Again: if St. John, speaking of one who does not relieve an indigent brother, asks with indignation, "How dwelleth the love of God in him?" May not I, with greater reason, say, "How dwelt the love of God in David?" who far from assisting Uriah, murdered his soul by drunkenness, and his body with the sword! And if David did not love God, how can you believe that a promise made to "those who love God," respected him in his state of impenitency? (2) When we extol free grace, and declare, that "God's mercy is over all his works," you directly answer, that the word ALL must be taken in a limited sense: but when you extol the profitableness of sin, *all*, ("in all things working for good," must be taken universally, and include "sin and corruption," contrary to the context. (3) I say, contrary to the context; for, just before the apostle declares, "If ye live after the flesh, ye shall die," ye shall evidence the truth of Ezekiel's doctrine, 'When the righteous turneth away from his righteousness, in his sin that he hath sinned shall he die"; and at the end of

the chapter, "the things that work for good" are enumerated, and they include "all tribulations and creatures,"
but not our own sin, unless you can prove it to be God's
creature, and not the devil's production. (4) It is nowhere promised, that *sin* shall do us good. On the contrary, God constantly represents it as the greatest evil in
the world, the root of all other temporal and eternal evils:
and as he makes it the object of his invariable disapprobation, so, till they repent, he levels his severest threatenings at sinners without respect of persons. But the
author of *Pietas Oxoniensis* has made a new discovery.
Through the glass of Dr. Crisp, he sees that one of the
choicest promises in Scripture respects the commission
of sin, of thefts and incest, adultery and murder! So
grossly are threatenings and promises, punishments and
rewards, confounded together by this fashionable divinity!

(5) I grant that, in some cases, the *punishment* inflicted upon a sinner has been overruled for good: but
what is this to the *sin itself*? Is it reasonable to ascribe
to *sin* the good that may spring from the *rod* with which
sin is punished? Some robbers have, perhaps, been
brought to repentance by the gallows, and others deterred from committing robbery by the terror of their
punishment; but by what rule in logic, or divinity, can
we infer from thence, either that any robbers love God,
or that all robberies shall work together for their good?

But "Onesimus robbed Philemon his master; and flying from justice, was brought under Paul's preaching and
converted." Surely, sir, you do not insinuate that Onesimus' conversion depended upon robbing his master!
Or that it would not have been better for him to have
served his master faithfully, and stayed in Asia to hear
the Gospel with Philemon, than to have rambled to
Rome for it in consequence of his crime! The heathens
said, "Let us eat and drink, for tomorrow we die." It will
be well if some do not say, upon a fairer prospect than

theirs, "Let us steal and rob, for tomorrow we shall be converted."

(P) *You add, that "The royal and holy seed was continued by the incest of Judah with Tamar, and the adultery of David with Bathsheba."* And do you really think, sir, God made choice of that line to show how incest and adultery "work together for good?" For my part, I rather think that it was because, if he had chosen any other line, he would have met with *more* such blots. You know that God slew David's child conceived in adultery; and if he chose Solomon to succeed David, it was not because the adulterous Bathsheba was his mother, but because he was then the best of David's children: for I may say of God's choosing the son, what Samuel said of his choosing the father, "the Lord looketh on the heart," I Sam. 16: 7.

(Q) *You proceed in your enumeration of the good that sin does to the pleasant children.* "How has many a poor soul, who has been faithless through fear of man, even blessed God for Peter's denial!" Surely, sir, you mistake: none but the fiend, who desired to have Peter "that he might sift him," could bless God for the apostle's crime; nor could any one, on such a horrible account, bless any other God but "the god of this world." David said, "My eyes run down with water, because men keep not thy law"; but the author of *Pietas Oxoniensis* tells us, that "many a poor soul has blessed God" for the most horrid breaches of his law! Weep no more, perfidious apostle! thou hast "cast the net on the right side of the ship"; thy three *curses* have procured God multitudes of *blessings!* Surely, sir, you cannot mean this! "Many a poor soul has blessed God" for *granting a pardon to Peter,* but never *for Peter's denial.* It is extremely dangerous thus to confound *a crime* with *the pardon* granted to a penitent criminal.

(R) *Upon the same principle you add, "How have
many others been raised out of the mire, by considering
the tenderness shown to the incestuous Corinthian!"* I
am glad you do not say, "by considering *the incest* of
the Corinthian." The good received by many did not
then spring from this horrid crime, but from the tenderness of the apostle. This instance, therefore, by your
own confession, does not prove that sin does any good
to believers.

But as you tell us with what "tenderness" the apostle
restored that man, when he was swallowed up in godly
sorrow, you will permit me to remind you of the severity
which he showed him while he continued impenitent.
"In the name of our Lord Jesus Christ," said he, "when
ye are gathered together, deliver such a one unto Satan
for the destruction of the flesh, that his spirit may be
saved in the day of the Lord." Hence it appears, the
apostle thought his case so desperate, that his body must
be solemnly delivered to Satan, in order, if possible, to
bring his soul to repentance. Now, if the incestuous
man's sins "had been for ever and for ever cancelled";
if he had not forfeited the Divine favour, and cut himself off from "the general assembly of the first born" by
his crime; what power could the apostle, who acted under
the influence of the Spirit, have had to cut him off from
the visible Church as a corrupt member? What right to
deliver the body of one of "God's pleasant children" to
destruction? Was this "finished salvation"? For my part,
as I do not believe in a *two-fold*, I had almost said *Jesu-
itical*, will in God, I am persuaded he would have us
consider things as they are; an impenitent adulterer as a
profligate heathen; and a penitent believer as his "pleasant child."

XIX. *You add*, (1) *A "grievous fall serves to make
believers know their place."* No, indeed, it serves only to
make them *forget* their place; witness David, who, far

from knowing his place, wickedly took that of Uriah; and Eve, who, by falling into the condemnation of the devil, took her Maker's place, in her imagination, and esteemed herself as wise as God. (2) "It drives them nearer to Christ." Surely, you mistake, sir; you mean nearer the devil: for a fall into pride may drive me nearer Lucifer, a fall into adultery and murder may drive me nearer Belial and Moloch; but not nearer Jesus Christ. (3) "It makes them more dependent on his strength." No such thing. The genuine effect of a fall into sin, is to stupefy the conscience and harden the heart: witness the state of obduracy in which God found Adam, and the state of carnal security in which Nathan found David, after their crimes. (4) "It keeps them more watchful for the future." Just the reverse: it prevents their watching for the future. If David had been made more watchful by falling into adultery, would he have fallen into treachery and murder? If Peter had been made more watchful by his *first* falling into perjury, would he have fallen *three times* successively? (5) "It will cause them to sympathize with others in the like situation." By no means. A fall into sin will naturally make us desirous of drawing another into our guilty condition. Witness the devil and Eve, Eve and Adam, David and Bathsheba. The royal adulterer was so far from sympathizing with the man who had unkindly taken his neighbor's favorite ewe lamb, that he directly swore, "As the Lord liveth, the man that has done this thing shall surely die."

(6) "It will make them sing louder to the praise of restoring grace throughout all the ages of eternity." I demand proof of this. I greatly question whether Demas, Alexander the coppersmith, Hymeneus, Philetus, and many of the fallen believers mentioned in the Epistles of our Lord to the Churches of Asia, in the Epistle to the Hebrews, and in those of St. Peter, St. James, and St.

Jude, shall sing restoring grace at all. The apostle, far
from representing them all as singing louder, gives us to
understand, that many of them shall be "thought worthy
of a much sorer punishment" than the sinners consumed
by fire from heaven; and that "there remaineth therefore no more sacrifice for their sins"; (a sure proof that
Christ's sacrifice availed for them, till they "accounted
the blood of the covenant an unholy thing";) for, adds
the apostle, "The Lord will judge his people"; and, notwithstanding all that Dr. Crisp says to the contrary,
"there remaineth [for apostates] a certain fearful looking for of judgment, and fiery indignation, which shall
devour the adversaries. Weeping, wailing, and gnashing
of teeth," and not "louder songs," await "the unprofitable servant."

But supposing some are "renewed to repentance, and
escape out of the snare of the devil"; can you imagine
they will be upon the footing of those who, standing
"steadfast and immovable, always abounded in the work
of the Lord?" Shall then "the labour of these be in vain
in the Lord?" Are not our works to follow us? Shall
the unprofitable servant, if restored, receive a crown of
glory equal to his, who, from the time he listed, has always "fought the good fight, and kept the faith"? The
doctrine you would inculcate, at once bears hard upon
the equity of the Divine conduct, and strikes a fatal blow
at the root of all diligence and faithfulness, so strongly
recommended in the oracles of God.

You will be sensible of your error, if you observe, that
all the fine things which you tell us of a fall into sin, belong not to *the fall,* but to *a happy recovery from it:*
and my honoured correspondent is as much mistaken,
when he ascribes to *sin* the effects of *repentance and
faith,* as if he ascribed to a frost the effects of a thaw, or
to sickness the consequence of a recovery.

And now that we have seen how you have done a *pious* man's strange work, permit me, sir, to tell you, that, through the prevalence of human corruption, a word spoken *for* sin generally goes farther than ten thousand spoken *against* it. This I know; that if a fall, in an hour of temptation, appears only half so profitable as you represent it, thousands will venture after David into the whirlpool of wickedness. But alas! *facilis descensus Averni,* etc.: it is easier to follow him when he plunges in, than when he struggles out, with his eyes wasted, his flesh dried up, and his bones broken.

(S) *I gladly do you the justice, honoured sir, to observe, that you exclaim against sin in the next page; but does not the antidote come too late?* You say, "Whatever may be God's secret will, we are to keep close to the declaration of his own written word, which binds us to resist sin." But, alas, you make a bad matter worse, by representing God as having two wills, a secret, effectual will that we should sin, and a revealed will, or written word, commanding us to resist sin! If these insinuations are just, I ask, Why should we not regard God's *secret,* as much as his *revealed* will? Nay, why should we not regard it more, since it is the more efficacious, and consequently the stronger will?

You add, "He would be mad who should wilfully fall down, and break a leg or an arm, because he knew there was a skilful surgeon at hand to set it." But I beg leave to dissent from my honoured opponent. For, supposing I had a crooked leg, appointed to be broken for good, by God's secret will intimated to me; and supposing a dear friend strongly argued, not only that the surgeon is at hand, but that he would render my leg straighter, handsomer, and stronger than before; must I not be a fool, or a coward, if I hesitate throwing myself down?

O sir, if "the deceitfulness of sin" is so great that thousands greedily commit it, when the gallows on earth, and horrible torments in hell, are proposed for their just wages; how will they be able to escape in the hour of temptation, if they are encouraged to transgress the Divine law, by assurances that they shall reap eternal advantages from their sin? O how highly necessary was it that Mr. Wesley should warn his assistants against talking of a state of justification and sanctification in so unguarded a manner as you and the other admirers of Dr. Crisp so frequently do!

You conclude this letter by some quotations from Mr. Wesley, whom you vainly try to press into the doctor's service, by representing him as saying of established Christians what he speaks of babes in Christ, and of the commission of adultery and murder, what he only means of evil desire resisted, and evil tempers restrained: but more of this in a "Treatise on Christian Perfection."

Your most obedient and obliged servant in the bonds of a peaceful gospel, J. FLETCHER.

TO ALL CANDID CALVINISTS
CHURCH OF ENGLAND

HONOURED AND DEAR BRETHREN—A student from Geneva, who has had the honour of being admitted a minister of your Church, takes the liberty of dedicating to you these strictures on GENEVA LOGIC, which were written both for the better information of your candid judgment, and to obtain tolerable terms of peace from his worthy opponents.

Some, who mistake blunt truth for sneering insolence, and mild ironies for bitter sarcasms, will probably dissuade you from looking into this FOURTH CHECK TO ANTINOMIANISM. They will tell you that *"Logica Genevensis* is a very bad book," full of "calumny, forgeries, vile slanders, accrimonious sneers, and horrid misrepresentations." But candour, which condemns no one before he is heard, which weighs both sides of the question in an impartial balance, will soon convince you, that, if every irony proceeds from spleen and acrimony of spirit, there is as much of both in these four words of my honoured opponent, *Pietas Oxoniensis* and *Goliath Slain,* as in all the four Checks; and that I have not exceeded the apostolic direction of my motto, "Rebuke them sharply," or rather, αποτομως, *cuttingly,* but "let brotherly love continue."

I do not deny, that some points of doctrine, which many hold in great veneration, excite pity or laughter in my Checks. But how can I help it? If a painter, who knows not how to flatter, draws to the life an object excessively ridiculous in itself, must it not appear excessively ridiculous in his picture? Is it right to exclaim against his pencil as *malicious,* and his colours as *unfair,* because he impartially uses them according to the rules of his art? And can any unprejudiced person expect that he should draw the picture of the night without using any black shades at all?

If the charge of "bitterness" do not entirely set you against this book, they will try to frighten you from reading it, by protesting that I throw down the foundation of Christianity, and help Mr. Wesley to place works and merit on the Redeemer's throne. To this dreadful charge I answer, (1) That I had rather my right hand should lose its cunning to all eternity, than use it a moment to detract from the Saviour's real glory, to whom I am more indebted than any other man in the world. (2) That the strongest pleas I produce for holiness and good works, are quotations from the homilies of our own Church, as well as from the Puritan divines, whom I cite preferably to others, because they held what you are taught to call *the doctrines of grace.* (3) That what I have said of those doctrines recommends itself to every unprejudiced person's reason and conscience. (4) That my capital arguments in favour of practical Christianity are founded upon our second justification by the evidence of works in the great day; a doctrine which my opponent himself cannot help assenting to. (5) That from first to last, when the *meritorious cause* of our justification is considered, we set works aside; praying God 'not to enter into judgment with us," or "weigh our merits, but to pardon our offences" for Christ's sake; and gladly ascribing the whole of our salvation to his alone merits, as much as Calvin or Dr. Crisp does. (6) That when the word *meriting, deserving,* or *worthy,* which our Lord himself uses again and again, is applied to good works, or good men, we mean absolutely nothing but *rewardable,* or qualified for the reception of a gracious reward. And, (7) That even this *improper* merit or rewardableness of good works is entirely derived from Christ's *proper* merit, who works what is good in us, and from the gracious promise of God, who has freely engaged himself to recompense the fruits of righteousness, which his own grace enables them to produce.

I hope, honoured brethren, these hints will so far break the waves of prejudice which beat against your candour, as to prevail upon you not to reject this little means of information. If you condescend to peruse it, I trust it will minister to your edification, by enlarging your views of Christ's prophetic and kingly office; by heightening your ideas of that practical religion which the Scriptures perpetually enforce; by lessening your regard for some well-meant mistakes, on which good men have too hastily put the stamp of orthodoxy; and by giving you a more favourable opinion of the sentiments of your remonstrant brethren, who would rejoice to live at peace with you in the kingdom of grace, and walk in love with you to the kingdom of glory. But whether you consent to give them the right hand of fellowship or not, nobody, I think, can be more glad to offer it to you, than he who, with undissembled respect, remains, honoured and dear brethren, your affectionate brother, and obedient servant in Christ,

J. FLETCHER.

A FOURTH CHECK TO ANTINOMIANISM

A LETTER

To Richard Hill, Esq.

HON. AND DEAR SIR: My entering the field of controversy to defend St. James' "pure religion," procured me your Five Letters, which I compare to a shower of rain, gently descending from the placid heaven. But the six which have followed resemble a storm of hail, pouring down from the lowering sky, ushered by some harmless flashes of lightning, and accompanied by the rumbling of distant thunder. If my comparison is just, it is no wonder that when I read them first I was almost thunderstruck, and began to fear, lest, instead of adding light, I had only added heat, to the hasty zeal which I endeavoured to check.

But at the second perusal, my drooping hopes revive: the disburdened clouds begin to break: the air, discharged of the exhalations which rendered it sultry or hazy, seems clearer or cooler than before; and the smiling plains of evangelical truth, viewed through that defecated medium, appear more gay after the unexpected storm. Methinks even *moderation,* the phœnix consumed by our polemic fires, is going to rise out of its ashes: and that, notwithstanding the din of a controversial war, "the voice of the turtle is *still* heard in our land."

May the gentle sound approach nearer and nearer, and tune our listening hearts to the melodious accents of Divine and brotherly love! And thou Prince of Peace, thou true Solomon, thou pacific Son of warlike David, should an evil spirit come upon me as it did upon Saul, to make me dip my pen in the envenomed gall of discord, or turn it into a javelin to strike my dear opponent through and through; mercifully bow the heavens, gently touch the strings of my heart, and play upon them the melting tune of forgiving love! Teach me to check the rapid growth of Antinomian errors, without hindering the slow progress of thy precious truth; and graciously instruct me how to defend an insulted, venerable father, without hurting an honoured, though, alas! prepossessed brother. If the latter has offended, suffer me not to fall upon him with the whip of merciless revenge; and if I must use the rod of reproof, teach me to weigh every stroke in the balance of the sanctuary with tender fear, and yet with honest impartiality.

Should I, in this encounter gracious Lord, overcome by *thy wisdom* my worthy antagonist, help me by *thy* meekness to give him an example of Christian moderation; and while I tie him with the cords of a man and a believer, while I bind him with reason and Scripture to the left wheel of thy Gospel chariot, which, alas! he mistakes for a wheel of antichrist's carriage; let me rejoice to be tied by him with the same easy bonds to the *right* wheel, which he, without reason, fears I am determined to stop. And when we are thus mutually bound to thy triumphant car, draw us with double swiftness to the happy regions where the good, as well as "the wicked, cease from troubling," and those who are "weary *of contention* are at rest." So shall we leave for ever behind the deep and noisy "waters of strife," in which so many bigots miserably perish; and the barren mountains of Gilboa, where harried Saul falls upon the point of his own controversial sword, and lovely Jonathan himself receives a mortal wound.

You remember, honoured sir, that I opened the Second Check to Antinomianism by demonstrating that in the day of judgment we shall be justified by works, that is, by the evidence of works. A person of your penetration could not but see, that if this legal proposition stood, your favourite doctrine of finished salvation, and *Calvinian* imputation of righteousness to an impenitent adulterer, would lose their exorbitant influence.

Our first and second justification differ, (1) With respect to *time:* the time of the one is the hour of conversion; and the time of the other the day of judgment. (2) With respect to *place:* the place of the former is this earth; and the place of the latter the awful spot, in the new heaven or on the new earth, where the tribunal of Christ shall be erected. (3) with respect to the *witnesses:* the witnesses of the former are the Spirit of God and our own conscience; or, to speak in Scripture language, "The Spirit bearing witness with our spirits that we are the children of God": but the witnesses of the latter will be the countless myriads of men and angels assembled before Christ. (4) With respect to the *Justifier:* in the former justification "one God justifies the circumcision and the uncircumcision"; and in the latter, "one Mediator between God and man, even the man Christ Jesus," will pronounce the sentence: for, "the Father judgeth no man, but hath committed all judgment to the Son." (5) With respect to the *justified:* in the day of conversion, *a penitent sinner* is justified; in the day of judgment, *a persevering saint.* (6) With respect to *the article upon which justification will turn:* although the meritorious cause of both our justifications is the same, that is, the blood and righteousness of Christ, yet the instrumental cause is very different; by FAITH we obtain (not purchase) the first, and by WORKS the second. (7) With respect *to the act of the Justifier:* at our conversion God covers and pardons our sins; but in the day of judgment Christ uncovers and approves our righteousness. And, (lastly,) with regard to *the consequences of both:* at the first justification we are enlisted by the Friend of sinners to "fight the good fight of faith" in the Church militant; and at the second we are admitted by the righteous

Judge to "receive a crown of righteousness, and shine like the sun" in the Church triumphant.

Is it not strange that the enchanting power of Calvinian logic should have detained us so long in Babel, where things so vastly different are perpetually confounded? Is it not deplorable that when Mr. Wesley has the courage to call us out of mystic Geneva, so many tongues and pens should be sharpened against him? Shall foreign logic for ever prevail over English good sense, and Christian brotherly kindness? Have we so "leaned toward Calvinism" as to be totally past recovery? And is the balance between St. Paul's and St. James' justification lost among pious Protestants for ever? O ye regenerate Britons, who have unhappily fallen in love with the Genevan Delilah, "awake! awake! put on strength," and leap out of the arms of that enchantress! If she rocks you asleep in her bosom, it is only to bind you fast with cords of Antinomian errors, and deliver you up to the horrors of Antinomian practices. Has she not already cut off the locks, and put out the eyes of thousands? And does not Samson publicly grind for the Philistine? Have we not seen Mr. Hill himself tell the world that 'all sins work for good to the pleasant children," who go on frowardly from adultery to treachery, and from treachery to murder?

J. FLETCHER.

A LETTER

To Richard Hill, Esq.

HONOURED AND DEAR SIR: An assertion of yours seems to me of greater moment than the quotation from Bishop Cowper, which I answered in my last. You maintain, (p. 11,) "that the doctrine of a two-fold justification is not to be found in any part of the liturgy of our Church."

I. Not to mention again the latter part of St. Athana-

sius' Creed; *permit me, sir, to ask you, if on the thirteenth and fourteenth Sundays after Trinity you never
considered what is implied in these and the like petitions?*
"Grant that we may so *faithfully* serve thee in this life,
that we *fail not finally* to attain thy heavenly promises,
through the merits of Jesus Christ. Make us to *love*
that which thou dost *command,* that we may *obtain* that
which thou dost *promise.*" Again: on St. Peter's day,
"Make all pastors *diligently* to preach thy holy word,
and the people *obediently* to follow the same, *that they
may receive the crown* of everlasting glory, through
Jesus Christ." And on the third Sunday in Advent:
"Grant that thy ministers may so prepare thy way, by
turning the hearts of *the disobedient,* that at *thy second
coming to judge the world,* we may be found *an acceptable people* in thy sight."

St. James' justification by works, consequent upon
justification by faith, is described in the service for Ash
Wednesday: "*If* from henceforth we walk in his ways:
if we follow him in lowliness, patience, and charity, and
be ordered by the governance of his Holy Spirit, seeking
always his glory, and serving him duly with thanks-
giving":—Then comes the description of our final justification, which is but a solemn and public confirmation
of St. James' justification by works.—"This *if we do,*
Christ will deliver us from the curse of the law, and from
the extreme malediction which shall light upon them that
shall be set on the left hand; and he will set us on his
right hand, and give us the gracious benediction of his
Father, commanding us to take possession of his glorious
kingdom."—*Commination.*

II. *As final justification by the evidence of works is
clearly asserted in our liturgy, so it is indirectly maintained in our articles.* You know, honoured sir, that the
eleventh treats of *justification by faith* at our conversion,
and you yourself very justly observe, (p. 11,) "That

our reformers seem to have had an eye to the words of our Lord, 'The tree is known, [that is, is evidenced,] by its fruits,' when they drew up our twelfth article, which asserts, that a lively faith may be as evidently known by good works as a tree discerned by its fruit." This, honoured sir, is the very basis of Mr. Wesley's "rotten" doctrine; the very foundation on which St. James builds "his pure and undefiled religion." This being granted, it necessarily follows, to the overthrow of your favourite scheme, that a living, justifying faith may degenerate into a dead, condemning faith, as surely as David's faith, once productive of the fruits of righteousness, degenerated into a faith productive of adultery and murder.

You are aware of the advantage that the twelfth article gives us over you; therefore, to obviate it, you insinuate, in your Five Letters, that David's faith, when he committed adultery, was the same as when he danced before the ark. It was justifying faith still, only "in a winter season." This argument, which will pass for a demonstration in Geneva, will appear an evasion in England, if our readers consider that it is founded merely upon the Calvinian custom of forcing rational comparisons to go *upon all four* like brutes, and then driving far beyond the intention of those by whom they were first produced. We know that a tree on the banks of the Severn may be good in winter though it bear no good fruit; because no trees bear among us any fruit, good or bad, in January. But this cannot be the case either of believers or unbelievers—they bear fruit all the year round—unless you can prove that like men in an apoplectic fit they neither think, speak, nor act "in a winter season." Again:

Believers who commit adultery and murder are not good trees, even in a negative sense, for they *positively* bear fruit of the most poisonous nature. How then can either their faith or their persons be evidenced a *good* tree, by such bad fruit, such *detestable evidence?* While you put your logic to the rack for an answer, I shall take the liberty to encounter you a moment with your own weapons, and making the degraded comparison of our twelfth article walk upon all four against you, I promise you, that if you can show me an apple tree which bears poisonous crabs in summer, much more one that bears them "in a winter season," I will turn Antinomian, and believe that an impenitent murderer has justifying faith, and is complete in Christ's righteousness.   J. FLETCHER.

A LETTER

To Richard Hill, Esq.

HON. AND DEAR SIR: While my engine, common sense, stands yet firm upon the point of our *justification by the evidence of works,* which you have so fully granted me, permit me to level it a moment at the basis of the main pillars which support Antinomianism and Calvinism.

1. If righteous Lot had died when he repeated the crimes of drunkenness and incest, his justification would have been turned into condemnation, according to St. Paul's plain rule, *If thou be a breaker of the law, thy circumcision is made uncircumcision:* for neither the holy God, nor any virtuous man, can possibly justify a sinner upon the evidence of drunkenness and incest.

2. If old Solomon, doating upon heathenish young women, and led away by them into abominable idolatries, had died before he was brought again to repentance, he could never have seen the kingdom of God. He should have perished in his sin, unless Geneva logic can make it appear, in direct opposition to the word of God, that the *impenitent* shall not perish, and that *idolaters* shall inherit the kingdom of God, Luke 13:3; I Cor. 6:9.

3. If the incestuous Corinthian had been cut off while he defiled his father's bed, the justification granted him at his first conversion, far from saving him in the

day of judgment, would have aggravated his condemnation, and caused him to be *counted worthy of a much severer punishment* than if he never had *known the way of righteousness*—never been justified; unless you can prove that Christ would have acquitted him upon the horrid evidence of apostasy and incest, which appears to me as difficult a task as to prove that Christ and Belial are one and the same filthy god.

4. If David and Bathsheba had been run through by Uriah, as Zimri and Cosbi were by Phinehas; and if they had died in their flagrant wickedness, no previous justification, no Calvinian imputation of righteousness, would have secured their justification in the last day. For, upon the evidence of adultery and premeditated murder, they would infallibly have been condemned; according to those awful words of our Lord, *I come quickly to give* EVERY MAN, [here is no exception for the "pleasant children,"] *according as* HIS *work shall be*, not according as my work has been. *Blessed are they that do his commandments, that they may enter in through the gates into the city; for without are dogs,* WHOREMONGERS, *and* MURDERERS, Rev. 22:12, etc.

Should you say, honoured sir, It is provided in the decree of absolute election that adulterers, who once walked with God, shall not die till they have repented:

1. I demand proof that there ever was such a decree. In the second Psalm, indeed, I read about God's decree respecting Christ and mankind; but it is the very reverse of Calvin's decree, for it implies general redemption and conditional election. *I will declare the decree. Thou art my son. I will give thee the* HEATHEN *for thine inheritance, and the* UTTERMOST *parts of the earth for thy possession. Kiss the son, lest he be angry, and ye perish from the way.*

2. This evasion is founded upon a most absurd supposition, which sews pillows to the arms of backsliders

and apostates, by promising them immortality if they persevere in sin. But setting aside the absurdity of supposing that old Solomon, for example, might have kept himself alive till now by assiduously worshipping Ashtaroth; or, which is the same, that he might have put to death by putting off repentance, because he could not die till he had repented: I ask, Where is this strange Gospel written? Certainly not in the Old Testament; for God asks there with indignation, "When the righteous turneth away from his righteousness, and committeth iniquity, SHALL HE LIVE?" No: "in his sin that he has sinned SHALL HE DIE," Ezek. 18:24. Much less in the New, where Christ protests, that he will *spue lukewarm believers out of his mouth,* and that *every branch in him which bears not fruit, shall be taken away* or *cut off.* An awful threatening this, which was executed even upon one of the twelve apostles! For our Lord himself says, *Those that thou* GAVEST *me I have kept, and none of* THEM *is lost but Judas,* who fell finally, since he died in the very act of self murder, and is particularly called *the son of perdition.*

But granting you, that lest Lot, David, and Solomon should be condemned by works in the day of judgment, they were to be immortal till they repented and did their first works; this very supposition indicates, that till they repented they were *sons of perdition, according to that* solemn declaration of truth manifest in the flesh, *Except ye repent, ye shall all perish.*

As if you were aware of this difficulty, (p. 149,) you have recourse to a noted distinction in Geneva logic, by which you hope to secure your favourite doctrine, as well as fond Rachel once secured her favourite teraphim. You say, "that though a sinner [David, for instance, or Solomon] be justified *in the sight of God* by Christ alone, he is declaratively justified by works both here and at the day of judgment."

Now, honoured sir, this necessarily implies, that though David in Uriah's bed, and Solomon at the shrine of Ashtaroth, are justified in the sight of God by Christ's chastity and piety imputed to them; yet, before men, and before the Judge of quick and dead, they are justified by the evidence of their own chastity and piety. This distinction, one of the main supports of Calvinism, is big with absurdities; for if it be just, it follows,

1. That while God says of Solomon, worshipping the goddess of the Zidonians, he is still a true believer, "he is justified from all things"; Christ says, *By his fruit ye shall know him;* he is an impenitent, unjustified idolater; and St. James, siding with his Master, says roundly, that Solomon's *faith* being now *without works is a dead,* unjustifying faith; by which, as well as by his bad works, he is condemned already. Now, sir, it remains that you should give up Antinomian Calvinism, or tell us who is grossly mistaken, God or Christ. For, upon your scheme, God says of an impenitent idolater, who once believed in him, "He is fully justified by the perfect law of liberty." And Christ says, "He is fully condemned by the same law!" And reason dictates, that both parts of a full contradiction cannot be true.

Do not say, honoured sir, that, upon the Calvinian plan, the Father and the Son never contradict one another in the matter of a sinner's justification; for if the Father justifies by the imputation of an external righteousness, which constitutes a sinner righteous while he commits all sorts of crimes; and if the Son, on the other hand, condemns a sinner for his *words,* much more for the commission of adultery, idolatry, and murder; their sentence must be as frequently different as a believer acts or speaks, contrary to the law of liberty. For Christ being *the same yesterday, today, and for ever,* cannot justify: he must condemn now, as well as in the day of judgment, every man who now acts or speaks wickedly.

Should you attempt to account for the Father's imaginary justification of an impenitent idolater, by bringing in Calvin's decrees, and saying that God reckoned Solomon a converted man at the shrine of Ashtaroth, because he had absolutely decreed to give him restoring grace; I reply, supposing such decrees are not imaginary, is it not absurd to say, God reckons that cold is heat, and confounds January with July, because he has decreed that summer shall follow winter? Therefore, which way soever you turn, absurdities or impieties stare you in the face.

2. The unreasonableness of Calvinism will appear to you more glaringly still, if you suppose for a moment that David died in Uriah's bed. For then, according to Dr. Crisp's justification by the imputation of Christ's chastity, he must have gone straight to heaven; and, according to our Lord's condemnation, by the evidence of personal adultery, he must have gone straight to hell. Thus, by the help of Geneva logic, so sure as the royal adulterer might have died before Nathan stirred him up to repentance, I can demonstrate, that David might have been saved and damned, in heaven and in hell, at the same time!

3. Your distinction insinuates, that there will be two days of judgment; one to try us secretly *before God,* by imputed sin and imputed righteousness; and the other to try us publicly *before men and angels,* by personal sin and personal righteousness. A new doctrine this, which every Christian is bound to reject, not only because the Scripture is silent about it, but because it fixes a shocking duplicity of conduct upon God; for it represents him, first, as absolutely saving or damning the children of men, according to his own capricious imputation of Christ's righteousness, or of Adam's sin; and then as being desirous to make a show of justice before men and angels, by pretending to justify or condemn people "ac-

cording to their works," when in fact he has already justified or condemned them without the least respect to their works; for, say Bishop Cowper and Mr. Hill, "In the act of justification, good works have no place"; and, indeed, how should they, if free grace and free wrath have unalterably cast the lot of all, before the foundation of the world?—or, in other terms, if finished salvation and finished damnation have the stamp of God, as well as that of Calvin?

4. According to your imaginary distinction, Christ, as King of Saints, frequently condemns for inherent wickedness, those whom he justifies, as a Priest, by imputed righteousness; and so, to the disgrace of his wisdom, he publicly recants, as a Judge, the sentence of complete justification, which he privately passes as a God. Permit me, honoured sir, to enforce this observation by the example of Judas, or any other apostate. I hope nobody will charge me with blasphemy, for saying that our Lord called Judas with the same sincerity with which he called his other disciples. Heaven forbid that any Christian should suppose the Lamb of God called Iscariot to get him into the pit of perdition, as the fowler does an unhappy bird which he wants to get into a decoy. Judas readily answered the call, and undoubtedly believed in Christ as well as the rest of the apostles; for St. John says, 'This beginning of miracles did Jesus in Cana of Galilee, and manifested forth his glory, and his disciples [of whom Judas was one] believed in him." His faith was true so far as it went; for he was one of "the little flock to whom it was God's good pleasure to give the kingdom," Luke 12:32. Our Lord pronounced him "blessed," with the rest of his disciples, Matt. 13:16, and conditionally promised him one of the twelve apostolic crowns in his glory, Matt. 19:28.

If you say, that "he was always a traitor and a hypocrite," you run into endless difficulties; for, (1) You make

Christ countenance, by his example, all bishops, who knowingly ordain wicked men—all patrons, who give them livings—and all kings, who prefer ungodly men to high dignities in the Church. (2) You suppose that Christ, who would not receive an occasional testimony from an evil spirit, not only sent a devil to preach and baptize in his name, but at his return encouraged him in his horid dissimulation, by bidding him "rejoice that his name was written in heaven." (3) You believe, "that the faithful and true Witness," in whose mouth no guile was ever found, gave this absurd, hypocritical charge to a goat, an arch hypocrite, a devil: "Behold, I send you forth as sheep in the midst of wolves; but fear not, the hairs of your head are all numbered. A sparrow shall not fall to the ground without your Father, and ye are of more value than many sparrows. Do not premeditate, it shall be given you what you shall speak: for it is not you that speak, but the Spirit of your Father which speaketh in you."

When our Lord spoke thus to Judas, he was a sheep, i.e. "he heard Christ's voice, and followed him." But, alas! he was afterward taken by the bright shining of silver and gold, as David was by the striking beauty of Uriah's wife. And when he had admitted the base temptation, our Lord, with the honesty of a Master, and tenderness of a Saviour, said, "Have not I chosen you twelve, and one of you is a devil?" He has let the tempter into his heart. This severe, though indirect reproof, reclaimed Judas for a time; as a similar rebuke checked Peter on another occasion. Nor was it, probably, till near the end of our Lord's ministry that he began to be 'unfaithful in the mammon of unrighteousness": and even then Christ kindly warned, without exposing him.

Some, indeed, think that our Lord was partial to Peter; but I do not see it: for with equal love and faithfulness he warned all his disciples of their approaching fall, and mentioned the peculiar circumstances of Judas' and Peter's apostasy. "Aye, but he prayed for Peter that his faith might not fail." And is this a proof that he never prayed for Judas? That he always excepted him, when he prayed for his disciples, and that he would have excepted him, if he had been alive when he interceded for all his murderers? "However, he looked at Peter, to cover him with a penitential shame." Nay he did more than this for Judas; for he pointed at him, first indirectly, and then directly, to bring him to a sense of his crime. But, supposing our Lord had not at all endeavoured to stop him in his dreadful career, would this have been a proof of his reprobating partiality? Is it not said, that "the Lord weigheth the spirits?" As such, did he not see that Judas offended of malicious wickedness and calm deliberation; and that Peter would offend merely through fear and surprise? Supposing, therefore, he had made a difference between them, would it be right to account for it by Calvinian election and reprobation, when the difference might so naturally be accounted for from the different state of their hearts, and nature of their falls? Was it not highly agreeable to the notions we have of justice, and the declarations we read in the Scripture, that our Lord should reprobate, or give up Judas, when he saw him immovably fixed in his apostasy, and found that the last hour of his day of grace was now expired?

From all these circumstances, I hope I may conclude, that Judas was not always a hypocrite; that he may be properly ranked among apostates, that is, among those who truly fall from God, and therefore were once truly in him; and that our Lord spoke no untruth, when he called the Spirit of God the Spirit of Judas' Father, without making any difference between him and the other disciples.

If you ask, How he fell? I reply, That overlooking an important part of our Lord's pastoral charge to him, "He

that endureth unto the end the same shall be saved,"
he dallied with worldly temptations till the evil spirit,
which was gone out of him, entered in again, with seven
other spirits more wicked than himself, and took possession of his heart, which was once swept from reigning
sin, and garnished with the graces which adorn the Christian in his infant state. Thus, like Hymeneus, Philetus,
Demas, and other apostates, "by putting away a good
conscience, concerning faith he made shipwreck," and
evidenced the truth of God's declaration: "When the
righteous turneth away from his righteousness, all his
righteousness that he hath done shall not be mentioned:
in his sin that he hath sinned he shall die."

"Nay, Judas kept his Master's money, and was a thief;
therefore he was always a hypocrite, an absolute reprobate."

To show the weakness of this objection, I need only
retort it thus: David set his heart upon his neighbour's
wife, as Judas did upon his Master's money, and like
him betrayed innocent blood; therefore he was always
a hypocrite, an absolute reprobate. If the inference is
just in one case, it is undoubtedly so in the other.

"But David repented, and did his first works."

I thank my objector for this important concession.
Did Judas perish? It was then because he did not do his
first works, though he repented. And is David saved?
It is because he not only repented, but did also his first
works; or, to use your own expressions, because he recovered "justifying faith, which cannot be without good
works." Thus, when he had recovered justifying faith
before God, he could again be justified by the evidence of
works, both before his fellow mortals, and that God who
"judges the world in righteousness," and who sentences
every man according to *his own* works, and not merely
according to works done by *another* near 6000 or 1800
years before they were born. Thus the royal adulterer,

who died a justified, chaste penitent, can, through the merits of Christ, stand before the throne in a better and more substantial righteousness than the fantastic robe in which you imagine he was clothed, when his eyes were full of adultery, and his hands full of blood: an airy, loose, flimsy robe this, cut out at Geneva and Dort, not at Jerusalem or Antioch; a wretched contrivance, the chief use of which is to cover the iron-clay feet of the Calvinian Diana, and afford a safe asylum, a decent canopy to "the pleasant children," while they debauch their neighbours' wives, and hypocritically murder them out of the way.

O ye good men, how long will ye inadvertently represent our God, who is glorious in holiness, as the pander of vice? and Christ's immaculate righteousness as the unseemly cloak of such wickedness as is not so much as named among the Gentiles? "O that salvation, *from this evil*, were given unto Israel out of Sion!" O that the Lord would deliver his people from this preposterous error! O that the blast of Divine indignation, and the sighs of thousands of good men, lighting at once on the great image, might tear away the loose robe of righteousness which Calvin put upon her in a "winter season!" Then could all the world read the mark of the beast and the fiend, which she wears on her naked breast: "Free adultery, free murder, free incest, any length of sin for the pleasant children, the little flock of the elect: free wrath, free vengeance, free damnation for the immense herd of the reprobates!"

But to return to Judas, the first of all Christian apostates: waiving the consideration of his justification in his infancy, I observe, that as he had once true faith, he undoubtedly "believed to righteousness," and consequently "it was imputed to him for righteousness." Now, if this mean that God put upon him a loose robe of righteousness, which for ever screened him from condemnation, and under which he could conceal a bag of stolen money, as easily as you suppose David hid the ewe lamb which he conveyed away from Uriah's pasture, it follows, upon your scheme, that "justification being one single immutable act, in which works have no place," Judas is still completely justified before God by Calvinian imputation of righteousness; although Christians have hitherto believed works have so important a place in justification, that the apostate is no less condemned before God, than before men and angels, by his avarice and treason.

Let those who can split a hair as easily as an eagle can find her passage between east and west, take the chosen apostle, who did not make his election sure by the works of faith, and let them split him asunder: so shall happy Iscariot, the dear elected child of God, wrapped in imputed righteousness, and carried by everlasting love, infallibly go to heaven without works, in consequence of his Calvinian justification before God; while poor reprobated Judas, for accomplishing God's decree, shall infallibly go to his own place, in consequence of his condemnation by the evidence of wicked works.

Thus, honoured sir, by fixing my plain engine, common sense, upon the immovable point which you have granted me, i. e. St. James' justification by works, I hope I have not only removed the rock of offence from off Mr. Wesley's anti-Crispian propositions, but heaved also your great Diana, and her brother Apollo, (I mean unconditional election and absolute reprobation) from off the basis of orthodoxy, on which you suppose they stand firm as the pillars of heaven. May the God of pure, impartial love, whom they have so long indirectly traduced, as a God of blind dotage to hundreds, and implacable wrath to millions of his creatures, in the very same circumstances—the God whom those unscriptural doctrines have represented as fond Eli, and grim Apollyon; may he, I say, arise for his name's sake, and touch the Geneva colossus with his own omnipotent finger; so shall it in a moment fall from the amazing height of reverence to which Calvin, the Synod of Dort, and Elisha Coles have raised it; and its undeceived votaries shall perceive, they had no more reason to call Geneva impositions 'the doctrines of grace," than good Aaron and the mistaken Israelites to give the tremendous name of JEHOVAH to the ridiculous idol, which they had devoutly set up in the absence of legal Moses; so, giving glory to God, they shall confess that the robe of their image, with which some so officiously cover impenitent adulterers and murderers, is no more like the true wedding garment, than the imaginary appearances of armed men in the clouds are like the multitude of the heavenly host.

While you try to defend this robe, and I to tear it off the back of Antinomian Jezebel, let us not neglect "putting off the old man, putting on Christ Jesus, and walking in him" as St. Paul, or with him as Enoch, "arrayed in fine linen, clean and white, which is the righteousness *imparted* to the saints, when Christ is formed in their hearts by faith," and imputed to them so long as they walk, in their measure, "as he also walked." That, notwithstanding our warm controversy, we may "walk in love" with each other, and all the people of God, is the prayer of, honoured and dear sir, your obedient and devoted servant, in St. James' Gospel,   JOHN FLETCHER.

A LETTER

To Richard Hill, Esq.

HONOURED AND DEAR SIR: The fourth letter of your Review you produce as "a full and particular answer" to what I have advanced against Dr. Crisp's scheme of finished salvation, and finished damnation. But to my great surprise, you pass in profound silence over my strongest arguments. Had I been in your place, I would have paid some regard to my word, printed in capitals in my title page: I would have tried to prove, that, upon the doctor's scheme, St. Paul might, consistently with wisdom, exhort the Philippians "to work out their [finished] salvation with fear and trembling." And if I could not have made it appear, that our Lord has finished his work, as an interposing Mediator, a teaching Prophet, and a ruling King; I would either have given up the point, or endeavoured to show, that he has finished it at least as a Priest.

But even this you could not do without setting aside two important parts of his priestly office: for the same Jesus, who offered up himself as the true paschal Lamb, is now exalted at the right hand of God, to bless us as our Melchisedec, and "make intercession for us" as our Aaron, saying daily concerning a multitude of barren fig trees in his vineyard, "Let them alone this year also, till I shall dig about them; and if they bear fruit, well: and if not, then after that thou shalt cut them down." Now if he daily carries on his own personal work of salvation, not only as a Prophet and a King, but also as a Mediator and a Priest, common sense dictates, that "his personal work" is no more finished than our own; and that the doctrine of finished salvation is founded upon a heap of palpable mistakes, if by that expression you mean any thing more than a finished atonement.

But, overlooking these insurmountable difficulties, you open your "full and particular answer" by saying, pp. 62, 63, "Finished salvation is a grand fortress, against which all your artillery is played, and at which your heavy bombs of bitter sneer and cutting sarcasm are thrown. Yet this very expression, in its full extent, I undertake to vindicate, and in so doing shall fly to the sword of the Spirit; and the Lord enabling me to wield it aright, I doubt not I shall put to flight the armies of the aliens." Let us now see how you manage your sword, put us to flight, and establish finished salvation.

I. Page 63. *"When the Lord of glory gave up the ghost, he cried, 'It is finished.' And what was finished? Not merely his life, but 'the work which was given him to do.' And what was this work, but the salvation of his people? One would have imagined, that the Lord's own use of this expression might have silenced every cavil."*

The Lord's own use of this contested expression, "finished salvation!" Pray, dear sir, where does he use it? Certainly not in the two passages you quote, "I have finished the work thou gavest me to do," previously to my entering on my passion; and "It is finished"; that is, all the prophecies relative to what I was to do, teach, and suffer *before* my death, are accomplished. These scriptures do not in the least refer to the work of salvation on our part; nor do they even take in the most important branches of salvation's work on Christ's part. To assert it, is to take a bold stride into Socinianism, and maintain, it was not needful to our salvation that Christ should die, and rise again. For when he said, "I have finished the work thou gavest me to do," he was not yet entered upon his passion: nor had he died for our sins, much less was he yet risen for our justification, when he said upon the cross, "It is finished." To suppose, then, that salvation's work on Christ's part was finished, not only before his resurrection, but also before his death, is to set aside some of his most important works, in direct opposition to the Scriptures, which testify, that "he died, the just for the unjust"; and affirm, that "if he is not raised, our faith is vain, we are yet in our sins." Thus, sir, you have so unhappily begun to "wield your sword," as to cut down, at the first stroke, the two grand articles of the Christian faith—the death and resurrection of Jesus Christ.

II. Page 33. *To mend the matter, you have recourse to the mysterious doctrine of the decrees; and because "all events are present unto God, and were so from eternity to eternity," you affirm that "the glorification of the elect is as much finished as their predestination."* By the same rule of Geneva logic, I may say, that because God has decreed the world shall melt with fervent heat, the general conflagration is as much finished as the deluge. Were ever more strange assertions obtruded upon mankind?

If this illustration does not convince you of your mistake, I turn the tables, and make your blood run cold with the dreadful counterpart of your own proposition. The damnation of the non-elect "born or unborn," is as much finished as their predestination. And are these "the good tidings of great joy which shall be to all people?" and is this the comfortable Gospel of free grace, which we are "to preach to every creature?" Alas, my dear sir, you wield your sword so unskilfully, as absolutely to cut down all hopes and possibilities of mercy for millions of your fellow creatures; even for all the poor reprobates on the left side of the ship, who, "from eternity to eternity were irresistibly enclosed in the net of finished damnation!"

III. Page 63. *To support your unscriptural assertion, you produce Rom. 8:29, "Whom he did predestinate, them he called: and whom he called, them he also justified; and whom he justified, them he also glorified."* Indeed, sir, the apostle no more meant to insinuate by these words, that David was justified and glorified when he wallowed in the filth of adultery and murder, than that Judas was condemned and damned when he left all to follow Christ. He only lays before us an account of the method which God follows in the eternal salvation of obedient, persevering believers; who are the persons that, as such, he predestinated to life, "according to his foreknowledge, *and* the counsel of his *holy* will." These "he called," but not these alone. When they made their calling sure, by believing in the light of their dispensation, these "he also justified." And when they made their justification sure, by "adding to their faith virtue," etc., these "he also glorified"; for the souls of departed saints are actually glorified in Abraham's bosom; and living saints are not only called and justified, but also in part glorified; for, by "the Spirit of glory and of God, *which* rests upon them, *they are* changed into the Divine image from glory to glory"; yea, they are already "all glorious within."

How much more reasonable and scriptural is this sense of the apostle's words than that which you fix upon them, by which you would make us believe, that, on the one hand, Solomon's salvation including his justification and glorification) was finished, "in the full extent of the expression," when he worshipped the abomination of the Zidonians, and gloried in his shame: while, on the other hand, Demas' damnation was finished when he was St. Paul's zealous "companion in the kingdom and patience of Jesus Christ!" O sir, have you not here also inadvertently used the "sword of the Spirit," to oppose the "mind of the Spirit," and make way for barefaced Antinomianism? You proceed:

IV. Page 63. "*The same apostle, in his Epistle to the Ephesians, speaking to believers, addresses them as already (virtually) 'seated in heavenly places in Christ Jesus.'*" Hence you infer, that their salvation was finished, "in the full extent of the expression." But your conclusion is not just; for the apostle, instead of supposing their salvation finished, exhorts them "not to steal, not to be drunk with wine, and not to give place to the devil," by fornication, uncleanness, filthiness, or covetousness; "for this ye know," adds he, "that no unclean person, etc., hath any inheritance in the kingdom of

Christ"; so far is he from being "already virtually seated in heavenly places in Christ Jesus."

What need is there of "darkening counsel by a word without knowledge?" By the dark word "virtually?" While the Ephesians kept the faith, did they not 'set their affections on things above?" Were not their hearts in heaven with Christ agreeably to our Lord's doctrine, "Where your treasure is, there will your heart be also?" And by a lively faith, which is "the substance of things hoped for," did they not already share the glory of their exalted Head? Will you still endeavour to persuade the world, that when David defiled his neighbour's bed, he was "seated in heavenly places in Christ"? Is it not evident that these, and the like expressions of St. Paul, must not be understood of idle Antinomian speculations; but of such a real change as our Church mentions in her collect for Ascension day? "Grant, that as Christ ascended into the heavens, so we may also in heart and mind thither ascend, and continually dwell." Such powerful exertions of faith, hope, and love, as are described in the 77th hymn of the Rev. Mr. Madan's collection?

> By *faith* we are come
> To our permanent home;
> By *hope* we the rapture improve:
> By *love* we still rise,
> And look down on the skies—
> For the heaven of heaven is *love!*

But this is not all: if the elect, whether they be drunk or sober, chaste or unclean, "are already virtually seated in heavenly places in Christ," according to the doctrine of finished salvation; are not poor reprobates, whether they pray or curse, repent or sin, already virtually seated in hellish places in the devil, according to the doctrine of finished damnation? O sir, when you use the sword of the Spirit to storm the New Jerusalem, and cut the way through law and Gospel before an adulterer *in flagrante delicto,* that he may *virtually* [that is, I fear, *comfortably and securely*] "sit in heavenly places in Christ," do you not dreadfully prostitute God's holy word? Inadvertently fight the battle of the rankest Antinomians, and secure the foundation of Mr. Sandiman's, as well as Dr. Crisp's increasing errors? But you have an excuse ready:

V. *Page 63. "Christ has purchased the Spirit, to work mortification of sin, etc., in the hearts of his children: and in this respect their sanctification is really as much finished as their justification."* I reply, (1) If their justification by works is not finished before the day of judgment, as our Lord informs us, Matt. 12:37, your observation proves just nothing. (2) The Scriptures, in direct opposition to your scheme, declare, that the Spirit strives with, and consequently was purchased for all; those who "quench" it, and "sin against the Holy Ghost," not excepted. Therefore, neither the sanctification nor salvation of sinners is absolutely secured by the purchase you mention. If it were, all the world would be saved. But, alas! many "deny the Lord that bought them," and by "doing despite to the Spirit of grace" purchased for them, "bring upon themselves swift destruction," instead of finished salvation. Here, then, the sword which you wield flies again to pieces, by clashing with the real sword of the Spirit, brandished by St. Peter and St. Paul.

VI. Page 64. *You bring in "the immutability of God's counsel confirmed by an oath," and add, "The will and testament is signed, sealed, and properly attested. The whole affair is finished. There remains nothing to do but to take possession."* I thank you, dear sir, for this concession; something then "remains to do": we must, at least, "take possession"; and if we neglect doing it, farewell finished salvation. We shall as much fall short of the heavenly, as the Israelites, who perished in the wilderness, because they refused to take possession, fell short of the earthly Canaan.

Again: we grant that God's "will and testament is finished, and sealed by Christ's most precious blood": and that "the everlasting covenant is ordered in all things, and sure." But if part of that will and covenant runs thus: "Ye are saved by grace through faith. You are kept by the power of God through faith. If ye continue in the faith. Faith without works is dead. Wherefore work out your own salvation with fear and trembling. For him that sinneth I will blot out of my book. If ye walk contrary to me, I will walk contrary to you. I will cut my staff, beauty, asunder, that I may break my covenant which I have made with all the people, Zech. 11:10. And ye shall know my breach of promise, Num. 14:34. I will therefore put you in remembrance, though ye once knew this, how that the Lord, having saved the people out of the land of Egypt, afterward destroyed them that believed not; although through faith they kept the passover, and the sprinkling of blood, lest the destroyer should touch them. And did all drink the same spiritual drink, (for they drank of that spiritual rock that followed them; and that rock was Christ.) Now all these things happened to them for examples: and they are written for our admonition. Wherefore let him that thinketh he standeth take heed lest he fall." If part of God's will and covenant, I say, runs thus, is it not absurd to suppose, that any man's salvation is finished while he not only does not comply with the gracious terms of God's "sure covenant," but notoriously incurs the dreadful threatenings recorded in his unalterable "will and testament?" Here, then, instead of "turning to flight the armies of the aliens," you have given us weapons to beat you out of the field. But you soon come back again to say,

VII. Page 64. *"Certain it is, that the salvation of every soul given by the Father to the Son, in the eternal covenant of redemption, is as firmly secured as if those souls were already in glory."* The certainty which you speak of, exists only in your own imagination. Judas was given by the Father to the Son; and yet Judas is lost. If the salvation of some people "was as firmly secured from the beginning as if they had already been in glory," all the Gospel ministers who have addressed them at any time as children of wrath, have been preachers of lies, and the Holy Spirit witnesses to an untruth, when he testifies to the unregenerate elect that they are in danger of hell. But this is not all: upon your dangerous scheme, the foundations are thrown down; man is no more in a state of trial; the day of judgment will be a mere farce; and the Scriptures are a farrago of the most absurd cautions, and the most scandalous lies: for they perpetually speak to believers as to persons in danger of "falling," and "being cut off," if they do not "walk circumspectly"; and they assert that some "perish for whom Christ died"; and that others, by "denying the Lord who bought them, bring upon themselves swift destruction."

But pray, sir, when you tell us, "The salvation of every soul given by the Father to the Son, in the eternal covenant of redemption, is as firmly secured as if those souls were already in glory," do you not see the cloven foot on which your doctrine stalks along? Permit me to uncover it a moment, and strike my readers with salutary dread, by holding forth the inseparable counterpart of your dangerous opinion, "Certain it is, that the damnation of every soul given by the Father to the devil, in the eternal covenant of reprobation, is as firmly secured as if those souls were already in hell." Shame on the man that first called such horrid tenets "the doctrines of grace, and the free Gospel of Jesus Christ!" Confusion on the lying spirit, who broke out of the bottomless pit, thus to blaspheme the Father of mercies, delude good men, and sow the tares of Antinomianism! O, sir, when you plead for such doctrines, instead of wielding aright "the sword of the Spirit," do you not plunge it in muddy, Stygian waters, till it is covered with sordid rust, and reeks with poisonous error? But you pursue:

VIII. Page 64. *"To scruple the use of that expression, finished salvation, argues the greatest mistrust of the Mediator's power, and casts the highest reflection upon his infinite wisdom, by supposing that he did not count the cost before he began to build, and therefore that either his own personal work, or that which he does in his members, (for they are only parts of the same salvation,) is left unfinished."* If we do not admit your doctrine, honoured sir, it is not because we mistrust the Mediator's "power," and have low thoughts of his "wisdom"; but because we cannot believe that he will use his power in opposition to his wisdom and truth, in taking the elect by main force into heaven, as a strong man takes a sack of corn into his granary; much less can we think that he will use his omnipotence in opposition to his mercy and justice, by placing millions of his creatures in such forcible circumstances, as absolutely necessitate them to sin and be damned, according to the horrible doctrine of finished damnation.

Nor do we suppose that Christ unwisely forgot to "count the cost." No: from the beginning he knew that some would abuse their liberty, and bury their talent of good will, and gracious power to come unto him, "that they might have more abundant life." But far from being disappointed, as we are when things fall out contrary to our fond expectation, he declared beforehand, "I have laboured in vain, yet surely my work is with my God," Isa. 49: 4. As if he had said, "If I cannot rejoice over the obstinate neglecters of my great salvation; if my kindly dying for their sins, excepting that against the Holy

Ghost, and my sincerely calling upon them to 'turn and live,' prove useless to them, through their 'doing despite to the Spirit of grace,' and committing 'the sin unto death'; yet my work will not be lost with respect to my God. For my impartial, redeeming love will effectually 'stop every mouth,' and abundantly secure the honour of all the Divine perfections, which would be dreadfully sullied, if, by an absolute decree that all should necessarily fall in Adam, and that millions should never have it in their power to rise by me, I had set my seal to the horrible doctrine of finished salvation."

Here, then, in flourishing with your sword, you have "beaten the air," instead of "turning to flight the armies of"—those who are not clear in the doctrine of absolute predestination, whom you call—"aliens"; and in a quotation, p. 37, "absolutely place among the numerous hosts of the Diabolonians, who by the best of laws must die as election doubters."

IX. Page 64. *"If any thing be left unfinished, Christ would never have said, 'He that believeth hath everlasting life'; it is already begun in his soul."* Well, if it is but begun, it is not yet finished. But you add, "It is so certain in reversion, that nothing shall deprive him of it." True, "if he continues in the faith *and* abides in Christ, hearing his voice *and* following him"; for who "shall pluck you out of *the Redeemer's* hand?" "Who shall harm you, if ye be followers of that which is good?" But if the believer "make shipwreck of his faith," and "ends in the flesh," after having "begun in the Spirit," with all apostates he shall "of the flesh reap destruction." Again:

"Everlasting life," in the passage you quote, undoubtedly signifies a title to eternal bliss, as it appears from these words of our Lord "He that has left brethren, etc., for my sake, shall receive in the world to come eternal life." And from these words of St. Paul, "Ye have your fruit unto holiness, and the end everlasting life." Now if we give over following after holiness, and do not continue to leave all for Christ's sake, may we not forfeit our title to glory, as the servant who had ten thousand talents forgiven him, forfeited his pardon and the privilege annexed to it, by "taking his fellow servant by the throat," and arresting him for a "hundred pence?" But supposing the expression "everlasting life," means, as you intimate, "the life of God, already begun in the soul," agreeably to these scriptures: "The life that I live, I live by faith in the Son of God; for the just shall live by faith"; how can you infer that the life of faith is inamissible? If you can believe that every child quickened in the womb grows up to be a man, because he has human life in embryo, I will grant that no soul, quickened by the seed of grace, can miscarry, and that the seed of the word brings forth fruit to maturity in every sort of ground.

Should you reply, "That the life of faith, or spiritual life, cannot be lost, because it is of an eternal nature," I deny the consequence. Suppose I have lost an everlasting jewel, do I not quibble myself out of my invaluable property, if I say "I have not lost it, for it is everlasting?" Did not Satan and Adam lose their spiritual life? Do not all apostates lose it also? Is there a damned soul but what has lost it twice? Once in Adam, and the second time by his own personal transgressions? Are not all men who burn "in fire unquenchable, trees plucked up by the roots"; not because they "died in Adam," but because they "are twice dead"; because they personally "destroyed themselves," and, when Christ gave them a degree of life, "would not come to him that they might have it more abundantly?" Thus, by resisting to the last the quickening beams of the Spirit that "strove with them," they "quenched him" in themselves, and became apostates. If Christ is "the light and the life of men," and if he "enlightens every man that comes into the world," are not all the damned apostates? Have they not all fallen from some degree or other of quickening grace? Have they not all buried one or more talents? And is it not Satan's masterpiece of policy, to make good men assure quickened sinners that they cannot lose their life, no, not by plunging into the whirlpools of adultery, murder, and incest? The ancient serpent deceived our first parents by saying, "Ye shall not surely die," if ye eat of the forbidden fruit. But now, it seems, he may take his rest, for, O astonishing! Gospel ministers do his work; they inadvertently "deceive the very elect," and "overthrow the faith of some," by making them the very same false promise.

I have already observed, that he "who believeth" is said to "have everlasting life"; not only because, while he keeps the faith, he has a title to glory, but because living "faith *always* works by love," the grace that "never faileth," the grace that "lives and abides for ever"; not indeed in this or that individual, during his state of probation, but in the kingdom of heaven, "among the spirits of just men made perfect in love," and confirmed in glory. However, you still urge, "To say that everlasting life can be lost, is a contradiction in terms: if it is everlasting, how can it be forfeited or lost?" How? Just as the Jews forfeited the land which God gave to Abraham for an everlasting possession, Gen. 17:8. Just as the seed of Phinehas lost "the everlasting priesthood," Num. 25:13. Just as the Israelites "broke the everlasting covenant," Isaiah 24:5. Just as Hymeneus and Philetus forfeited the everlasting privileges of believers; that is, by "making shipwreck of faith and a good conscience." Here, then, the edge of your own sword is again blunted, and the stroke given to the "aliens" easily parried with the unbroken "sword of the Spirit": I mean the word of God illustrated by itself, and taken in connection with itself. However, you proceed:

X. Page 64. *"The chosen vessel, Paul, tells his beloved Timothy, that God 'hath saved us, and called us with a holy calling,'"* etc. Hence you conclude, that if we are elect, our salvation is finished. I grant, that God hath saved us from hell, placed us in a state of salvation begun, and "called us with a holy calling, to work out our salvation with fear and trembling"; under some dispensation of that "grace which was given us in Christ before the world began; according to God's own purpose, *that Christ should be* the Saviour of all men, especially of them that believe." But alas! though "many are thus called, yet but few are chosen; because few walk worthy of their high vocation, few make their calling and election sure." Numbers, like David and Solomon, Demas and Sapphira, believe for awhile, and "in time of temptation fall away"; some of whom, instead of rising again, "draw back unto perdition."

Hence "the chosen vessel, Paul," himself cries to halting believers, "How shall we escape if we neglect so great salvation?" So far was he from imagining that the salvation of some, and the damnation of others "were as firmly secured" as if the one were already in heaven, and the other in hell! So little did he think that to preach the Gospel was to present the elect with nothing but the cup of finished salvation, even when they take away the wives and lives of their neighbours; and to drench the reprobates with the cup of finished damnation, even while they ask, seek, knock, and endeavour to make their mock calling sure!

Certain it is, that if the apostle spoke of your finished salvation, when he said, "God hath saved us, and called us with a holy calling," reprobated myriads may reasonably give over wrestling with almighty, everlasting wrath, and cry out, "He hath damned us, and called us with an unholy, hypocritical, and lying calling, according to his own purpose and wrath, which was given us in Adam before the world began." O sir, by this frightful doctrine you give a desperate thrust to the hopes which millions entertain, that God is not yet absolutely merciless toward them, and that they may yet repent and be saved; but happily for them, it is with the dagger of error, and not with "the sword of the Spirit."

XI. Page 65. *"But farther. Believers are said to be 'saved by faith,' and to be 'kept by the power of God through faith unto salvation.' Now true faith and salvation are here inseparably linked by the apostle."* Inseparably linked! Pray, sir, where is the inseparable link? I see it not. Nay, when I consult the apostles, on whose strained words you raise your argument, they rise with one consent against your doctrine. The one says, Some branches in Christ "were broken off because of unbelief; thou standest by faith; [undoubtedly true faith;] nevertheless, fear, lest he also spare not thee. Behold his goodness toward thee, if thou continue in his goodness; otherwise thou also shalt be cut off." The other declares, "If after they [fallen believers, whom he does not call "pleasant," but cursed children] have escaped the pollutions of the world, through the knowledge of the Lord and Saviour Jesus Christ, (that is, through true faith,) they are again entangled therein, and overcome; the latter end is worse with them than the beginning, II Peter 2:20, compared with II Peter 1:2, 8, 9, 10. Thus, sir, St. Paul and St. Peter, whom you call to your assistance, agree to wrench your sword out of your own hand. But you soon take it up again.

XII. Page 64. *"Christ being styled not only the author, but the finisher of our faith, he must be, consequently, the finisher of our salvation."* So he undoubtedly is, when we are 'workers together with him," that is, when using the gracious talent of will and power, which he freely gives us, we "work out our own salvation with fear and trembling." But if we bury that talent, "do despite to the Spirit of grace, forget that we were washed from our sins," and wallow again in the mire of iniquity; "Christ," the author of the faith which we destroy, "profiteth us nothing; we are fallen from grace."

Is it right to rock feeble believers in the cradle of carnal security, by telling them they can never lose the faith; when part of St. Paul's triumphant song, just before he received the crown of martyrdom, was, "I have kept the faith?" What wonder was it that he should have kept, what even the carnal, incestuous Corinthian could never lose! When the Scriptures mention, not only those who "have kept the faith," but those who 'have made shipwreck of it, and of a good conscience; those who "believe for awhile, and in time of temptation fall away"; and those who one day believe, another day have little faith, and by and by have no faith; are we not "wise above what is written," and sow we not Antinomian tares, when we give lukewarm Laodiceans to understand they can never lose what, alas! they have already lost?

If Christ was to believe in his own blood for us, I grant, that the work of faith and salvation could not miscarry. But what ground have we to imagine that this is the case? Did the apostles charge Christ or sinners to believe under pain of damnation? If believing is entirely the work of Christ, why did he marvel at the unbelief of the Jews? Did you ever marvel at the sessions that the constables in waiting did not act as magistrates? Did you ever send them to jail for not doing your work, as you suppose Christ sends unbelievers to hell for not believing, that is, upon your scheme, for not doing his work?

While we readily grant you, that the talent of faith, like that of industry, is the 'free gift of God," together with the time, opportunity, and power to use it; should you not grant us, that God treats us as rational, accountable creatures? That he does not use the gift of faith for us: that we may bury our talent of faith, and perish; as some bury their talent of industry and starve? And that it is as absurd to say, the faith of every individual in the Church is inadmissible, because Christ is the author and finisher of our faith, as to affirm that no individual ear of corn can be blasted, because Christ (who upholds all things by the word of his power) is the unchangeable author and finisher of all our harvests?

Once more, permit me, honoured sir, to hang the mill stone of reprobation about the neck of your Diana, to cast her back with that cumbrous weight into the sea of error, from whose scum she, like another Venus, had her unnatural origin. If the salvation of the elect is finished, because "Christ is the author and finisher of their faith," it necessarily follows, that the damnation of the reprobates is also finished, because "Christ is the author and finisher of their unbelief." For he that absolutely withholds faith, causes unbelief as effectually, as he that absolutely withholds the light, causes darkness.

If, in direct opposition to the words of our Lord, John 3:18, you say, with some Calvinists, that "Christ does not damn men for unbelief, but for their sins," I reply, This is mere trifling. If Christ absolutely refuses them power to believe in the light of their dispensation, how can they but sin? Does not Paul say, that "without faith it is impossible to please God?" Is not unbelief at the root of every sin? Did not even Adam eat the forbidden fruit through unbelief? And is not "this our only victory, even our faith?"

An illustration will, I hope, expose the emptiness of the pleas which some urge in favour of unconditional reprobation, or, if you please, non-election. A mother conceives an unaccountable antipathy to her sucking child. She goes to the brink of a precipice, bends herself over it with the passive infant in her bosom, and,

withdrawing her arms from under him, drops him upon
the craggy side of a rock, and thus he rolls down from
rock to rock, till he lies at the bottom beaten to pieces,
a bloody instance of finished destruction. The judge asks
the murderer what she has to say in her own defence.
The child was mine, replies she, and I have a right to do
what I please with my own. Beside, I did neither throw
him down nor murder him: I only withdrew my arms
from under him, and he fell of his own accord. In mystic
Geneva she is honourably acquitted; but in England the
executioner is ordered to rid the earth of the cruel monster. So may God give us commission to rid the Church
of your Diana, who teaches that he, the Father of mercies,
does by millions of his passive children, what the barbarous mother did by one of hers; affirming, that he unconditionally withholds grace from them; and that, by
absolutely refusing to be "the author and finisher of their
faith," he is the absolute author and finisher of their unbelief, and consequently of their sin and damnation.

XIII. *However, without being frightened at these
dreadful consequences, you conclude as if you had won
the day*: p. 65, "Now I appeal to any candid judges,
whether I have not brought sufficient authority from the
best of authorities, God's unerring word, for the use of
that phrase, finished salvation," which, p. 63, "in its full
extent, I undertook to vindicate." I cordially join in your
appeal, honoured sir, and desire our unprejudiced readers to say, if you have brought one solid proof from
God's unerring word in support of your favourite scheme,
which centers in the doctrine of finished salvation: and if
that expression, when taken "in its full extent," is not
the stalking horse of every wild Nicolaitan ranter; and the
dangerous bait, by which Satan, transformed into an
angel of light, prevails upon unstable souls to swallow
the silver hook of speculative, that he may draw them
into all the depths of practical, Antinomianism.

XIV. *I do not think it worth while to dwell upon the lines you quote from Mr. Charles Wesley's hymns.* He is yet alive to tell us what he meant by "It's finished; it's past," etc. And he informs me that he meant "the sufficient sacrifice, oblation, and satisfaction, which Christ made upon the cross for the sins of the whole world, except 'doing despite to the Spirit of grace,' or the sin against the Holy Ghost." The atonement, which is a considerable part of the Redeemer's work, is undoubtedly finished; and if by a figure of poetry, that puts a part for the whole, you choose to give the name of finished salvation to a finished atonement, I have already observed, in the Third Check, that we will not dispute about the expression. We only entreat you so to explain and guard it, as not to give sanction to "Antinomian dotages," and charge the God of love with the blasphemy of finished damnation.

XV. *The Calvinistical passage which you produce from the Christian Library is unguarded, and escaped Mr. Wesley's or the printer's attention.* One sentence of it is worthy of a place in the *Index Expurgatorius,* which he designs to annex to that valuable collection. Nevertheless, two clauses of that very passage are not at all to your purpose. "Christ is now thoroughly furnished for the carrying on of this work: he is actually at work." Now if Christ is actually at work, and carrying on his work, that work is not yet finished. Thus, even the exceptional passage which you, or the friends who gave you their assistance, have picked out of a work of fifty volumes, shows the absurdity of taking the expression, "finished salvation," in its full extent.

Should you say, "Christ is thoroughly furnished for his work, (namely, the salvation of the elect,) therefore that work is as good as finished," I once more present you with the frightful head of Geneva Medusa, and reply, "Christ is thoroughly furnished for his work, (namely, the damnation of the reprobates,) therefore that work is as good as finished." Thus all terminates still in uncovering the two iron-clay feet of your great image, absolute election and absolute reprobation, or, which is all one, finished salvation and finished damnation.

O sir, the more you fight for Dr. Crisp's scheme of free grace, the more you expose his scheme of free wrath. I hope my judicious readers are shocked at it, as well as myself. Your "sword" really "puts us to flight." We start back, we run away: but it is only from the depths of Satan, which you help us to discover in speculative Antinomianism, or barefaced Calvinism.

XVI. *If you charge me with "calumny," for asserting that speculative Antinomianism and barefaced Calvinism are one and the same thing; to clear myself, I present you with the creed of an honest, consistent, plain-spoken Calvinist.* Read it without prejudice, and say if it will not suit an abettor of speculative Antinomianism, and, upon occasion, a wild Ranter, wading through all the depths of practical Antinomianism, as well as an admirer of "the doctrines of grace."

Five Letters, 1st edit. pp. 33, 34, 27. "I most firmly believe, that the grand cause of so much lifeless profession is owing to the sheep of Christ being fed in barren pastures and muddled waters of a legalized Gospel. The doctrines of grace are not to be kept out of sight for fear men of corrupt minds should abuse them. I will no more be so fearful to trust God with his own truths, as to starve his children and my own soul: I will make an open confession of my faith."

"1. I believe in God the Father Almighty, who from all eternity unconditionally predestinated me to life, and absolutely chose me to eternal salvation. Whom he once loved he will love for ever; I am therefore persuaded, (pp. 28, 31,) that as he did not set his love on me at first for any thing in me, so that love, which is not at all dependent upon any thing in me, can never vary on account of my miscarriages: and for this reason; when I miscarry, suppose by adultery or murder, God ever considers me as one with his own Son, who has fulfilled all righteousness for me. And as he is 'always well pleased' with him, so with me, who am absolutely 'bone of his bone and flesh of his flesh.' (pp. 26, 31.) There are no lengths, then, I may not run, nor any depths I may not fall into, without displeasing him; as I see in David, who, notwithstanding his repeated backslidings, did not lose the character of the man after God's own heart. I may murder with him, worship Ashtaroth with Solomon, deny Christ with Peter, rob with Onesimus, and commit incest with the Corinthian, without forfeiting either the Divine favour or the kingdom of glory. 'Who shall lay any thing to the charge of God's elect?' to the charge of a believer? to my charge? For,

"2. (Pages 26, 27, 32.) I believe in Jesus Christ, that 'by one offering has for ever perfected' me, who am 'sanctified' in all my sins: in him I am complete in all my iniquities. What is all sin before his atoning blood? Either he has fulfilled the whole law, and borne the curse, or he has not. If he has not, no soul can be saved; if he has, then all debts and claims against his people and me, be they more (suppose a thousand adulteries, and so many murders) or be they less, (suppose only one robbery,) be they small or be they great, be they before or be they after my conversion, are for ever and for ever cancelled. I set up no more mountainous distinctions of sin, especially sins after conversion. Whether I am dejected with Elijah under the juniper tree, or worshipping Milcom with Solomon; whether I mistake the voice of the Lord for that of his priest, as Samuel, or defile my neighbour's bed, as David, I am equally accepted in the Beloved. For in Christ I am chosen, loved, called, and unconditionally preserved to the end. All trespasses are

forgiven me. I am justified from all things. I already
have everlasting life. Nay, I am now (virtually) set down
in heavenly places with Christ; and as soon shall Satan
pluck his crown from his head, as his purchase from his
hand."

Pages 27, 28. "Yes, I avow it in the face of all the
world; no falls or backslidings can ever bring me again
under condemnation; for Christ hath made me free from
the law of sin and death. Should I outsin Manasses himself, I should not be a less pleasant child; because God
always views me in Christ, and in him I am without spot
or wrinkle, or any such thing. Black in myself, I am still
comely through the comeliness put upon me: and therefore He 'who is of purer eyes than to behold iniquity,'
can, in the midst of all adulteries, murders, and incests,
address me with, 'Thou art all fair, my love, my undefiled; there is no spot in thee!' And,

"3. I believe in the Holy Ghost, the Spirit of grace,
against whom I can never sin, (p. 26,) whose light and
love I can never quench, to whom I can never do despite,
and who, in his good time, will irresistibly and infallibly
(Review, p. 38) work in me to will and to do. In the
meantime I am perfectly secure; for I can never perish,
my salvation being already finished in the full extent of
the expression." (Review, p. 63, etc.)

"Once, indeed, I supposed, that 'the wrath of God
came,' at least for enormous crimes, 'upon the children of
disobedience'; and I thought it would come upon me if I
committed adultery and murder: but now I discover my
mistake, and believe (p. 28 and 25) it is a capital error
to confound me and my actions. While my murders, etc.,
certainly displease God, my person stands always absolved, always complete, always pleasant in the everlasting righteousness of the Redeemer. I repeat it, (2d edit.
p. 37,) it is a most pernicious error of the schoolmen, to
distinguish sins according to the fact, and not according to

the person. He that believeth hath as great sin as the unbeliever: nay, his sins, (p. 32,) for the matter of them
are perhaps more heinous and scandalous than those of
the unbeliever; but although he daily sinneth, perhaps as
David and the Corinthian, by adultery, murder, and incest, he continueth godly.

"Before I was acquainted with the truth, I imagined
that sin would dishonour God and injure me: but since
the preachers of finished salvation have opened my eyes,
I see how greatly I was mistaken. And now I believe
that God will overrule my sin, (whether it be adultery,
murder, or incest,) for his glory and my good.

"(1) For his glory. (Pages 36, 30, 31, 32). God often
permits his own dearest children to commit adultery,
murder, and incest, to bring about his purposes. He has
always the same thing in view, namely, his own glory and
my salvation, together with that of the other elect. This
Adam was accomplishing when he put the whole world
under the curse; Onesimus when he robbed Philemon
his master; Judah when he committed incest with Tamar;
and David when he committed adultery with Bathsheba.
How has many a poor, faithless soul even blessed God
for Peter's denial! As for the incestuous Corinthian, the
tenderness shown him after his crime, has raised many
out of the mire, and caused them to recover their first
love.

(2) "For my good. (Page 32.) God has promised to
make 'all things work for good to me'; and if all things,
then my very sins and corruptions are included in the
royal promise. Should I be asked, What particular good
sin will do me in time and in eternity? I answer: A
grievous fall [suppose into adultery, murder, or incest]
shall serve to make me know my place, to drive me
nearer to Christ, to make me more dependent upon his
strength, to keep me more watchful, to cause me to sympathize with the fallen, and to make me sing louder to the

praise of free, sovereign, restoring grace, throughout all the ages of eternity. Thus, although I highly blame (p. 33,) those who roundly say, 'Let us sin that grace may abound,' I do not legalize the Gospel, but openly declare, (p. 27,) that if I commit adultery, murder, or incest, before or after my conversion, grace shall irresistibly and infallibly abound over these, and all my other sins, be they small or be they great, be they more or be they less. My foulest falls will only drive me nearer to Christ, and make me sing (p. 32) his praises louder than if I had not fallen. Thus [to say nothing of the sweetness and profit which may now arise from sin] adultery, incest, and murder shall, upon the whole, make me holier upon earth, and merrier in heaven."

I need not tell you, honoured sir, that I am indebted to you for all the doctrines, and most of the expressions of this dangerous confession of faith. If any one doubt of it, let him compare this creed and your Letters together. Some clauses and sentences I have added, not to "misrepresent and blacken," but to introduce, connect, and illustrate your sentiments. You speak, indeed, in the third person, and I in the first, but this alters not the doctrine. Beside, if the privileges of a lean believer belong to me as well as to David, I do not see why I should be debarred from the fat pastures you recommend, (p. 34,) which, I fear, are so very rich, that if the leanest sheep of Christ do but range, and take their fill in them, they will in a few days wax wanton against him, butt at the sheep which do not bleat to their satisfaction, attack the under shepherds, and grow so excessively fat as to outkick Jeshurun himself.

XVII. *Some half-hearted Calvinists, who are ashamed of their principles, and desirous to conceal their Diana's deformity, will probably blame you for having uncovered the less frightful of her feet, and shown it naked to the wondering world.* But to the apology which you have already made about it, I hope I may, without impertinence, add one or two remarks.

1. Whoever believes either the doctrine of unconditional election, or that of righteousness absolutely imputed to apostatizing believers, or that of the infallible perseverance of all who were saints yesterday, and today commit adultery, murder, or incest; and, in a word, whoever believes the doctrine of finished salvation implicitly receives two-thirds of the Antinomian creed which you have helped me to. And those who have so strong a faith, and so large a conscience, as to swallow so much, (together with the doctrine of finished damnation, eternal wrath flaming against myriads of unborn creatures, and everlasting fire prepared for millions of passive, sensible machines, which have only fulfilled God's secret and irresistible will,) might, one would think, receive the whole creed without any difficulty: for why should those who can swallow five or six camels as a glib morsel, strain at three or four gnats, as if they were going to be quite choked. Again:

2. If Calvinism is true, you are certainly, honoured sir, the honest and consistent Calvinist, so far as consistency is compatible with the most inconsistent of all schemes. Permit me to produce one instance, which I hope will abate the prejudices which some unsettled Calvinists have conceived against you for speaking quite out with respect to the excellent effects of sin in believers.

If man is not a free agent, (and undoubtedly he is not, if from all eternity he has been bound by ten thousand chains of irresistible and absolute decrees,) it follows, that he is but a curious machine, superior to a brute, as a brute is superior to a watch, and a watch to a wheelbarrow. Upon Calvin's principles this wonderful machine is as much guided by God's invisible hand, or rather by his absolute decrees, as a puppet by the unseen wire which causes its seemingly spontaneous motions. This being the case, it is evident that God is as much the author of our actions, good or bad, as a show-man is the author of the motions of his puppets, whether they turn to the right or to the left. Now as God is infinitely wise, and supremely good, he will set his machines upon doing nothing but what, upon the whole, is wisest and best. Hence it appears, that if the doctrine of absolute decrees, which is the fundamental principle of Calvinism, is true, whatever sin we commit, we only fulfil the absolute will of God, and do that which, upon the whole, is wisest and best; and therefore that you have not unadvisedly pleaded for Baal, but rationally spoken for God, when you have told us what great advantages result from the commission of the greatest crimes. In doing this strange work, then, you have acted only as a consistent predestinarian; and though some thoughtless Calvinists may, yet none that are judicious will blame you, for having spoken agreeably to the leading principle of "the doctrines of grace."

I have observed, that speculative Antinomianism, or barefaced Calvinism, stalks along upon the doctrine of finished salvation, and finished damnation, which we may consider as the two feet of your great Diana; and the preceding creed, which is drawn up for an elect, uncovers only her handsome foot, finished salvation. To do my subject justice, I should now make an open show of her cloven foot, by giving the world the creed of a reprobate, according to the dreadful doctrine of finished damnation. But as I flatter myself that my readers are already as tired of Calvinism as myself, I think it needless to raise their detestation of it, by drawing before their eyes a long chain of blasphemous positions, capable of making the hair of their heads stand up with horror. I shall, therefore, with all wise Calvinists, draw a veil over the hideous sight, and conclude by assuring you, few people more heartily wish you delivered from speculative Antinomianism, and possessed of salvation truly finished in glory, than, honoured and dear sir, your affectionate and obedient servant, in the bonds of what you call the "legalized Gospel,"   JOHN FLETCHER.

A LETTER
To Richard Hill, Esq.

HON. AND DEAR SIR: Having endeavoured, in my last, to convince you out of your own mouth, that undisguised Calvinism and speculative Antinomianism exactly coincide, before I turn from you to face your brother, I beg leave to vindicate good works from an aspersion, which zealous Calvinists perpetually cast upon them. For as practical Antinomianism destroys the fruits of righteousness, as a wild boar does the fruit of the vine; so speculative Antinomianism besprinkles them with filth, as an unclean bird does the produce of our orchards.

Hence it is, that you charge me (Review, p. 69,) with "vile slander," for insinuating that our free-grace preachers do not "raise the superstructure in good works." Page 41, as if you wanted to demonstrate the truth of my "vile slander," you say, "Though we render the words χαλα εργα, 'good works,' yet the exact translation is 'ornamental works'; and truly, when brought to the strictness of the law, they do not deserve the name of 'good.' But, however grating the expression may sound to those who hope to gain a second justification by their works, yet we have Scripture authority to call them dung, dross, and filthy rags."

Now, sir, if Scripture authorizes us to call them thus, they are undoubtedly very useless, loathsome, and abominable; and the Minutes, which highly recommend them, are certainly dreadfully heretical. I must then lose all my controversial labour, or once more take up the shield of truth, and quench this *fiery* (should I not say, this

"filthy") dart, which you have thrown at St. James'
undefiled religion: I begin with your criticism.

I. *"Though we render the words* χαλα εργα, *good
works, yet the exact translation is ornamental works."*
I apprehend, sir, you are mistaken. The Greek word
χαλος exactly answers to the Hebrew which conveys
the joint ideas of *goodness* and *beauty.* Before there
was any "filthy rag" in the world, "God saw every thing
that he had made; and behold it was very good," which
the Septuagint very exactly renders χαλα λἳαν. Fully to
overthrow your criticism, I need only to observe, that good
works are called *good,* with the **very** same word by
which the *goodness* of the law, and the *excellence* of the
lawgiver are expressed. For St. Paul, speaking of the
law, Rom. 7:16, says that it is χαλος, "good"; and our
Lord, speaking of himself, says "I am ο ω′οιμην οχαλος,
the GOOD Shepherd." Now, sir, as you are too pious to
infer from the word χαλος; that neither the law nor
Christ "deserved to be called *good,*" I hope you will be
candid enough to give up your similar inference concerning *good works.*

Inconsistency is the badge of error. You give us, if I
mistake not, a proof of it, by telling us with one breath
that "good works do not deserve the name of *good,*" but
that of *"ornamental";* and, with the next, that Scripture
authorizes us to call them "dung, dross, and filthy rags."
Are then dung, dross, and filthy rags *ornamental* things?
or did you try to render Geneva criticism as famous as
Geneva logic? But,

II. *You have recourse to divinity as well as to criticism: for you say,* "When good works are brought to the
strictness of the law, they do not deserve the name of
good." I answer: If our Lord himself called them *good,*
it does not become us to insinuate that in so doing he
passed a wrong judgment, and countenanced "proud
justiciars" in their legal error. With respect to the

"strictness of the law," which you so frequently urge, your frightful notions about it cannot drive us into Antinomianism; because we think that Christ and St. Paul were better acquainted with the law than Calvin and yourself. If 'all the law and the prophets hang on the grand commandment of love," as our Lord informs us; and if "he that loveth another hath fulfilled the law," as the apostle declares, we see no reason to believe that the law condemns as "dung" the labour of that love by which it is fulfilled, and rejects as "filthy rags" works which Christ himself promises to crown with eternal rewards. You probably reply:

III. *"Many Pharisees go to church without devotion, and many fornicators give alms without charity, fancying that such good works make amends for their sins, and merit heaven."* Good works, do you call them? The Scriptures never gave them that honourable name. They are the hypocritical righteousness of unbelief, and not "works meet for repentance," or "the fruits of the righteousness of faith." Treat *them* as you please, but spare *good works.* It is as unjust to asperse good works on their account, as to hang the honest men who duly carry on the king's coinage at the mint, because the villains who counterfeit his majesty's coin evidently deserve the gallows.

IV. *Should you object that "the best works have flaws, blemishes, and imperfections; and therefore may properly be called dung, dross, and filthy rags,"* I deny the consequence. The best guineas may have their flaws: nay, some dust or dirt may accidentally cleave to them; but this does not turn them into dross. As therefore a good guinea is gold, and not dross, though it has some accidental blemishes; so, God himself being judge, a good work is *a good work,* and not a filthy rag, though it is not free from all imperfections.

V. *Not so, do you say? "We have Scripture authority*

to call good works filthy rags." You build, it seems, your mistakes upon Isaiah 64: 6, "All our righteousnesses are as filthy rags": a passage which, upon mature consideration, I beg leave to rescue from the hands of the Calvinists. The Jews were extremely corrupted in the days of Isaiah: hence he opens his prophecy by calling the rich, "Ye rulers of Sodom," and the poor, "Ye people of Gomorrah." And what says he to them? "How is the faithful city become a harlot! Righteousness lodged in it, but now murderers!" Yet these murderers hypocritically went on keeping their Sabbaths and new moons. They "fasted," but it was "for strife," and "to smite with the fist of wickedness." They "made many prayers," and offered multitudes of sacrifices, but "their hands were full of blood." Nor did they consider that he who, under these circumstances, "sacrifices an ox, is as if he slew a man."

This corruption of the Jews, though general, was not universal: for the Lord of hosts had left to them a remnant, though very small. Now Isaiah, one of that very little flock, being humbled at the sight of the general wickedness of his people, confesses it in the first person (*we*) as ministers always do on such occasions; and he uses the word *all*, because the small remnant of the righteous was as lost in the multitude of the wicked. The verse, taken in connection with the context, runs thus: "Thou meetest him that rejoiceth, and worketh righteousness, those that remember thee in thy ways." But, alas! we are not the people. "Behold, thou art wroth, for we have sinned. We are all as an unclean thing, and all our righteousnesses are as filthy rags." Therefore, instead of meeting us, as thou dost the righteous, thou hast hid thy face from us, and hast consumed us because of our iniquities. "We all do fade as a leaf; and our iniquities, like the wind, have taken us away": so far are we from resembling the righteous, who "are like a tree planted by the water side, whose leaf does not wither." Who does not see that the prophet here opposes the happiness of the righteous to the misery of the wicked? And that it is the hypocritical righteousness of the ungodly, and not the precious obedience of believers, which he compares to filthy rags?

VI. *However, "We have Scripture authority to call good works dross."* Your mind, I suppose, runs upon Isaiah 1:22, 25, where God expostulates with the obstinate Jews, by saying, "Thy silver is become dross," thy righteousness is all hypocrisy: yet, if thou returnest, "I will purge away thy dross," I will make thee truly righteous. Is it not evident, that it is hypocrisy and *bad* works, not *good* works, which God here calls *dross?* Will he, think you, purge away *good* works from his people? Is it not enough that armies of Antinomians do the devil that service? Must we also suppose that God promises to be his drudge?

VII. *But, "we have Scripture authority to call good works dung."* Not at all: for the two passages you probably think of, are against you. In the first, God speaks to the disobedient Jews, and says, "If ye will not hear, and give glory unto my name, I will send a curse upon you: yea, I have cursed your blessings already. Behold, I will spread upon your faces the dung of your solemn feasts," Mal. 2:2, 3. Now, sir, who does not see by the context that festivals kept by cursed hypocrites are called dung, and not the solemn worship performed by penitent believers?

If you quote Phil. 3:8, it will be to as little purpose. Do you rightly understand that passage? "I count all things but loss, for the excellency of the knowledge of Christ, for whom I have suffered the loss of all things, and do count them but dung, that I may win Christ, and be found in him, not having mine own righteousness, which is of the law, but that which is through the faith of Christ." You know, sir, that the apostle once made far too much of his privileges as a Jew, his morals as an honest man, and his observance of the law as a strict disciple of Moses. And you remember that when he wrapped himself up in that kind of external righteousness, his heart breathed nothing but contempt toward Christ, and slaughter against his people. What wonder is it that he should count such a righteousness, together with all earthly, perishing things, loss and dung, for Christ? Who does not see that it was not the precious righteousness of faith, which consists in pardon, acceptance, and power to do good works, but the paltry righteousness of an unbeliever, a blasphemer, a murderer?

Should you say that when the apostle declares, "he counts all things but dung, that he may be found in Christ," he certainly includes good works, and counts them dung: I reply, You have as good reason to say that he certainly includes repentance, faith, obedience, grace, and glory, and counts them dung also!

Some gentlemen invite you to go a hunting, or play at cards, to keep you from the sessions; and you answer, "I am determined to do my duty. Once your sports were gain to me, but now I count them but loss of time: yea, doubtless, I count all things, that stand in competition with my office, vile and contemptible as dung: they no more tempt me to pursue them, than yonder dung hill tempts me to take my rest; I am ready to trample upon them as filthy dust, rather than not to be found upon the bench doing my duty as a magistrate: not according to my own former mistaken notions of justice, but according to the equitable laws of my country."

Now, sir, should I not very much wrong you if I inferred from your very generous answer that you call doing justice dung? And do you not greatly wrong St. Paul, when, upon a pretence equally frivolous, you insinuate that he gave to good works such an injurious name? That he called the will of God, done in faith by the Spirit of Christ, dung?

Again: when the apostle prayed to "be found in Christ, not having his own *Pharisaic* righteousness, which was of the *letter of* the law, but the righteousness which is of God by faith"; is it not evident that (beside the desire of being pardoned and accepted through faith in Christ) he wished to be found to the last a branch grafted "in the true vine," by faith? A living branch, filled with the righteous sap of the root that bore him? A branch made fruitful by the principle of all acceptable righteousness, which is "Christ in us, the hope of glory?" And, to use his own words in this very epistle, a branch "filled with the fruits of righteousness, which are by Jesus Christ to the glory of God?" Phil. 1:11, compared with 3:9.

Let men of reason and religion say if this sense is not more agreeable to the letter of Scripture in general, and the apostle's words in particular, than the fantastic imputation of righteousness, which Calvinists build upon them. An imputation this, which constitutes a man righteous, while he commits adultery, murder, or incest. Is it not deplorable that such an unscriptural and unnatural idea should ever have entered the minds of pious men? Especially when St. John says, "Little children, let no man deceive you: he that does righteousness," and not barely he for whom Christ hath done righteousness, "is righteous?" Is it not lamentable that good men, influenced by prejudice, should be able to persuade thousands that St. John meant, "Let not Mr. Wesley deceive you; he that actually liveth with another man's wife, worships abominable idols, and commits incest with his father's wife, may not only be righteous, but complete in imputed righteousness; in a righteousness which exceeds, not only the righteousness of the Pharisees, but the personal righteousness of converted Paul, and of the brightest angel in glory!"

O sir, if you have told it in Paris, tell it not in Constantinople, lest the daughters of the Mohammedans bless God, that, lewd and bloody as their prophet was, he never so far lost sight of morality and decency as to give Mussulmen a cloak, under the specious name of a "robe of righteousness," under which they can curse, swear, and get drunk, commit adultery, robbery, murder, and incest, without being less righteous than if they had kept all the commandments of God; less in favour with the Most High than if they had personally abounded in all the works of piety, mercy, and self denial, which adorned the life of Jesus Christ; and less interested in finished salvation than if they were already in glory. O sir, is not this doctrine more dangerous than that of transubstantiation? It is not more dishonourable to Christ, more immoral, and consequently more pernicious to society? And would it not absolutely destroy the morals of all those who receive it, if our Lord, for his name's sake, did not in mercy deny to thousands of them sense or attention, to draw a dreadful conclusion from their dreadful premises; while he graciously gives to thousands more hearts infinitely better than their immoral principles!

Having thus endeavoured to rescue the passages on which you found your assertion concerning good works, and proved that there is not one scripture which gives you the least authority to call them either dung, dross, or filthy rags; to convince you that a heap of impious absurdities lies concealed under that doctrine, permit me to produce some of the scriptures where good works are mentioned; and to substitute to that phrase the hard names which, you tell us, the Scripture authorizes you to call them.

"Let your light so shine before men, that they may see your good works, [i. e. your dung,] and glorify your Father who is in heaven." "She has wrought a good work [i. e. filthy rag,] upon me, against my burial." "Dorcas was full of good works," [i. e. of dung and rags.] "God make you to abound in every good work," i. e. in every sort of dung and dross. "We are created in Christ Jesus to good works," i. e. to filthy rags, "which God hath prepared for us to walk in." "Walk worthy of the Lord, being fruitful in every good work," i. e. in every filthy rag. "God establish you in every good work," i. e. in dung of every sort. "Provoke one another to love and good works,"i. e. to dross and rags. "Be zealous of good works," i. e. of filthy rags. "Be rich in good works," i. e. in dross. "Be careful to maintain good works," i. e. dung. "Let the Gentiles by your good works," i. e. your dung. "Let they shall behold, glorify God in the day of visitation." "Be thoroughly furnished to every good work: be perfect in every good work," i. e. in dung and dross of every kind. "Blessed are they that die in the Lord, for their works," i. e. their dung and rags, "follow them." "God is not unrighteous, to forget your works," i. e. your dung, "that proceedeth of love." "The Gentiles should do works," i. e. dung, "meet for repentance." "Esteem ministers highly in love for their work's [i. e. their dung's,] sake." "If he have not works," i. e. dung, "can faith save him?" "Faith without works," i. e. without filthy rags, "is dead." "By works," i. e. dung, "was Abraham's faith made perfect." "He and Rahab were justified by works," by filthy rags. "He that believeth in me, the works that I do shall he do also, and greater works than these," i. e. filthier rags, and more ornamental dung, "shall he do." "This is the work," i. e. the dung, "of God, that you believe," etc.

Indeed, sir, I am almost ashamed to take up the "filthy rag" of this bad divinity, though it is only with the point of my pen, to hold it out a moment to public view, that the world may be sick of barefaced Antinomianism. I drop it again into the sink of defiled religion, out of which Dr. Crisp raked it; and beg for the honour of Christ and your own, that you will no more recommend it as pure Gospel.

And now, dear sir, permit me to expostulate a moment with you. Against whom have you employed your pen, when you have taught the world to call good works dung, dross, and filthy rags; pretending to have authority from the Scripture thus to revile the best thing under heaven? Is it only against the "proud justiciars?" Is it not also indirectly, though I am persuaded undesignedly, against the adorable trinity? Has not the Father "created us to good works"? Did not the Son "redeem us, that we might be a people zealous of good works?" And does not the Holy Ghost sanctify us, that "all our works being begun, continued, and ended in him, we may glorify God's holy name," and cause it to be glorified by all around us?

What harm did good works ever do you, or any one, that you should decry them in so public a manner as you have done? Did you ever duly consider their nature and excellence? Or have you condemned them in a hurry, without so much as casting an attentive look upon them? Permit me to bring them to you, as God brought the beasts of the field to Adam, that he might give them names according to their nature; and tell me which of them you will call dung, which dross, and which filthy rags?

First, then, what objection have you against the *good works of the heart*? Against the awaking out of sin, returning to God, repenting, offering the sacrifice of a contrite spirit, and believing unto righteousness? What objection against trusting in the Lord Jehovah, in whom is everlasting strength? casting the anchor of our hope within the veil? loving God for himself, and all mankind for God's sake? Do you see any of these good works of the heart that look like a "filthy rag?"

No sooner is the "inward man of the heart" truly engaged in any one of the preceding works, than the outward man is all in motion. The candle of the Lord is not lighted in the soul to be "put under a bushel," and extinguished, but to be set as "on a candlestick" of the body, "that it may give light to all" around, and that men "seeing our light, may glorify our heavenly Father." Hence arise several classes of external good works.

Consider the man of God as he is clothed with a corruptible body, which must be nourished without being pampered. He "keeps it under," by moderate fasting or abstinence. He "daily denies himself, and takes up his cross." He works with cheerful diligence. He eats, drinks, or sleeps, "with gladness and singleness of heart"; and if he is sick, he bears his pain with joyful resignation, doing or suffering "all to the glory of God," in the spirit of sacrifice, and "in the name of the Lord Jesus."

View him in his family. Not satisfied with mental prayer, he bends the knee "to his Father who sees in secret"; and not contented with private devotions, he reads to his assembled household select portions of God's word, and solemnly worships him with them "in spirit and in truth." Nor does he think, that doing his duty toward God excuses him from fulfilling it toward his neighbour. Just the reverse. Because his soul is all reverence to his heavenly Father, it is all respect to his earthly parents. Because he ardently loves the Bridegroom of souls, he feels the warmest regard for his wife, he bears the tenderest, and yet the most rational affection to his children. Nor is he less desirous that his servants should serve God and "work out their salvation," than he is that they should serve him and do his work. Hence arise his familiar instructions, mild reproofs, earnest entreaties, encouraging exhortations. His strict honesty and meekness of wisdom, his moderation and love of peace are known to all around him; and even those who despise his piety are forced to speak well of his morals.

Behold his works as a member of society in general. In his little sphere of action he makes his star "to shine upon the just and the unjust," his charity is universal. To the utmost of his ability he opposes vice, countenances virtue, promotes industry, and patronizes despised piety. Humble faith kindles him into "a burning and shining light"; he is a minister of the God of all mercies, he is a flaming fire. He feeds Christ in the hungry, gives him drink in the thirsty, clothes him in the naked, entertains him in strangers, attends him on sick beds, visits him in prisons, and comforts him in the mournful apartments, where the guilty are stretched on the rack of despair, or where the godly, forsaken of their friends, pledge their dying Lord with the dregs of the cup of sorrow. How easily does he overlook the unkindness of his neighbours! How readily does he forgive injuries! How cordially heaps he coals of melting fire upon the heads of his enemies! How sincerely does he pray for all his slanderers and persecutors! And how ardently desire "to grow in grace," and endeavour "to adorn" more and more "the doctrine of God our Saviour in all things!"

Consider him as a member of a religious society. How excellent, how Divine are his works! He respectfully holds up the hands of his minister, and kindly bears the burdens of his brethren. He watches over them for good, "rejoices with those that rejoice," and "mourns with those that mourn." He compassionately sympathizes with the tempted, impartially reproves sin, meekly restores the fallen, and cheerfully animates the dejected. Like undaunted Caleb, he spirits up the fearful; and, like valiant Joshua, he leads them to the conquest of Canaan; and goes on "from conquering to conquer."

And suppose he "went on *even* unto perfection," and "took the kingdom of heaven by violent" faith, and humble, patient, importunate prayer; would you call him a filthy rag man, and insinuate that he had only done a dung work? O, sir, if you can so publicly call good works, dross, dung, and filthy rags; and (what is worse still) assert, that the Holy Ghost in the Scriptures, authorizes you so to do; who will wonder to see you represent the doctrine of Christian perfection as a pernicious Popish heresy, which turns men "into temporary monsters?" Would you be consistent, if you did not rise against it with the collected might of credulous uncharitableness, and barefaced Antinomianism? For,

What is, after all, the perfection that Mr. Wesley contends for? Nothing but two good works, productive of ten thousand more; or, if you please, two large filthy rags, in which ten thousand other filthy rags are wrapped; that is, "loving God with all our hearts, and our neighbour as ourselves." It is nothing but "perfect love shed abroad in our hearts by the Holy Ghost given unto us," making us 'steadfast, immovable, always abounding in the work of the Lord," always "zealous of good works," always the reverse of the easy elect, who, by means of Calvin's contrivance, are "all fair and undefiled," while they wallow in the adulterer's mire, and the murderer's gore. Or, in other terms, it is nothing but Christ, through the Holy Spirit, "dwelling in our hearts by faith," and making us always "zealous of good works." Now, if good works are dross, dung, and filthy rags; it is evident that perfection is a rich mine of dross; a heap of dung, as immense as that which Hercules got out of Augeas' stables; and a vast store house of filthy rags, spun by "proud justiciars," as cobwebs are by venomous spiders.

In this wrong view of Christian perfection, I no more wonder to see multitudes of careless professors agree, like Pilate and Herod, to destroy it out of the earth; nor am I surprised to hear even good, mistaken people cry out, "Down with it! down with it!" While I complain of their want of candour, I commend their well-meant zeal, and wish it may flame out against objects worthy of their detestation; against perfection itself, suppose it is what they imagine. Yes, if it is a mine of "dross," let them drown it: I give my consent; but let them do it with the floods of Scripture and argument. If it is a dung hill in the Church, let them carry it out, and permit even the swine, which come "from wallowing in the mire," to shake themselves upon it: I will not say it is improper. If it is a repository of filthy rags, more infectious than those which convey the jail distemper or the plague; let them agree to set fire to it, and burn it down to the ground: but let them do it with "fire from the altar," and not with "tongues set on fire" of prejudice or malice.

But if Christian perfection is (next to angelic perfection) the brightest and richest jewel which Christ purchased for us by his blood; if it is the internal kingdom of God ruling over all; if it is Christ *fully* formed in our hearts, the *full* hope of glory; if it is the fulfilment of the promise of the Father, that is, "the Holy Ghost given unto us," to make us abound in righteousness, peace, and joy, through believing"; and in a word, if it is the Shekinah, filling the Lord's human temples with glory; is it right, sir, to despise it as some do, or to expose it as you have so frequently done?

Should you apologize for your conduct, by saying, "I have only treated YOUR perfection as you have treated OUR finished salvation, and OUR imputed righteousness": I reply, The case is widely different. I hope I have made it appear, that you have not one single text in all the Bible to prove that a bloody adulterer (*in flagrante delicto*) stands complete in imputed righteousness; or that the salvation of idolatrous and incestuous apostates, who now work out their damnation with both hands, is actually finished, in the full extent of the expression. The whole stream of God's word runs counter to these "Antinomian dotages." Nor are they less repugnant to conscience and common sense, than to the law and the prophets. But you cannot find one word in all the Scriptures against the pure love of God and our neighbour, against perfect love, which is all the perfection we encourage believers to press after. The law and the Gospel, the Old and the New Testament, are equally for it. All who are "filled with the Spirit," sweetly experience it. A heathen, that fears God and regards man, cannot speak evil of it, but through misapprehension. And even while, through the amazing force of prejudice, you write against it with so much severity, it recommends itself to your own reason, and conscience. Are you not then, dear sir, under a mistake, when you think you may take the same liberty with God's undeniable truth, which I have taken with Dr. Crisp's indefensible error?

Permit me to state the case more fully still. Mr. Wesley cries to believers: "It is your privilege so to believe in Christ, and receive the Spirit, as to 'love God with all your hearts, and your neighbours as yourselves.'" And you say to them: "Mr. Wesley is blinder than a Papist, regard not his heretical words. Your salvation is finished. Whatever lengths you go in sin, you are as sure of heaven as if you were already there. It is your privilege to commit adultery, murder, and incest, not only without fearing that the Lord will be displeased with you; but conscious that, black as ye are in yourselves by the actual commission of these crimes, through Christ's comeliness put upon you, God can address each of you with, Thou art all fair, my love, my undefiled, there is no spot in thee!" (*Five Letters*, p. 28.) Now, sir, are you not a partial judge, when, by way of retaliation, you serve the holy doctrine maintained by Mr. Wesley, as I have served the unholy tenet propagated by Calvin and yourself?

Think you, really, that because a judge, after a fair trial, justly condemns a notorious robber to be hanged; another judge, to retaliate, has a right to quarter a good man, after a mock trial, or rather without any trial at all? And do you suppose, that because Jehu deservedly made "the house of Baal a draught house"; or because Josiah burned dead men's bones upon the unhallowed "altar in Bethel," to render it detestable to idolaters, Antiochus had a right to turn the temple of the Lord into a stye, and to pollute "the altar of incense," by burning "dung and filthy rags" upon it, that true worshippers might abominate the offering of the Lord, and loathe the holy of holies? Thus, however, have you (inadvertently I hope) treated good works and Christian perfection, which are ten thousand times more sacred and precious in the sight of God than the holy, and the most holy place in the temple of Jerusalem.

And now, dear sir, please to look at the preceding list of the good works, which adorn the Christian's breast, or blazon his shining character; and tell us if there is one, which, upon second thoughts, you object against as a nuisance: one, which you would put away like "dross"; one, which you would have carried out of his apartment as "dung," or remove from his pious breast as a "filthy rag."

Methinks I hear you answer, "Not one. May they all abound more and more in my heart and life, and in the hearts and lives of all God's people!" Methinks that all the Church militant and triumphant cry out, "Amen!" A Divine power accompanies their general exclamation. The veil of prejudice begins to rend. Your honest heart relents. You acknowledge that Calvinism has deceived you. You retract your unguarded expressions. The Spirit of holiness, whom you have grieved, returns. The heavenly light shines. The Antinomian charm is broken. "Dross" is turned into fine gold; "dung" into savoury meat, which every believer loveth next to the bread of life; and "filthy rags," into the "linen, fine and white, which is the righteousness of the saints, and the robe made white in the blood of the Lamb." Far from pouring contempt, through voluntary humility, upon this precious garment, you give praise to God, and in humble triumph put it on, together with the Lord Jesus Christ.

In that glorious dress you "walk with Christ in white," and in love with Mr. Wesley. Paris, and the convent of Benedictine monks, disappear. The "New Jerusalem," and "the tabernacle of God, come down from heaven. Leaving the things that are behind, *you solemnly* hasten unto the day of the Lord. Following peace with all men, and holiness, without which no man shall see the Lord, *you daily* perfect it in the fear of God." You feel the amazing difference there is between a real and an imaginary imputation of righteousness. You tear away with honest indignation the pillow of finished salvation from under the head of Laodicean backsliders, who sleep in sin; and of bloody murderers, who defile their neighbour's bed. You set fire to the fatal canopy, under which you have inadvertently taught them to fancy that the holy and righteous God calls them "my love, my undefiled!" even while they wallow in the poisonous mire of the most atrocious wickedness. And to undo the harm you have done, or remove the offence you have given by your letters, you show yourself reconciled to St. James' pure religion; you openly give Mr. Wesley the right hand of fellowship, and gladly help him "to provoke" believers to uninterrupted "love and good works," that is, to Christian perfection.

Such is the delightful prospect which my imagination discovers through the clouds of our controversy; and such are the pleasing hopes that sometimes soothe my polemical toil, and even now make me subscribe myself, with an additional pleasure, honoured and dear sir, your affectionate brother and obedient servant, in the bonds of a pure Gospel,   JOHN FLETCHER.

A LETTER

To Richard Hill, Esq.

Hon. and Dear Sir: Although I reserve for two separate tracts my answer to your objections against "the monstrous doctrine of perfection," and my reply to the argument which you draw from our seventeenth article, in favour of the doctrine of unconditional election; the already exorbitant length of this Check calls for a speedy conclusion; and I hasten toward it, by laying before my readers the present state of our controversy, enlarging chiefly upon imputed righteousness and free will, two points which I have not yet particularly discussed in this piece.

Imputed righteousness, as it is held by the Calvinists, I have endeavoured to expose in the Second Check, by the most absurd, and yet (upon your plan) most reasonable plea of a bare-faced Antinomian, who expects to be justified in the great day by Christ's imputed righteousness without works. To this you have answered, (Review, p. 68, etc.,) by exclaiming, "Shocking slander, slanderous banter," etc., and I might reply only by crying out, *Logica Genevensis!* But, as honest inquirers after the truth would not be benefited, for their sakes I shall in this letter show how far we agree, wherein we disagree, and what makes us dissent from you, about the doctrine of imputed righteousness.

We agree that all the righteousness which is in the spiritual world is as much Christ's righteousness, as all the light that shines in the natural world at noon is the light of the sun. And we equally assert that, when God justifies a sinner who believes in Christ, he freely pardons his past sins, graciously accounts him righteous, and, as such, admits him to his favour, only through faith in the Redeemer's meritorious blood and personal righteousness.

To see clearly wherein we disagree, let us consider both your doctrine and ours; touching, as we go along, upon the capital arguments by which they are supported.

Consistent Calvinists believe, that if a man is elected, God absolutely imputes to him Christ's personal righteousness, that is, the perfect obedience unto death which Christ performed upon earth. This is reckoned to him for obedience and righteousness, even while he is actually disobedient, and before he has a grain of inherent righteousness. They consider this imputation as an unconditional and eternal act of grace, by which, not only a sinner's past sins, but his crimes present and to come, be they more or be they less, be they small or be they great, are for ever and for ever covered. He is eternally "justified from all things." And therefore, under this imputation, he is perfectly righteous before God, even while he commits adultery and murder. Or, to use your own expressions, whatever lengths he runs, whatever depths he falls into, "he always stands absolved, always complete in the everlasting righteousness of the Redeemer." (Five Letters, pp. 26, 27, 29.) In point of justification, therefore, it matters not how unrighteous a believer actually is in himself; because the robe of Christ's personal righteousness, which, at his peril, he must not attempt to patch up with any personal righteousness of his own, is more than sufficient to adorn him from head to foot; and he must be sure to appear before God in no other. In this rich garment of finished salvation, the greatest apostates shine brighter than angels, though they are "in themselves black" as the old murderer, and filthy as the brute that actually wallows in the mire. This "best robe," as it is called, is full trimmed with such phylacteries as these, "Once in grace, always in grace: once justified, eternally justified: once washed, always fair, undefiled, and without spot." And so great are the privileges of those who have it on, that they can range through all the bogs of sin, wade through all the puddles of iniquity, and roll themselves in the thickest mire of wickedness without contracting the least spot of guilt, or speck of defilement.

This scheme of imputation is supported, 1. By scripural metaphors, understood in a forced, unscriptural sense. Thus when a sound Calvinist reads about "the breastplate of righteousness," and "the garment of salvation"; or about "putting on Christ, walking in him, being in him, being found in him, or being clothed with righteousness," his prepossessed mind directly runs upon his imputation. And if he reads in the Psalms, "I will make mention of thy righteousness, and thine only," he immediately concludes that the psalmist meant the personal righteousness of the man Christ: as if David really made mention of no other righteousness but that in all the Psalms! or God had had no righteousness, before the Virgin Mary "brought forth her first-born Son!"

2. By the parable of the man who "was bound hand and foot, and cast into outer darkness, because he had not on a wedding garment"; that is, upon your scheme, because Christ's personal righteousness was not imputed to him: as if the Prince of Peace, the mild Jesus, who says, "Learn of me, for I am meek," had kindly invited a man to the feast, and then commanded him to be thrust into hell, merely because he had not on a garment which he never could procure; a robe which none but God could clothe him with; and which God determined should never be for him, when he decreed that Christ should never work out an inch of righteousness for one single reprobate. Does not this exceed Ovid's description of the iron age? *Non hospes ab hospite tutus.* The bare mention of such a dreadful reflection cast upon God's goodness, and our Lord's hospitality, will amount to a strong argument against your imputation, with those who are

yet concerned for God's adorable perfections, and our Lord's amiable character.

3. By the parable of the prodigal son, who, it is supposed, was clothed with the "best robe" of Christ's personal righteousness. But this notion is overturned by the context itself: for the father had met, forgiven, and embraced his returning son in his own ragged garment, before the "best robe" was called for, and put upon him. Whence it would follow, that a sinner may be forgiven without the garment of righteousness; and as completely accepted out of Christ, as the prodigal was without the "best robe."

4. By the goodly raiment of Esau, in which Jacob got his father's blessing. But Moses' account of the cheat put upon the short-sighted Isaac, entirely overthrows the scheme of the Calvinists. The robe which they recommend is made of Christ's complete and personal righteousness; it is long and wide enough perfectly to cover even a giant in sin; nor must it be patched with any thing else. But Jacob's dress, far from being all of a-piece, was a mongrel sort of human and beastly garment. For, when Rebekah had clothed his body with Esau's raiment, "she put goat skins upon his hands, and upon the smooth of his neck," to make them feel like Esau's hairy hands and shaggy neck. And the worst is, that the goat skins, and not Esau's borrowed dress, deceived the aged patriarch, and got the blessing. Hear the historian. "Jacob went near to his father, and he felt him, and said, The voice is Jacob's voice, but the hands are the hands of Esau; and he discerned him not because his hands were hairy; so he blessed him," Gen. 37:22. Thus the skin of a goat, the emblem of a reprobate, unfortunately comes in to patch up your best robe. And I doubt not but, as the typical garment was too scanty to cover Jacob's hands andneck; so the fancied antitype will prove too short to cover the hands of those, who, like "Onesimus, rob their

masters"; and the neck and heels of those, who, like David, are "swift to shed blood," and climb up into their neighbour's bed; if they do not get a more substantial righteousness than that in which you suppose they stand complete, while they commit their enormous crimes.

5. Plain Scripture is also brought to support this imputation. David says, "Blessed is he whose sin is covered: blessed is the man unto whom the Lord imputeth not iniquity," Psalms 32:1, 2. But, alas for your scheme! it is thrown down by the very next words, "And in whose spirit there is no guile." Thus, although you would make us believe the contrary, David's own doctrine shows that he was not the "blessed man whose sins are covered by non-imputation of iniquity," when his spirit was full of guile, adultery, and murder. And, indeed, he tells us so himself in this very Psalm: "When I kept silence," says he, when I harboured guile and impenitency, "day and night thy hand was heavy upon me: but when I acknowledged my sin unto thee," when I parted with my guile, "thou forgavest the iniquity of my sin."

6. However, if David's words are flatly against your imputation, it is supposed, that as prefaced by St. Paul, they make greatly for it: "David describeth the blessedness of the man to whom God imputeth righteousness without works," Rom. 4: 6. I have already observed, that as the apostle cannot contradict David and himself, he only means without the works of the law, as opposed to faith and to the work of faith. That this is the true meaning of St. Paul's words, is evident by those which introduce them: "To him that worketh not, but believeth, his faith is counted for righteousness." Who does not see here, that believing, which is the good work that begets all others, is opposed to the faithless works, about which the Pharisees made so much ado to so little purpose? Who does not perceive, that a man must believe, that is, do the work of God before his faith can be "counted for

righteousness"? and consequently, that righteousness is imputed to him who believes, not absolutely without any sort of works; but only without the works of the law, emphatically called by the apostle, works, or "deeds of the law," when he contradistinguishes them from faith, and "the work of faith."

7. To the preceding scriptures our Calvinist brethren add a plausible argument. "God," say they, "may as well impute to us Christ's perfect righteousness in all our sins, and account us completely righteous without one grain of inherent righteousness; as he imputed the horrid crimes of the elect to Christ in all his obedience, and accounted him completely guilty without one single grain of inherent sin. To deny, therefore, that God imputes righteousness to an elect, while he is full of unrighteousness, or to suppose that he imputes sin to an apostate, who 'is sold under sin,' is but a decent way of denying the imputation of our personal sins to Christ, and the vicarious satisfaction which he made on the cross."

To detect the fallacy of this argument, we need only observe, (1) That God never accounted Christ "completely guilty." Such expressions as these, "He made him sin for us; he laid upon him the iniquities of us all," etc., are only Hebrew idioms, which signify that God appointed Christ a sacrifice for sin; and that "the chastisement of our forfeited peace was upon him"; which no more implies that God put on his back, by an absolute imputation, a robe of unrighteousness, woven with all the sins of the elect, to make him completely guilty, than St. Luke, when he informs us that the Virgin Mary offered two young pigeons for her purification, suppose her ceremonial uncleanness was, somehow, woven into a couple of little garments, and put upon the back of the two young pigeons, which, by that mean, were made completely unclean.

I hope the following illustration will convince you, sir, that such refinements as these are as contrary to sober reason as to Scripture duly compared with itself. Gallio gets drunk, and as he reels home from his midnight revels, he breaks thirty-six lamps in the streets, and sends out volleys of curses to the number of two hundred. He is brought before you, and you insist on his going to the house of correction, or paying so much money to buy three dozen of lamps, beside the usual fine for his profane language. As he is not worth a groat, his sober brother Mitio kindly offers to lay down the sum for him. You accept of the "vicarious satisfaction," and binding the rake to his good behaviour, you release him at his brother's request. Now, sir, would you be reasonable if you reckoned Mitio completely guilty of getting drunk, swearing two hundred oaths, and breaking thirty-six lamps? Far from supposing him guilty of breaking one lamp, or swearing one oath, even while he makes satisfaction for his brother's wildness, do you not esteem him according to his own excellent character?

And will you defend a doctrine which charges God with a mistake ten thousand times more glaring than that you would be guilty of, if you really reckoned Mitio an abandoned rake, and Gallio a man of an exemplary conduct? Will you indeed recommend still as Gospel an opinion which supposes that the God of everlasting unchangeable love once loathed and abhorred his beloved Son? and that the God of invariable truth could once say to the holy Jesus, "Thou art all foul, O thou defiled object of my hatred, there is no purity in thee": while he addresses a bloody adulterer with, "Thou art all fair, my love, my undefiled, there is no spot in thee?"

A variety of Scriptural and rational arguments I have, directly or indirectly, advanced in every Check against that capital doctrine of yours, "the absolute imputation of Christ's personal righteousness to believers"; whether they live chastely with their own wives, or entice away other men's wives: whether they charitably assist their neighbours, or get them treacherously murdered. All those arguments centre in this: If that doctrine is true, the Divine perfections suffer a general eclipse; one half of the Bible is erased; St. James' epistle is made void; defiled religion justly passes for "pure Gospel"; the Calvinian doctrine of perseverance is true; and barefaced Antinomianism is properly recommended as the "doctrine of grace."

Having thus considered your doctrine of imputed righteousness, permit me, honoured sir, to submit to your inspection the harmonizing views that we have of God's perfections; while we see him impute righteousness to a man (i. e. reckon a man righteous) so long as he actually believes with a faith working by obedient love; and impute iniquity to an apostate (i. e. reckon him unrighteous) as soon as he departs from the faith, to work iniquity, and walk in the ways of unrighteousness.

We firmly believe that God's imputation, whether of sin or righteousness, is not founded upon sovereign caprice, but upon indubitable truth. As we are partakers by generation of Adam's original pollution before God imputes it to us, that is, before he accounts us really polluted; so are we partakers by regeneration of Christ's original righteousness before God imputes righteousness to us, that is, before he accounts us really righteous. And therefore a positive and substantial communication of Christ's righteousness, apprehended by faith, no less precedes God's imputation of righteousness to a believer, than Bartimeus' receiving his sight, and admitting the light, were previous to God's reckoning that he actually saw.

Although we grant the Almighty "calls the things that are not, as though they were," and that, according to his foreknowledge, he frequently speaks of them in the prophetic style, as if they were now, or had been already; yet when he reckons what is, in order to pass sentence of absolution or condemnation, he cannot deny his truth, and reckon a man actually chaste and charitable that actually commits adultery and murder. We dare not impute this flagrant unrighteousness to God. And as "no guile was found in the Lord's mouth" while he was upon earth, we cannot admit the most distant thought of his being full of guile in heaven; which we apprehend would be the case, if he reckoned that a man who actually falls from adultery into murder is actually undefiled, and completely righteous.

Again: as Christ bore no manner of vicarious punishment for us; or, which is the same, as our iniquities were not actually laid upon him till he partook of our frail nature, and was positively interested in our corruptible blood; so, by a parity of reason, we are not indulged with the pardon and acceptance which he merited for us till we partake of his light and righteousness. Hence appears the weakness of that argument, "righteousness may as well be imputed to us, without any participation of the Divine nature, as sin was imputed to Christ, without any participation of our fallen nature." We absolutely deny the fact on which this argument is founded; and assert, with St. Paul, that Christ "was made sin for us," (i. e. a proper sacrifice for our sins,) not by an imaginary robe of unrighteousness put upon him according to your imputation; but by being really "made of a *fallen, mortal* woman," and "sent in the likeness of sinful flesh," that he might suffer and die for us; which he could not have done, if he had not assumed our fallen nature—unfallen man being quite above the reach of pain and death. It is not less certain, therefore, that "he was made in the likeness of sinful flesh," than it is indubitable that "he was in all points tempted like as we are, yet without sin."

As sure then as Christ was not "made sin [i. e. a sin offering] for us," by a speculative imputation of our personal sins; but by being actually made flesh, clothed with our mortality, and "sent in the likeness of sinful flesh"; so sure are "we made the righteousness of God in him," not by a speculative imputation of his personal good works, but by being "made partakers of the Divine nature, begotten of God, and clothed with essential righteousness"; which is the case when we "put on the new man, who after God is created in righteousness and true holiness." Thus it appears to us that your imputation may be demolished, only by retorting II Cor. 5:21, the scripture with which it is chiefly supported; and, if we are not mistaken, the venerable fabric raised upon that passage, like Mohammed's venerable tomb, hangs in the air without one single prop.

That the seed of righteousness, by which we are first interested in Christ, is universal in all infants, appears to us evident from St. Paul's words: "As by one man's [Adam's] disobedience the many [the multitudes of mankind] were made sinners," by a seed of sin; "so by the obedience of one [Christ] shall the many [the multitudes of mankind] be made righteous," by a seed of righteousness, to the end of the world, Rom. 5:19. Hence it is that righteousness is imputed to all infants; and that, as I have proved, Letter X, they stand justified before God, according to the inferior dispensation they are under.

When they grow up, and "hold the truth in unrighteousness," by sinning against their light, personal iniquity is imputed to them; and till they believe again in the light, and renounce the evil deeds which it reproves, they are condemned already." But the moment they truly repent, and unfeignedly believe the Gospel belonging to their dispensation, condemnation vanishes; God again imputes righteousness to them—that is, for Christ's sake he again pardons their sins, accepts their persons, and considers them as branches that admit the righteous sap of the true vine, and bear "the fruits of righteousness."

Once more: If these branches do not believingly abide in Christ, the vine, they become such branches in him as bear not fruit. Nay, they bear the poison of unrighteousness. Iniquity therefore is again imputed to them; and so long as they continue in their sin and unbelief, they are every moment liable to be "taken away, cast into the fire, and burned," John 15. Nevertheless, through the Redeemer's intercession, God "bears long with them"; and if they despise not to the last the "riches of his forbearance and long suffering," duly considering how "his goodness leadeth them to repentance," their backslidings are healed. They believe again "with the heart unto righteousness." The righteous sap of the true vine has again a free course in their hearts. They again receive Christ, who "is the end of the law," and the sum of the Gospel, "for righteousness to every one that believeth": and their faith, which once more admits the beams of the Sun of righteousness, is once more "imputed to them for righteousness."

This, honoured sir, is the holy imputation of righteousness, which we read of in the oracles of God; and we prefer it to yours for three reasons. (1) It hath truth for its foundation; but your imputation stands upon a preposterous supposition, that Christ the righteous was an execrable sinner, and that an elect is perfectly righteous, while he commits execrable iniquity. (2) Because it perfectly agrees with St. James' undefiled religion, which your scheme entirely overthrows. And (3) Because it is supported by the plainest scriptures.

The popes have at least the letter of one passage to countenance their monstrous doctrine of transubstantiation. They save appearances when they make their dupes believe that a bit of bread is really the body of Christ: for, say they, Christ took bread, and declared, This is my body. But, O tell it not in Paris, lest the subjects of the triple crown triumph over us in their turn! The personal righteousness of Christ is not so much as once mentioned in all the Bible with the doctrine of imputation; and yet some divines can make whole congregations of men, who protest against the impious absurdities of the Church of Rome, believe that the imputation of Christ's personal righteousness is a Scriptural doctrine, and the very marrow of the Gospel! This garment of their own weaving they cast over adulterers and murderers, and then represent the filthy, bloody wretches, as complete in Christ's obedience, perfect in righteousness, and "undefiled" before God!

If I had a thousand tongues, could I employ them more to the glory of Christ, and the good of souls, than by crying to the thousands who are still "sold under sin," and still take their carnal ease in that imaginary garment of righteousness, "Awake to *true* righteousness, and sin not"? Search the Scriptures. Where is it said, that Christ's personal righteousness was ever imputed to either man or angel? And where is it written that righteousness was ever imputed to any one, farther than he was possessed of, and actuated by, a living, powerful inherent principle of righteous faith?

"To the law and the testimony!" Can any thing be plainer than the two following positions, on which all our doctrine of imputation is founded? (1) Faith is a powerful, quickening, justifying, sanctifying, working, victorious, saving grace. (2) This faith, as it springs from and receives Christ, and his righteous power, "is imputed to us for righteousness."

Does not the first of these propositions stand unshaken upon such scriptures as these? "Faith is the evidence of things not seen, and the substance of things hoped for: all things are possible to him that believeth: whosoever believeth is born of God: all that believe are justified;

purifying their hearts by faith: sanctified through faith that is in me: this is the victory that overcometh the world, even our faith: ye are saved through faith: faith worketh by love: remembering your work of faith: faith without works is dead: he that believeth hath everlasting life: holding the mystery of faith in a pure conscience, which some having put away concerning faith have made shipwreck," etc. Is it not evident from these scriptures, that all who have a living faith have not only a pardon, but works, especially love, which is "the fulfilling of the law";—love, the most excellent "fruit of righteousness," in which all others are contained? And surely, if they have a pardon, and true inherent righteousness in their Christ accepting, loving, and obedient faith, that faith may well be "imputed to them for righteousness," or God may well account them righteous.

Nor is the second proposition, upon which our imputation stands, less clearly laid down in the Scriptures. "Abraham believed in the Lord, and he counted, [or imputed] it to him for righteousness," Gen. 15:6. What says the Scripture? "Abraham believed God, and it was imputed unto him for righteousness," i. e. for preceding righteousness, through the remission of his past sins; for present acceptance in the Beloved, whom he received; and for present righteousness through the righteous exertions of a "faith that worketh by love." Again: 'To him that believeth, his faith is imputed for righteousness: we say that faith was imputed to Abraham for righteousness: that he might be the father of all them that believe, that righteousness might be imputed to them also. He was strong in faith, giving glory to God; and therefore it was imputed to him for righteousness. Now it was not written for his sake alone, that it was imputed to him; but for us also, to whom it shall be imputed, if we believe," Gal. 3:6; Rom. 4:3, etc.

As Moses had led the van of these testimonies in favour of our scriptural imputation, and St. Paul the main body, permit St. James to bring up the rear. "Seest thou," says he, "how faith wrought with Abraham's works, and by works was faith made perfect, and the scripture was fulfilled, which says, Abraham believed God, and it was imputed to him for righteousness?" James 2:23. The whole is thus summed up by the great defender of free grace: "The Gentiles which followed not after righteousness have attained to righteousness, even the righteousness which is of faith. But Israel, which followed after the law of righteousness, hath not attained to it. Wherefore? Because they sought it not by faith; but, as it were, by [the faithless] works," which they did in self-righteous obedience to the letter of the law; trampling under foot the righteousness of faith, which speaketh on this wise: "If thou shalt confess with thy mouth the Lord Jesus, and shalt believe in thy heart that God hath raised him from the dead, thou shalt be saved: for with the heart man believeth unto righteousness, and with the mouth confession is made unto salvation," Rom. 9, and 10.

Who does not see, in reading these words, that we must do something unto righteousness, as well as unto salvation? Is it not evident that we must now "believe with the heart," in order to the former, and "make confession with the mouth," as we have opportunity, in order to the latter; and, consequently, that righteousness imputed, as well as salvation finished, without any thing done on our part, is a doctrine that is not less contrary even to St. Paul's Epistle to the Romans, fairly taken together, than to that strong rampart of undefiled religion, the Epistle of St. James.

However, a cloud of objections arises, to keep the light from a prejudiced reader: and as he thinks that three of them are remarkably strong, I beg leave to consider them with some degree of attention.

I. OBJECTION. "Your doctrine of justifying, sanctifying, and working faith imputed to us for righteousness, I bear my loud testimony against; because it confounds righteousness with sanctification, two Gospel blessings, which are clearly distinguished, I Cor. 1:30."

ANSWER. It would be much better to confound, than to destroy them both; as I fear you do, when you cast a robe of finished salvation, i. e. of complete righteousness and finished holiness, over impenitent adulterers and murderers. But be that as it will, your objection is groundless. I have already observed, and I once more declare, that when we speak of the righteousness of faith we understand three things: (1) The non-imputation, or "forgiveness of the sins that are PAST," Rom. 3:25. (2) Present "acceptance in the Beloved!" Eph. 1:6. And, (3) A principle of universal righteousness, by which we are interested in Christ's righteousness; just as a branch is interested in the excellence of the vine, by receiving the generous sap which it actually derives from it; and not by an imaginary imputation of the fine grapes which the vine bore seventeen hundred years ago. "Let no man deceive you; he that DOES righteousness," is a righteous branch; even as Christ is a righteous vine! I John 3:7; John 15:5.

On the other hand, when we speak of sanctification we understand the wonderful change wrought in us by the working of the above-mentioned principle of righteousness; and the internal fruits which it produces, till, by "growing up into Christ in all things, we come in the unity of the faith, and of the knowledge of the Son of God, unto a perfect man, unto the measure of the stature of the fulness of Christ." It is evident therefore, that, considering righteousness and sanctification even in their most intimate union, we do not confound them at all; but maintains as clear a distinction between them as that which subsists between the derivation of a sap by a wild branch from the good olive tree, and the change produced in that branch upon such a derivation.

II. OBJECTION. "Your doctrine is Popery refined. By paying saving honours to a Christian grace, and taking the crown from Christ to set it upon faith, you shake the very foundation of the Mediator's throne. If this is not high treason against him, what crime deserves that name?"

ANSWER. Your fears are laudable, though absolutely groundless. (1) Faith, the humble grace that will know nothing but Christ, for "wisdom, righteousness, sanctification, and redemption," can never dishonour his person, claim his crown, or shake the foundation of his throne. Is it not ridiculous to make so much ado about faith robbing Christ of saving honours, when Christ himself says, "Thy FAITH hath SAVED thee"; and when the apostle cries out, "Believe, and thou shalt be saved!" Were then Christ and St. Paul two refined Papists, and guilty of high treason against the Redeemer?

(2) If some will be "wise above what is written," we dare not. If they are ashamed of the oracles of God, we are not: therefore, whatever they think of us, we must say, with the evangelical apostle, "Faith was imputed to Abraham for righteousness: and to him that believeth, HIS FAITH is imputed for righteousness."

(3) Should you say that Abraham's faith, or his believing God, signifies either Christ's person or his personal righteousness, we reply, *Credat Judœus Apella!* There was indeed a time when Calvinist divines could make simple Protestants believe it, as easily as the pope can make credulous Papists believe that a wafer of the size of half a crown is the identical body of our Lord:

but as many Romanists begin to shake off the yoke of
Popish absurdities, so many Protestants will cast away
that of Calvinian impositions. And as our fathers taught
us to protest that the hocus pocus of a Popish priest cannot turn bread into flesh, so will we teach our children
to protest that the bare assertion of a Calvinist minister
cannot turn Abraham's faith into Christ's person, or into
his personal righteousness; which must however be the
case if those words, "Abraham's faith," or his believing
God, "was imputed for righteousness," do only mean, as
we are confidently told, that "Christ, or his personal
righteousness, was imputed to Abraham for righteousness."

(4) Does it reflect any dishonour upon Christ to
say, with St. Paul, that "FAITH is imputed to us for righteousness"; when believing includes its object, (Christ
the way, the truth, and the life,) as necessarily as eating
supposes food, and drinking, liquor? Is it not as impossible to "believe in the light," without Christ the light;
or to believe in the truth, without Christ the truth, as it
is to breathe without air, and hear without sounds?
Again: if you affirm "that we warm ourselves by going
to the fire," do you sap the foundation of natural philosophy because you do not say ten times over that the
warming power comes from the fire, and not from our
motion toward it? And do we destroy the foundation of
Christianity, when we assert that "faith working by love"
instrumentally saves us, because we do not spend so
much time as you in saying over and over that the saving
merit and the saving power flow from the Saviour, and
not from our own act of believing? Is not this as clear as
it is that the light flows in upon us from the sun, and
not from (though it is through the opening of our eyes?

Lastly: would not physicians make themselves appear
very ridiculous if they distressed their patients when
they were going to take a medicine, with the fear of

ascribing their recovery to their taking the remedy, i. e. to "their own doing," rather than to the virtue of the remedy itself? And are those divines alone partakers of heavenly wisdom who puzzle sinners that are coming to Christ, and place a lion in their way, by perpetually injecting into their minds a fear lest they should ascribe their salvation to faith rather than to the Saviour whom faith receives? Where does the apostle, whose evangelical sentiments they do so deservedly extol, set them the example of such refinements? Is it Rom. 4, where he says, directly or indirectly, seven times, that "FAITH is imputed for righteousness?" Is it not strange that at last "orthodoxy" should consist in fairly setting aside, or explaining away the doctrine of St. Paul, as well as that of St. James?

III. OBJECTION. "Your mind is full of carnal reasonings. You do not know either Christ or yourself. If you did you would never set up the inherent righteousness of faith, which is nothing but our own righteousness, in opposition to imputed righteousness. If you were not quite blind, or 'very dark,' you would see that all our righteousnesses are as filthy rags; and you would humbly acknowledge that the holy breastplate and robe of righteousness, which we may with safety and honour appear in before God, are the breastplate and robe of Christ's personal righteousness freely imputed to us, without any of our doings. This best robe, which you so horribly bespatter, we must defend against all the Arminians, Pelagians, and Papists in the world."

ANSWER. To do this grand objection justice, it will be proper to consider it in its various parts, and give each a full answer.

1. We acknowledge that we cannot think nonsense is any more compatible with the wisdom of God, and flat contradiction with his sacred oracles, than adultery is

compatible with undefiled religion, and murder with common morality. If these sentiments are "carnal reasonings," we beg leave to continue carnal reasoners, till you can recommend your spiritual reasonings, either by common sense or plain Scripture.

2. You confound, without reason, the inherent righteousness of faith with Pharisaic self righteousness. I have already proved that the latter, which is the partial, external, and hypocritical righteousness of unbelieving formalists, is the only righteousness which the prophet compares to filthy rags. With respect to the former, that is our own righteousness of faith, far from setting it up in opposition to imputed righteousness rightly understood, we assert that it is the righteousness of God, the very thing which "God imputes to us for righteousness"; the very righteousness which has now the stamp of his approbation, and will one day have the crown of his rewards.

3. You affirm that the breastplate of righteousness which St. Paul charges the Ephesians to have on, is Christ's personal righteousness imputed to us; and we prove the contrary by the following arguments. The apostle, who is the best illustrator of his own expressions, exhorts the Thessalonians to "put on the breastplate of faith and love." Now, as we never heard of soldiers having two breastplates on; the imaginary breastplate of their general, which they wear by imputation; and the solid plate of metal, which actually covers their breasts; we conclude, that the "breastplate of righteousness," which St. Paul recommends to the Ephesians, together with the "shield of faith," is nothing but the "breastplate of faith and love," which he recommends to the Thessalonians.

To help my readers to see your doctrine in a proper light, I might say, If the breastplate of our Lord's personal obedience has no more to do with our breasts than the personal dinner which he took in the Pharisee's house has to do with our empty stomachs; and the personal garment in which he shone upon Mount Tabor has to do with our naked shoulders; the judicious apostle would probably have called it a brainplate rather than a breastplate, as having far less to do with the breast and heart than with the brain and imagination. But as this argument would rather turn upon our translation than upon the original, I drop it, and present you with one that has more solidity.

If the breastplate of a Christian warrior is as far from him, in time and place, as the personal righteousness wrought by our Lord in Judea seventeen hundred and sixty years ago, his shield may be at the same distance; and so undoubtedly may his helmet and sandals, his belt and sword. Thus, by Calvin's contrivance, you have a soldier of Christ armed cap-a-pee, without one single piece of armour from head to foot. And will you say of these imaginary accoutrements, in which the elect can with all ease commit adultery and incest, that they are "the armour of righteousness on the right hand and on the left," in which St. Paul fought his battles, and subdued so many kindreds and nations to his Lord's triumphant cross? O! if that champion were yet alive, who said, in the midst of Corinth, "The kingdom of God is not in word, but in power," how would he cry, in the midst of mystic Geneva, "The armour of God is not a Calvinian notion, but a Divine reality!"

What we are persuaded he would thunder out through the world, we are at last determined to proclaim on the walls of our Jerusalem. "Soldiers of Christ, have on the true breastplate of righteousness! Put on the solid breastplate of inherent faith and love. If Satan's temptations are not idle imputations of his dreadful assaults upon Christ; if his darts are really fiery and terrible, throw away Calvinian imputation: 'cast off the works of darkness and put on the real armour of righteousness, the armour of light, the whole armour of God:' so shall you be 'able to stand in the evil day; and having DONE ALL, to stand with safety in judgment, and with honour in the congregation of the righteous.'"

4. We apprehend that you are not less mistaken about the ROBE than about the breastplate of righteousness. And we think we can prove it by the testimony of the three most competent judges in the universe, an apostle, an elder before the throne, and the Lamb in the midst of it. Hear we the apostle first.

1. If all the saints were clothed with the robe of Christ's personal righteousness, they would all be clothed exactly like Christ. But when St. John had a vision of the Redeemer's glory, he "saw him clothed with a vesture DIPPED IN BLOOD: and the armies which were in heaven followed him, clothed in fine linen WHITE and clean," Rev. 19:13, 14. Now, as the white robes worn by the soldiers that compose an army cannot be the red robe worn by the general at the head of the army, we so far give place to what you call "carnal reasonings," as to conclude, that so sure as white is not red, the robes of the saints are not the robes of our Lord's personal righteousness. Nay, we, who throw off the veil of prejudice, would be guilty of the very crime you charge us with, were we to entertain that daring idea. Christ's personal righteousness is the obedience of the Son of God, who by living and dying for us, became the "propitiation for the sins of the whole world;" now, if we pretended that this identical, 'all-meritorious "obedience of Christ unto death," this active and passive righteousness, which made an atonement for all mankind, is fairly made over to, and put upon us; would it not be pretending to merit with Christ, not only our own salvation, but the salvation of all mankind? O sir, it is you, we are afraid,

who affect the Saviour; for by presuming to put on his robes, you claim his mediatorial honours. For, after all your fears, lest we should make humble faith share the Saviour's glory, or his glorious apparel, you not only put it on yourself without ceremony, but throw it also over the shoulders of ten thousand elect, without excepting even those who add drunkenness to thirst, and cruelty to lust.

You will, I hope, see the great impropriety of this conduct, if you consider that the Redeemer's personal and peculiar righteousness is his personal and peculiar glory; and that those who fancy themselves clad with it, (if they do not sin ignorantly,) are as guilty of ridiculous, not to say treasonable presumption before God, as country clergymen would be before the archbishop of Canterbury and the king, if they seriously gave it out that the sleeves of their surplices are the very lawn sleeves of his grace; and their gowns and cassocks the identical coronation robes of his majesty.

The fanciful parsons would no doubt be pitied by all men of sense; and so are we by all our Calvinist brethren; but, alas! for a very different reason. They wonder at and kindly pity us, because we cannot fancy ourselves clothed with robes a thousand times more sacred than those which Aaron wore on the great day of atonement: with robes ten thousand times more incommunicable than the king's coronation robes: with a Divine garment, that, in the very nature of things, can absolutely suit none but him, "on whose head are many crowns, and who hath on his vesture and on his thigh a name written, King of kings, and Lord of lords;—the child born unto us of a virgin, the only begotten Son of the Father, given to put away sin by the sacrifice of himself:—the wonderful Counselor, the mighty God, the everlasting Father, the Prince of Peace."

O ye sons of men, how long will you become so "vain in your imagination," as to put on robes on which the very finger of God has embroidered such incommunicable names with adamant and gold! If you are "saviours of the world," and "mediators between God and man;" if you are "emmanuels" and "gods over all, blessed for ever," wear them; they fit you, and they are your right. But if "ye all shall die like men," who cannot atone for one sin; and if the flesh of every one of you "shall see corruption," touch them not, unless it be with the reverential faith of the Syro-Phenician woman. Like her you may indeed steal a cure through them: but O! do not steal them, as those who "come" in the Redeemer's dress, and say, "I am Christ," or those who tell you, "I am carnal, sold under sin," but no matter! I am safe. In the robes of Christ's righteousness, I am as righteous as Christ himself. If nevertheless you are bent upon putting them on by self-imputation, at the peril of your souls throw them not over the shoulders of impenitent sinners, lest you "turn the truth of God into a *flagrant* lie;" lest professing yourselves wise to salvation, you "become fools, and change the glory (the glorious robe) of the incorruptible God"-man into the infamous cloak of an incestuous adulterer.

2. Suppose that still despising the white robes, that is, the evangelical righteousness of the saints, you aspire at being clothed with the Redeemer's vesture dipped in blood; permit me to oppose to your error the testimony of one of the twenty-four elders who stand nearest the throne, and therefore know best in what robes the saints can stand before it with safety and honour.

"I beheld, (says the beloved disciple,) and lo, a great multitude which no man can number, of all nations, people, and tongues, stood before the throne, and before the Lamb, clothed with WHITE ROBES," Rev. 7:9. By comparing this verse with Rev. 19: 7, 8 it is evident, that great multitude was the Church triumphant, the wife of the Lamb, who has made herself ready. She is composed of souls who have fulfilled those awful commands, "O Jerusalem, wash thy heart from iniquity, that thou mayest be saved. Wash you, make you clean, put away the the evil of your doings from before my eyes. Come, and let us reason together; though your sins be as red as scarlet, they shall be as white as snow." They continued instant in prayer, that God would "wash them thoroughly from their iniquity, and cleanse them from their sins." Nor did they give over pleading his gracious promises, till the living water, the cleansing blood, the fuller's soap, and the refiners fire, had had their full effect upon them. Therefore, "to them it was granted, that they should be arrayed in fine linen, clean and white; for the fine linen is the righteousness of the saints."

Now the question between us is, whether the "fine linen, clean and white," and the "white robes" mentioned by St. John, are the evangelical, personal righteousness of the saints, or the mediatorial, personal righteousness of their Lord: but who shall help us to decide it? One of the elders before the throne, who advances and says unto John, "These who are arrayed in white robes, are they who came out of great tribulation, and have washed their robes and made them white in the blood of the Lamb." Rev. 7:14. Does not this information, given by one to whom the beloved disciple had just said, "Sir, thou knowest," make it indubitable that the righteousness which the saints appear in before God, is a righteousness which was once defiled, and therefore stood in need of washing? Now, what Christian will assert, that the personal righteousness of the immaculate Lamb of God had ever one spot of defilement?

Again: those robes were washed and made white by the saints: "THEY have washed their robes." It is evident, therefore, that if these robes were the personal righteousness of Christ, the saints had washed it. And who is the good man, that, upon second thoughts, will dare to countenance a preposterous doctrine, which supposes, that the saints have washed the defiled righteousness of the Lord, and made it white?

Once more: These robes are washed "in the blood of the Lamb," that is, "in the fountain opened for sin and for uncleanness." Now, if they were the robes of Christ's personal righteousness, does it not necessarily follow, that Christ opened a fountain to wash his own and spotted and sinful righteousness? Is it not strange, that those who pretend to a peculiar regard for the Redeemer's glory, should be such great sticklers for an opinion which pours such contempt upon him and his glorious apparel?

3. If the testimony of St. John, and that of one of the twenty-four elders, be not regarded, let our Lord's repeated declaration, at least, be thought worthy of consideration. All our righteousness flows from him, as all the sap of the branch flows from the vine. Therefore, speaking of righteousness, he says, "Buy of me white raiment, that thou mayest be clothed, and that the shame of thy nakedness do not appear," Rev. 3:18. But that this white raiment cannot be his personal righteousness, we prove, first, from his own words mentioned in the same chapter: "Thou hast a few names in Sardis, which have not defiled their garments," Rev. 3:4. Now, if these garments were the robes of Christ's personal obedience, which neither man nor devil can defile, how came our Lord to make it matter of praise to a few names, that they had not defiled them? If David could not in the least bespatter them by all his crimes, was it a wonder that some persons should have kept them clean? Is it not rather surprising that any names in Sardis should have had defiled garments, which remain "undefiled, and

without spot," even while those who wear them welter in the mire of adultery, murder and incest?

Once more: Our Lord says, "Behold, I come as a thief. Blessed is he that watcheth and keepeth his garments, lest he walk naked and they see his shame," Rev. 16:5. Who does not see here that the garments, which we are to keep with watchfulness, are garments which may be spotted or stolen? Garments of which we may be so totally stripped, as to be seen walking naked? Two particulars that perfectly suit our personal righteousness by faith, but can never suit the personal righteousness of Christ; that "best robe," which neither man nor devil can steal, neither adultery nor murder defile.

Having spent so much time with my objector, I beg leave to turn to you, honoured sir, and to conclude this essay upon imputed righteousness, by summing up the difference which subsists between us on that important subject; and inviting men of candour to determine who of us have reason, conscience, and Scripture on their side.

You believe that the uninterrupted good works and the atoning sufferings of Christ, which made up his personal righteousness while he was upon earth, are imputed to the elect for complete and eternal righteousness, be their own personal righteousness what it will: insomuch that, as you express it, (*Five Letters,* pp. 27 and 29,) "All debts and claims against them, be they more or be they less, be they small or be they great, be they before or be they after conversion, are for ever and for ever cancelled: they always stand absolved, always complete in the everlasting righteousness of the Redeemer." And you think that this imputed righteousness composes the robes of righteousness, in which they stand before God, both in the day of conversion and in the day of judgment.

On the other hand, we believe, that for the alone sake of Christ's atoning blood and personal righteousness, our personal faith, working by obedient love, is imputed to us for righteousness. And we assert, that this living faith, working by obedient love, together with the privileges annexed to it, (such as pardon through, and acceptance in the Beloved,) makes up the robe of righteousness "washed in the blood of the Lamb," in which true believers now walk humbly with their God, and will one day triumphantly enter into the glory of their Lord.

I hope, honoured sir, that when we speak of personal faith, love, and righteousness, you will do us the justice to believe, we do not mean that we can have either faith, love, or righteousness of ourselves, or from ourselves. No: they all as much flow to us from Christ, the true vine, and the Sun of righteousness, as the sap and fruit of a branch come from the tree that bears it, and from the sun that freely shines upon it. "Without him" we have nothing but helplessness; "we can do nothing" but sin; but with him we "can do all things." If we call any graces personal or inherent, it is not then to take the honour of them to ourselves, but merely to distinguish them from "imputed righteousness," which is nothing but the imputed assemblage of all the graces that were in our Lord's breast seventeen hundred and fifty years ago.

As some of my readers may desire to know exactly wherein the difference between personal and imputed grace consists, I shall just help their conception by three or four Scriptural examples. Joseph, struggling out of the arms of his tempting mistress, has personal chastity, a considerable branch of personal righteousness: and David, sparing his own flock and taking the ewe lamb that lay in Uriah's bosom, is complete in imputed chastity, which is a considerable part of imputed righteousness. Solomon choosing wisdom, and dedicating the temple, has inherent wisdom and piety: but when he chooses Pagan wives, and with them worships deformed idols, he has imputed wisdom and piety. Again: when Peter confesses that Jesus is the Christ, the Son of the living God, he personally wears the girdle of truth: but when he denies his Lord with oaths and curses, saying, "I know not the man," he wears it only by imputation. Once more: When David killed proud Goliath with his own sword, he stood complete in the personal righteousness we plead for: but when he killed brave Uriah with the sword of the children of Ammon, he stood complete in what our opponents extol as the "best robe."

And now, ye unprejudiced servants of the most high God, ye men of candour and piety, scattered through the three kingdoms, to you, under God, we submit our cause. Impartially weigh the arguments on both sides; and judge whether the robe recommended by our brethren deserves to be called "the best robe," because it is really better than the robes of "righteousness and true holiness" which we recommend; or only because it is best calculated to pervert the Gospel, dishonour Christ, disgrace undefiled religion, throw a decent cloak over the works of darkness, render Antinomianism respectable to injudicious Protestants, and frighten moral men from Christianity, as from the most immoral system of religion in the world.

By this time, honoured sir, you are perhaps ready to turn objector yourself, and say, "You slander our principles. 'The doctrines of grace' are doctrines according to godliness. Far from opposing inherent righteousness in its place, we follow after it ourselves, and frequently recommend it to others. Imputed righteousness is highly consistent with personal holiness."

To this I answer: I know a mistaken man, who believes he has a right to all his neighbour's property, because St. Paul says, "All things are yours;" and nevertheless he is so honest that you may trust him with untold gold. Just so it is with you, dear sir. You not only believe, but publicly maintain, that an elect who seduces his neighbour's wife "stands complete in the everlasting personal chastity of Christ," and that a fall into adultery will "work for his good:" and yet, I am persuaded that, if you were married, you would be as true to your wife as Adam was to Eve before the fall. But can you in conscience apologize for your errors, and desire us to embrace them, merely because your conduct is better than your bad principles?

Again: "You frequently recommend holiness," and perhaps give it out that the shortest way to it is to believe your doctrines of imputed righteousness and finished salvation: but this, far from mending the matter, makes it worse. As fishes would hardly swallow the hook, if a tempting bait did not cover it and entice them; so the honest hearts of the simple would hardly jump at imputed righteousness, if they were not deceived by fair speeches about personal holiness. Thus good food makes way for poison, and the right robe of decently wraps fig leaves and cobwebs.

Once more: Every body knows, that bad guineas are never so successfully put off, as when they are mixed with a great deal of good gold. But suppose I made it my business to pass them, either ignorantly or on purpose, would not the public be my dupes, if they suffered me to carry on that dangerous trade upon such a plea as this: "I am not against good gold. I pass a great deal of it myself. I have even some about me now. I frequently recommend it to others; neither did I ever decry his majesty's coin?" Would not every body see through such a poor defence as this? And yet, poor as it is, you could not, with any show of truth, urge the last plea: for, in order to pass your notions about imputed righteousness, you have publicly spoken against inherent righteousness, and all its fruits. In the face of the whole world you have decried the coin that bears the genuine stamp of the Lord's goodness. You have called good works, "dung, dross, and filthy rags;" and what is still worse, you have given it out that you had "Scripture authority" so to do.

Should you in the preceding objection add the following question: "If you were now dying, in which robe would you desire to appear before God; that of Christ's personal righteousness imputed to you, without any of your good works; or, that of your own self righteousness and good works, without the blood and righteousness of Christ?" My answer is ready.

I would be found in neither, because both would be equally fatal to me: for the robe of an Antinomian is not better than that of a Pharisee; and all are foolish virgins who stand only in the one or in the other. Were I then come to the awful moment you speak of, I would beg of God to keep me from all delusions, and to strengthen my heartfelt faith in Christ, that I might be found clothed, like a wise virgin, with "a robe washed and made white in the blood of the Lamb;" that is, with the righteousness of a living faith working by love: for such a faith is the blessed reality that stands at an equal distance from the Antinomian and Pharisaic delusion. And, I say it again, this righteousness of faith includes, (1.) A pardon through the blood and righteousness of Christ. (2.) Acceptance in the Beloved. And (3.) A universal principle of inherent righteousness. For the kingdom of God is not meat and drink, much less whim and delusion; but "righteousness, peace, and joy in the Holy Ghost."

But perhaps you ask, "Which would you depend upon for pardon and acceptance in a dying hour,—your own inherent righteousness of faith, of the atoning blood and meritorious righteousness of Jesus Christ?" If this is your question, I reply, that it carries its own answer along with it. For if I have the inherent righteousness of a living faith, and if the very nature of such a faith is (as I have already observed) to depend upon nothing but Christ for wisdom, righteousness, sanctification, and redemption," is it not absurd to ask, whether I would depend on any thing else? Suppose I have faith working by humble love, do not I know that the moment I rely upon myself, or my works, as the meritorious cause of my acceptance, I put off the robe "made white in the blood of the Lamb," and put on the spotted robe of a proud Pharisee?

However, it is by self-contradictory objections and false dilemmas that the hearts of the simple are daily deceived, as well as by fair speeches, which carry an appearance of great self abasement, and of a peculiar regard for the Redeemer's glory. Who can tell how many pious souls are driven by the tempter upon one rock, through an excessive fear of dashing against the other? Every judicious, moderate man,

> *Auream quisquis mediocritatem*
> *Diligit,*

sees their well-meant error, and can say to each of them,

> *Procellas*
> *Cautus horrescis, nimium premendo*
> *Littus iniquum.*

Lest you should be found in the odious apparel of a pharisee, you put on unawares the modish dress of an Antinomian.

But, O thou man of God, whosoever thou art, have nothing to do with the one or the other, except it be to decry and tear them both. In the meantime be thou really "found in Christ, not having thine own *Pharisaic* righteousness, which is the *letter* of the law;" nor yet notions about righteousness imputed to thee in the Antinomian way; but the substantial, evangelical "righteousness, which is through the faith of Christ: the righteousness which is of God by faith: the true armour of righteousness," with which St. Paul cut in pieces the forces of Pharisaism "on the right hand," and St. James those of Antinomianism "on the left."

Rejoicing, dear sir, that if our arguments should strip you of what appears to us an imaginary garment, you shall not be found naked; and thanking "the God of all grace" for giving you, and thousands of pious Calvinists, a more substantial robe than that for which you so zealously plead; in the midst of chimerical imputations of "calumny," I remain, with personal and inherent truth, honoured and dear sir, your affectionate brother, and obedient servant in our common Lord,

JOHN FLETCHER.

END